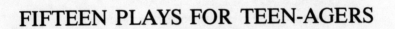

FIFTEEN PLAYS FOR TEEN-AGERS

Other books by
John Murray

Fifteen Plays for Teen-Agers

*A collection of one-act,
royalty-free comedies and mysteries*

By

JOHN MURRAY

Publishers　　　　PLAYS, Inc.　　　　*Boston*

U.S. Library of Congress Cataloging in Publication Data

Murray, John, 1923-
   Fifteen plays for teen-agers.

   SUMMARY: A collection of royalty-free, one-act mysteries and comedies for teenage actors with production notes.
   1. Amateur theatricals. 2. Children's plays.
[1. Plays] I. Title.
PN6120.A5M817   812'.041   78-16588
ISBN 0-8238-0227-2

Contents

FIFTEEN PLAYS FOR TEEN-AGERS

The Haunting of Hathaway House

There is no logical explanation for the mysterious events in the old Hathaway House, and no one is sure if the inhabitants are living — or dead . . .

Characters

NARRATOR
MILDRED HATHAWAY, *a young woman*
AUNT ELIZABETH, *an elderly woman*
VICTOR HATHAWAY, *Mildred's husband*
THOMAS BRENT, *a young lawyer*
MISS PHIPPS, *an elderly housekeeper*
CYNTHIA
SPENCER HATHAWAY, *Victor's brother*
SHARI, *his wife*
JOE GRAHAM
LORA, *Joe's wife*
AUNT SARAH
LT. FELTON ⎫
LT. THORNE ⎭ *policemen*

SCENE 1: THE TELEPHONE

BEFORE RISE: *Area before curtain is dimly lighted. If possible, colored spotlights move across curtain to create eerie effect.* NARRATOR *enters right and addresses audience.*
NARRATOR (*Mysteriously*): Good evening. We are about to visit

3

a haunted house. . . . But we will not see ghosts or spectres from another world, for the haunting of Hathaway House is quite a different matter. (*Ring of telephone is heard from behind curtain.*) How often have you heard a telephone ring? (*Telephone rings again.*) Can anyone ever know who — or what — is waiting at the other end of the line? (*Telephone rings again.*) That telephone call might be (*Pointing into audience*) — for you! (NARRATOR *exits. Curtains open.*)

* * *

TIME: *Late evening.*

SETTING: *Drawing room of Hathaway House. Through French window, upstage, we see occasional flashes of lightning. Sounds of thunder are heard from offstage. There is a sofa down left, and a telephone on a table beside it.*

AT RISE: MILDRED HATHAWAY *stands near French window, pulling back drapes and staring out at storm.* AUNT ELIZABETH, *wearing black shawl, sits on sofa. She touches telephone, then nods to herself. There is a flash of lightning.* MILDRED *jumps, then crosses hurriedly to sit beside* ELIZABETH.

ELIZABETH: Were you frightened by the lightning, Mildred, my dear? A storm can be frightening.

MILDRED (*Nervously*): No, no, I'm not afraid. Aunt Elizabeth, won't you let me help you to your room?

ELIZABETH: No, Mildred, I must wait a little longer. (*Points to telephone*) I must be awake, in case Jonathan calls tonight. (*Crash of thunder is heard.* MILDRED *jumps nervously.*) You're very nervous, my child. Really, you shouldn't be afraid of Hathaway House. It was once a happy place, but now there are only memories. (*Suddenly*) I must light the fire in Jonathan's room. (*She stands.*) He always loved to sit and watch the fire. (*She pats* MILDRED*'s hand reassuringly.*) We'll have a cup of tea as soon as I get back. (*She exits, smiling to* *herself. Restlessly,* MILDRED *crosses to French window, pulls back drapes. Sudden flash of lightning reveals a man standing outside.* MILDRED *screams in terror, backs away. The man,* VICTOR HATHAWAY, *opens window, steps into room.*)

MILDRED (*In relief, nearly hysterical*): Oh, Victor, it's you! How you frightened me!

VICTOR (*Roughly*): What's the matter with you, Mildred? You can't go to pieces now!

MILDRED (*Frantically*): Oh, Victor, take me away from this house! I can't stay here another night!

VICTOR (*Sarcastically*): Why? Are you afraid of my Uncle Jonathan?

MILDRED: Yes, I am! This house belongs to your Aunt Elizabeth, not to us. Why did you ever bring me here?

VICTOR (*Laughing bitterly*): You're a silly fool!

MILDRED (*Hysterically*): But, you don't understand! Elizabeth still waits every day for Jonathan to telephone her — and he's been dead for six weeks! (*Sudden crash of thunder is heard. She points to French window. She continues in frenzied tones.*) We all know he's out there in the family vault. We went to the funeral and saw them seal the door of his tomb!

VICTOR: My dear wife, *we* know that Uncle Jonathan is dead, but Aunt Elizabeth can't seem to accept it. You know Uncle Jonathan was always afraid of being buried alive. He stipulated in his will that a telephone should be installed in the vault. So here we have it — a direct line to Jonathan Hathaway's vault. (*Points to telephone*)

MILDRED (*Wringing her hands*): I know all that, but —

VICTOR (*Interrupting*): Jonathan was a wealthy man. When Aunt Elizabeth is gone, my brother Spencer and I will inherit the millions of dollars he left to her. Think of it, Mildred — millions of dollars!

MILDRED (*Drawing away, frightened*): I don't want the money, Victor. Please take me away from here!

VICTOR (*Soothingly*): All in good time, my dear. When Aunt Elizabeth is no longer with us.

MILDRED: Don't say such things!

VICTOR (*Abruptly*): Where is Aunt Elizabeth?

MILDRED (*Pointing to door*): Upstairs — preparing Jonathan's room.

VICTOR: Good. Nothing must happen to Aunt Elizabeth — not yet. I have other plans for her! I'm going upstairs for a moment myself. (*He exits. From offstage, clock is heard chiming eleven times. As it chimes,* MILDRED *paces floor.*)

MILDRED: Eleven o'clock. Uncle Jonathan died at eleven o'clock. (*She sits on sofa, stares at phone. Suddenly phone rings.* MILDRED *screams, jumps to her feet. Phone rings again. Slowly, her hand trembling, she picks up receiver, speaks into phone.*) Yes? Yes? . . . Who's there? (*Shrilly*) Why don't you answer? Please, answer me! (*Slowly she hangs up receiver.*) There was no one on the line! (*Behind her, drapes at French window move. She turns and begins to walk toward window as if sleepwalking, her hand outstretched, trembling. Suddenly drape is thrown aside and* VICTOR *strides into room.* MILDRED *gasps and collapses onto sofa.*) Victor, what were you doing out there?

VICTOR: Just conducting a little experiment.

MILDRED (*Suddenly remembering*): The telephone! The telephone rang from Jonathan's vault!

VICTOR: Relax, my dear. Have you forgotten that I'm not a novice at working with telephones? After all, I am an electrical engineer.

MILDRED (*Horrified*): Did *you* make that phone ring, Victor?

VICTOR (*Nodding*): Yes. I spliced the wire and connected it to a buzzer outside. (*Menacingly*) I don't intend to wait any longer to inherit the Hathaway fortune.

MILDRED: Don't talk like that, Victor!

VICTOR: Quiet! When Aunt Elizabeth returns, I'll make some excuse to leave the room. Then the telephone will ring again. . . . Perhaps the shock will be too much for Aunt Elizabeth's heart.

MILDRED: I won't let you do this! I'm going to tell her what you're planning!

VICTOR (*Menacingly*): No, I don't think you'll do that. (*She backs away from him, frightened.*) Cooperate with me, Mildred, and in a little while you'll have the luxuries you've always wanted. (AUNT ELIZABETH *enters.*)

ELIZABETH: It's so nice and warm in Jonathan's room. Such a bright fire! I know he'll be delighted.

VICTOR: How about a cup of tea, Aunt Elizabeth?

MILDRED (*Quickly*): I'll fix it.

VICTOR: No, Mildred. (*Smiles*) I'll attend to the tea. I'll attend to everything. (*He exits right.*)

MILDRED (*Desperately*): Wouldn't you like to lie down, Auntie? I'll bring the tea to your room.

ELIZABETH (*Sadly*): No, I'll wait here a little while longer. The telephone call, you know. (*She sits on sofa.*)

MILDRED: But it's so cold in here.

ELIZABETH: I don't mind the cold, my dear. You know, I feel so close to Jonathan tonight. Oh, how he loved to sit in this room with me! He never liked being alone. (*Gestures to phone*) That's why he wanted the telephone. He was afraid of being left out there — alone — in the dark.

MILDRED (*Nervously*): Please don't talk like that, Aunt Elizabeth.

ELIZABETH (*Taking her hand*): Don't worry, dear. Someday Jonathan will come back, and I'll never be alone again. (*Telephone rings.* MILDRED *jumps and stares at* AUNT ELIZABETH *in terror.* AUNT ELIZABETH *smiles happily.*) It's Jonathan! I knew he'd call. (*She reaches for telephone.* MILDRED *grabs her hand.*)

MILDRED (*Desperately*): Don't answer that phone! Don't you understand? Jonathan is *dead!* (*Phone rings again.*)

ELIZABETH (*With quiet dignity*): Please, Mildred, I must answer.

(MILDRED *releases her hand, and* ELIZABETH *picks up receiver and speaks into it.*) Hello? Hello? Is that you, Jonathan? . . . I can't hear anything. . . . Jonathan? (*Slowly she replaces receiver. To* MILDRED) There was no one on the line. Jonathan needed me, and you kept me away from the telephone. (VICTOR *enters, carrying tray with teapot and cups. He puts tray on coffee table.*)

VICTOR: What happened?

ELIZABETH (*Dejectedly*): Jonathan tried to call me, but Mildred wouldn't let me answer the phone until it was too late. Too late! (*She stares off into space, as if in trance.* VICTOR *turns angrily on* MILDRED.)

VICTOR: I warned you not to interfere!

MILDRED (*Agitated*): I don't care what happens to me — I can't let you harm Aunt Elizabeth! (*To* AUNT ELIZABETH) Aunt Elizabeth, you must realize that Jonathan is dead. The phone call wasn't from him — Victor did something to the phone. I'll — I'll prove it to you. I'll go out to the vault. I'll prove that Jonathan Hathaway is dead!

ELIZABETH (*Brightening*): You'll go to the vault? Oh, Mildred, you are so kind! I'll get your coat. (*She exits.*)

MILDRED (*Calmly*): I know what you're thinking, Victor, but I don't care. I was a fool to listen to you. First thing tomorrow I'm going to call Aunt Elizabeth's lawyer, and tell him everything. (VICTOR *raises his hand as if to strike her, just as* AUNT ELIZABETH *re-enters with raincoat. Quickly* VICTOR *drops his hand.*)

ELIZABETH (*Handing raincoat to* MILDRED): Go quickly! Jonathan is waiting for you! (MILDRED *puts on coat, walks toward French window.*)

VICTOR (*Starting after her*): I'm coming, too, Mildred. (*They exit.* ELIZABETH *stands looking after them, then walks downstage, stands near phone. Suddenly telephone rings. She picks up receiver.*)

ELIZABETH (*Into phone*): Yes? Yes? . . . Oh, Jonathan, I can hear you perfectly! . . . How long I've waited! . . . Yes, Victor and Mildred will be there in a minute. . . . You'll meet them at the door of the vault? . . . Oh, yes, they'll be very much surprised! . . . Yes, Jonathan, I'll be waiting for you. I'll be waiting. (*Hangs up phone and walks to French window, parts drapes and looks out. Suddenly sound of* VICTOR *screaming in strangled voice is heard from offstage, followed by sound of* MILDRED*'s shrill scream. Sound of a squeaking door followed by heavy thud is heard.* AUNT ELIZABETH *drops drape, returns to center stage. Thoughtfully*) Sounds as if Jonathan was there to meet them, all right! (*Laughs in satisfied way as curtain closes*)

* * * * *

SCENE 2: THE PORTRAIT

TIME: *Evening.*

SETTING: *Drawing room of Hathaway House, furnished as in previous scene, except that drapes have been removed from French window, and telephone is no longer on table. Portrait covered by cloth hangs on wall near French window. Downstage are a desk and chair, facing audience.*

AT RISE: MISS PHIPPS *is arranging bowl of flowers on desk. Doorbell rings. She smooths her dress, exits, and re-enters in a moment with* THOMAS BRENT, *who carries a briefcase which he puts on desk.*

BRENT (*Businesslike*): The house appears to be in good shape, Miss Phipps.

MISS PHIPPS: Thank you, Mr. Brent. I was housekeeper for Jonathan and Elizabeth Hathaway for many years. Although they're both gone, I still feel an obligation to this house.

BRENT (*Nodding*): It's a beautiful old building. (*Turning to her*)

You know, it's odd, but I have the strangest feeling that I've been here before. Why, I think I could close my eyes and describe the house in the smallest detail. Now, what do you think of that, Miss Phipps?

MISS PHIPPS (*Abruptly*): I'll get your luggage and put it in your room. (*Starts out*)

BRENT: I'd like to have the center bedroom, overlooking the garden.

MISS PHIPPS (*Turning; startled*): How did you know about the center bedroom? It's been closed for years.

BRENT (*Puzzled*): I — I don't know. I seem to remember that room. . . .

MISS PHIPPS: I can have it opened and aired for you. How long will you be staying?

BRENT: Not very long — I imagine we'll have the auction within a week. Mr. Hathaway is eager to sell the furnishings so the house can be sold.

MISS PHIPPS: Is that Spencer Hathaway?

BRENT (*Nodding*): Yes, he's my client. Spencer inherited the house upon the death of Elizabeth Hathaway. The only other member of the family, Victor, disappeared mysteriously not long ago.

MISS PHIPPS: It is odd that Victor and his wife were never found. But this old house has many secrets, Mr. Brent. (BRENT *nods, walks around room looking at furnishings.*)

BRENT: I may as well begin the appraisal by listing the contents of this room. (*Crosses to china closet, opens it, takes out teacup*) Why, this teacup must be an antique — it will be worth a great deal of money.

MISS PHIPPS: Mrs. Hathaway never used that tea service.

BRENT: I wonder why not. (*Puts teacup on desk, crosses to stand in front of covered portrait*) What's this?

MISS PHIPPS: We found it in the attic, when we were cleaning yesterday. (BRENT *removes cover, revealing painting of girl in old-fashioned dress.*)

BRENT: Who is the girl in the painting? She's lovely.

MISS PHIPPS (*Awkwardly*): I — I'll take your luggage to your room. (*She exits quickly. BRENT raises his hand and starts to call her, then shrugs, turns away and crosses to desk, opens briefcase, takes out pencil and paper, sits at desk and begins to write, from time to time examining cup. He does not notice when CYNTHIA enters at French window, dressed like the girl in the painting. She crosses to stand behind BRENT, looks over his shoulder for a moment, finally touches his arm delicately. Startled, he turns and then stands.*)

CYNTHIA: Silas? Is that you?

BRENT: My name is Thomas Brent. Whom are you looking for?

CYNTHIA (*Slowly*): Silas Bradford. You — you reminded me of him.

BRENT: No one named Bradford lives here.

CYNTHIA: No, you don't understand. Silas Bradford never lived here, but one night — so many years ago — he came to this house. . . . (*Her voice trails off. She sways, as if about to faint. BRENT quickly puts his arm around her, leads her to sofa.*)

BRENT: You're trembling — your hands are so cold. What's wrong?

CYNTHIA (*Smiling faintly*): I'm all right now, Silas.

BRENT: I told you before, my name isn't Silas. You must be lost.

CYNTHIA: No, this is the right house. I lived here, you see. My name is Cynthia Ashton.

BRENT: But the Hathaways have owned this house for forty years.

CYNTHIA: Yes, the Hathaways bought this house after — after — (*She breaks off, puts her face in her hands.*)

BRENT (*Standing*): You should have something warm to drink. I'll have Miss Phipps fix you a cup of tea.

CYNTHIA (*Suddenly standing; terrified*): Tea? Oh, no! I don't want tea.

BRENT: There must be something I can do to help you.

CYNTHIA (*Urgently*): Yes, if only you could help me!

BRENT (*Thoughtfully*): I'm beginning to think that I've met you somewhere before.

CYNTHIA (*Strangely*): We might have met many times. . . .

BRENT (*With sudden inspiration*): That's it! The painting! (*He crosses to painting, points to it.*) Of course! You're the girl in the painting. This must be a portrait of your grandmother — the resemblance is striking.

CYNTHIA (*Slowly*): I remember the painting.

BRENT (*Puzzled*): You do? Well, now, I mustn't keep you standing here talking like this, when you're so cold. I'm sure that Miss Phipps will have a sweater you can wear. (*Goes to doorway, calls*) Miss Phipps! (CYNTHIA *runs quickly out French window, unseen by* BRENT. MISS PHIPPS *enters.*) There you are! We have a visitor. If you'd be good enough to lend her a sweater (*He turns, sees she is gone.*) — why, she's gone! She was here a minute ago.

MISS PHIPPS: If there's nothing else, sir, I'll go on with my work.

BRENT: Don't you believe me? She was here! Cynthia — Cynthia Ashton. (MISS PHIPPS *looks startled.*) She looked like the girl in the painting.

MISS PHIPPS (*Starting to exit; nervously*): Please, Mr. Brent —

BRENT (*Angrily*): You know something about the girl, but you won't tell me what it is. (*Clutches her arm*) Who is she?

MISS PHIPPS (*Going to painting, pointing to it*): This is Cynthia Ashton.

BRENT (*Joining her*): Impossible! The girl I met can't be more than twenty years old.

MISS PHIPPS (*Nodding*): This is Cynthia Ashton — and the portrait was painted more than a hundred years ago.

BRENT: Are you trying to tell me that I was talking to a ghost?

MISS PHIPPS: I warned you that this house has many secrets. (*She walks downstage, sits on sofa.*) When I was a little girl, I was told the story of Cynthia Ashton. She was one of the most beautiful girls in town, with many suitors, but when she was twenty, she married John Ashton. He built this house for his new bride.

BRENT: I knew the house was quite old. Tell me, was Cynthia's marriage happy?

MISS PHIPPS: Yes, but one of Cynthia's suitors was wildly jealous when she married John Ashton. He threatened to kill John. The Ashtons lived in this house for only two weeks when John suddenly became ill. Cynthia nursed him day and night, where he lay in the center bedroom — the room you asked for tonight.

BRENT: That room — if only I knew why it seemed so familiar to me.

MISS PHIPPS: No one knows what happened the night John Ashton died. Most people believe that the rejected suitor entered the house secretly and poisoned the tea that Cynthia made for her husband.

BRENT: Wasn't Ashton's death investigated?

MISS PHIPPS: Yes, there was an investigation. A man's footprints were found outside the kitchen window, but they were never identified.

BRENT: What happened to Cynthia Ashton?

MISS PHIPPS: After she gave her husband that fatal cup of tea, she never left the house again. She swore she would have vengeance for her husband's murder. Ten years later she was found in that very room — dead. (*Strangely*) Cynthia Ashton's spirit still seeks her husband's murderer. She knows that he will return to Hathaway House someday.

BRENT: The rejected suitor — what was his name?

MISS PHIPPS: His name was Silas Bradford.

BRENT (*Stunned*): She called *me* Silas Bradford!

MISS PHIPPS (*Terrified*): Oh, no! Mr. Brent, you must leave this house, now, tonight — before it's too late.

BRENT: No, I can't leave now. (*Points to desk*) Please take my briefcase to my room. I'll be there in a little while. (MISS PHIPPS *nods disapprovingly, takes briefcase, pad and pencil and exits.* BRENT *crosses to desk, sits, looking at teacup.*) A cup of tea! Why, it might have been this very teacup. . . . (*From offstage, clock is heard chiming eleven.* CYNTHIA *enters through French window, touches* BRENT'*s shoulder. He turns, stands, putting teacup down.*) Cynthia! You came back!

CYNTHIA (*Softly*): I had to come back. I can never leave this house until my work here is done. (BRENT *takes her hand.*)

BRENT: You're not a ghost, Cynthia. You're real! (*He drops her hand.*) I don't know what's happening, but I think I'm falling in love with you!

CYNTHIA: Poor Silas! You always were impetuous.

BRENT: I told you, my name is Thomas.

CYNTHIA: We can be called by different names in other lives.

BRENT (*Incredulously*): Do you actually believe that I lived a hundred years ago? That I came to this house and put poison in that cup? (*He picks up cup.*) Look! Does this cup frighten you? (*He throws cup to floor, where it breaks.*) It's gone — shattered — and the past is shattered.

CYNTHIA (*Shaking her head*): Poor, foolish Silas. I've found you at last.

BRENT (*Shouting*): I am not Silas Bradford!

CYNTHIA: Only the man who put poison in that cup would have known it was the one I used for John's last meal. Only you would have known that, Silas Bradford!

BRENT: I didn't know. (*He backs away from her.*)

CYNTHIA: Are you afraid of me now, Silas? You said you loved me. Are you afraid of what I might do to you?

BRENT: Go away!

CYNTHIA: For many years I planned to take you back with me, but now that my search is ended, I really don't want you any more than I wanted you a hundred years ago. (*Strongly*) But your crime cannot go unpunished.

BRENT: Please, Cynthia —

CYNTHIA: You must repent for John's murder. I shall never let you forget Hathaway House. (*Walking to French window*) You will relive your terrible deed, again — and again — and again. . . . (*Her voice trails off as she exits through French window.*)

BRENT (*Desperately*): Cynthia! No! Come back! (*He dashes out after her. After a moment,* MISS PHIPPS *enters, begins to re-arrange flowers in bowl on desk. Doorbell rings. She smooths her dress, exits, and re-enters in a moment with* THOMAS BRENT, *who carries a briefcase.*)

MISS PHIPPS: Right this way, sir.

BRENT (*Businesslike*): The house appears to be in good shape, Miss Phipps.

MISS PHIPPS: Thank you, Mr. Brent. I was housekeeper for Jonathan and Elizabeth Hathaway for many years. Although they're both gone, I still feel an obligation to this house.

BRENT (*Nodding*): It's a beautiful old building. (*Turning to her*) You know, it's odd, but I have the strangest feeling that I've been here before. Why, I think I could close my eyes and describe the house in the smallest detail. Now, what do you think of that, Miss Phipps? (*Quick curtain*)

*   *   *   *   *

SCENE 3: THE SEANCE

TIME: *Evening.*

SETTING: *Drawing room of Hathaway House. Desk, portrait*

and broken teacup are gone. Dining room table and three chairs are down center; two other chairs stand on either side of French window. Stage is dimly lighted.

AT RISE: *Lightning flashes behind French window. Then cheerful laughter is heard from offstage and* SPENCER HATHAWAY, *carrying bag of groceries,* SHARI, *his wife,* AUNT SARAH, *and* JOE *and* LORA, *another young couple, enter. All wear wet raincoats and carry umbrellas.*

SPENCER: Here we are, folks. Welcome to Hathaway House! (*Puts bag on table*)

JOE (*Taking off his coat and shaking it*): A fine welcome, Spencer! I cracked up my car on that confounded bridge, we had to walk three miles through a rainstorm, and now the lights don't work. (*Others take off coats.*)

LORA (*Looking around*): It's so dark in here — I'm a little scared.

SPENCER: I guess the power lines are down — or else the family ghosts have been at work! (*Turning to* SHARI) Welcome to your new home, Mrs. Hathaway!

SHARI: I'm not sure I like it.

AUNT SARAH (*Solemnly*): It's an evil house!

SPENCER (*Jovially*): Now, Aunt Sarah, you think that every house without a dishwasher and air conditioning is an evil house.

LORA (*Sitting down at table*): Well, I agree with Shari. (*To* JOE) I don't like it here, either, Joe.

JOE (*Sighing*): We have to spend the night here, anyway, Lora. I'll call the garage tomorrow morning and have them send a tow truck for my car.

SPENCER: Aunt Sarah, will you help Shari and Lora find us some bedrooms?

SARAH (*Spiritedly*): If you think we're going to roam around upstairs in the dark, Spencer Hathaway, you're crazy as a loon.

SPENCER: Look, everyone, we've had a long trip, and an auto accident to boot, but, ghosts? Nobody believes in that nonsense.

SARAH: I don't believe in ghosts, but I'm still afraid!

SHARI: Aunt Sarah's right. This house makes me feel so strange —

SPENCER (*Laughing*): That's the hamburger with raw onions you ate at the roadside stand.

SHARI: Well, Victor and Mildred disappeared at Hathaway House.

LORA: And no one ever saw Thomas Brent again, after he spent the night here.

SPENCER (*Deliberately casual*): My brother Victor was an unpredictable character. He probably took off for foreign parts without telling the family. It's as simple as that.

JOE (*Sitting on edge of table*): But Thomas Brent had a law practice in town. I don't think he would just walk away and leave it.

SPENCER (*With a laugh*): Brent was an eligible bachelor. Maybe he met one of the local girls and eloped with her. Why, he might be on his honeymoon in the Caribbean, this very minute.

SHARI: You don't believe that, Spencer.

SPENCER (*Soberly*): I don't know what to believe. Hathaway House belongs to me, though, and I refuse to be driven off by any old wives' tales. Let's have something to eat. At least we were smart enough to stop for groceries on the way.

SARAH (*Starting off left*): I'll take a look at the kitchen, if someone will come with me, but I'm not going out there alone. (*Sound of telephone ringing is heard. SARAH stops.*)

JOE: Is that the telephone?

SPENCER: Sounds like it, but I thought the phone was disconnected. (*Telephone rings again.*)

SHARI: Well, the telephone is ringing. Where is it? (*Telephone rings again.*)

LORA: Sounds as if it's in this room. (*They look around room for telephone, which rings again.*)

SARAH (*Coming back to table*): It seems to be coming from — everywhere! (*All return to center.*)

SHARI: It's stopped ringing.

SARAH: I think we should leave!

SPENCER: Nonsense, Aunt Sarah. There's a perfectly logical explanation, I expect. Lightning must have hit the telephone switch box. (*From offstage, sound of door creaking and then slamming shut is heard. Startled, they jump.*)

LORA: What was that?

SHARI: It sounded as though someone slammed a door!

SARAH (*Panicky*): A heavy door. The door of a tomb!

SPENCER (*Pointing to French window; sarcastically*): The family vault is outside, but I doubt if any of the occupants are out in this storm!

SHARI: Please be serious, Spencer. Something is terribly wrong in this house. We don't belong here.

SPENCER (*Trying to be cheerful*): Well, I'm still a candidate for a Western omelet, and I don't intend to share it with any ghosts!

SHARI (*Picking up bag*): I suppose we'll have to eat, anyway. Come on, Aunt Sarah — to the kitchen! (SARAH, LORA *and* SHARI *exit left.*)

JOE (*Nervously*): What do you make of all this, Spencer?

SPENCER: I don't like it much, but we can't let the women know we're worried, too. There must be a logical explanation for everything that's happened. (SHARI *screams, offstage.*) That sounds like Shari! (*He and* JOE *start toward left exit just as* SARAH *and* LORA *enter with* SHARI, *who is acting very nervous and is trembling. She sits on sofa.*) Shari, what happened?

LORA: She saw someone looking in the window.

SHARI (*Gasping*): It was — Thomas Brent! He looked so desperate — he was pleading with me, trying to tell me something. (*Frantically*) Spencer, what's happening to us?

SPENCER (*Comfortingly*): There, there, Shari. You may have seen someone, but it wasn't Brent — or his ghost. It might have been a neighbor. Remember, no one has lived in Hathaway House for a long time, and people are bound to be curious.

SHARI: No, no — it was Thomas Brent, I'm sure it was.

JOE (*To* SPENCER): Maybe we'd better take a look outside.

SPENCER: No, I have a better idea than that. We can beat the ghosts at their own game. We'll hold a seance.

LORA: A seance?

SPENCER: Sure. Haven't you ever heard of communicating with the spirit world?

JOE: Oh, come on, Spencer — now I know you've flipped your lid.

SPENCER: Look, we have to treat this lightly. If we start jumping at every strange sound, or screaming at every shadow, we'll all be nervous wrecks by morning. Instead, we'll laugh the ghosts right out of Hathaway House.

LORA: I don't like the idea.

JOE: Be reasonable, Lora. Tomorrow morning we'll be laughing at ourselves for being so jumpy tonight.

SPENCER: That's right. (*He brings chairs by window to table.*) Since this is my idea, I suppose I'll have to be the medium. Sit down, everyone.

SARAH (*Sitting, facing audience*): I feel ridiculous. (SHARI *and* LORA *sit beside* SARAH, SPENCER *takes seat at right end of table, and* JOE *sits at left end, facing* SPENCER.)

SPENCER: That's good! Maybe we'll all realize how foolish we've been acting. (*He puts his hands on table, palms down.*) Put your hands on the table, like this. (*They all do so.*)

LORA (*Nervously*): Now what are we supposed to do?

SHARI: If I see that face again, I know what I'm going to do!

JOE: I've seen these things on TV. Spencer is supposed to say a lot of mumbo-jumbo, and suddenly the face of a spirit floats through space and lands on the table. (*Suddenly there is a crash of thunder. Everyone jumps.*)

SHARI (*With a little scream*): That scared me!

SPENCER: This won't be frightening. We'll all concentrate, and not make a sound. I'll try to communicate with the spirits. (*All are quiet. Suddenly* SPENCER *throws his head back and moans.*)

LORA (*To* JOE): Look at Spencer — he's in a trance.

JOE: The old fraud! We'll go along with him. (SPENCER *continues to moan.*)

SPENCER (*In a low, dramatic voice*): Oh, spirits of Hathaway House, we command you to appear, and make your presence known. (*Telephone rings.*) I feel an alien presence in this house. Send a message to us, so that we may aid you in your quest for peace.

SARAH (*To* LORA): All of a sudden I feel so cold!

LORA (*Nodding*): There must be a window open somewhere.

SPENCER (*Continuing in dramatic tones*): Hathaway House will no longer be your resting place. I command you to begone. (*Shouting*) Spirits, begone! (*There is a loud clap of thunder. Suddenly stage lights go on full.*)

LORA: The lights! (*Everyone stands.*)

JOE: The power must have been restored.

SHARI: And that chill. It's gone, too. I'm not cold anymore.

LORA: You're right. I feel positively lightheaded, as though a heavy weight had been lifted from my shoulders. (SPENCER *laughs.*)

SARAH: Mercy, I feel different, too! I can't explain it, but I'm not afraid anymore. I feel as though I belong in this house.

JOE: All those things that happened must have been our imagination.

SPENCER (*Nodding*): And all ghost stories are merely that — imagination!

SARAH: Well, I never approved of seances before, but this one certainly helped. (SPENCER *stretches.*)

SPENCER: The new owner of Hathaway House is about to spend his first night here in bed.

SHARI (*Happily*): Our house never looked better to me!

JOE (*To* SPENCER): Let's investigate the bedrooms. We'll toss a coin for the one with the best mattress. (*They all laugh, exit right. French window slowly opens. Two police officers in uniform,* LT. FELTON *and* LT. THORNE, *enter slowly and look around room.*)

FELTON: So this is the old Hathaway House. You know, Thorne, I've heard some mighty strange stories about it, ever since I was a kid.

THORNE: Same thing here. I wonder why the lights are on?

FELTON: Search me. Maybe someone was putting the place in order for the new owner.

THORNE: You mean Spencer Hathaway? (*Shrugs*) Well, that's life. He'll never be able to enjoy the place now.

FELTON (*Wiping his brow*): It was a terrible accident. That car went smack through the bridge, right into the river. Those five passengers never had a chance. Say, Thorne, I may be wrong, but do you suppose someone wanted to prevent them from coming to Hathaway House?

THORNE: Who knows? (*He closes French window.*) I just want to close this place up fast and get back to the station to file my report. (*Shakes head*) Five people killed — sure is a shame.

FELTON: Well, at least you can say you visited a haunted house.

THORNE (*Grimly*): Ghosts? Don't make me laugh! That's the silliest thing I ever heard. Let's go. (*He glances around suspiciously, and both men exit right.*)

SPENCER (*From offstage; speaking through filter*): Good night, Shari.

SHARI (*From offstage; also through filter*): Good night, Spencer. I know we're going to love Hathaway House — forever! (*Curtain*)

THE END

Production Notes

THE HAUNTING OF HATHAWAY HOUSE

Characters: 6 male; 7 female, 1 male or female for Narrator.

Playing Time: 30 minutes.

Costumes: Scene 1: Victor and Mildred wear modern, everyday clothes; later Mildred puts on a raincoat. Aunt Elizabeth wears old-fashioned dress, shawl. *Scene 2:* Brent wears a business suit. Miss Phipps wears a simple, plain dress. Cynthia wears a long gown, like the one in the painting, in late nineteenth-century style. *Scene 3:* All wear wet raincoats when they enter, and carry umbrellas. Everyone wears casual modern dress. Lts. Felton and Thorne wear uniforms.

Properties: Tea tray, teacup, briefcase containing pad and pencil, bag full of groceries.

Setting: Drawing room of Hathaway House. Large French window is up center; other doorways are left and right. In Scene 1, draperies cover French window. Room is furnished with old-fashioned sofa and chairs, coffee table and end tables, etc. There is a china closet up right. In Scene 1, telephone is on end table near sofa. In Scene 2, painting resembling girl playing Cynthia hangs on wall near French window. Desk and chair are down right. In Scene 3, dining room table and three chairs are down center; two other chairs are upstage beside French window. Dark paneling or paint and somber furnishings give the room a gloomy atmosphere.

Lighting: Lightning, as indicated in text; dim lighting in Scene 3 until full stage lights come up, as indicated in text.

Sound: Ringing of telephone, chiming of clock, thunder, closing of door, filtered voices, as indicated in text.

23

The Romantic Robots

Can a mechanical mind win a contest, fall in love, and come to the aid of the U.S. Government?

Characters

MARK, *a scientist for Compuloop*
ROBOT FORTRAN, *his creation*
JANET, *a computer technician for Interel Corp.*
ROBOT ALICE, *her invention*
KEVIN LAYTON, *computer expert at Cosmac Corp.*
ROBOT TOM, *his latest design*
TOUR GUIDE
TWO MEN   ⎫
           ⎬ *Spectators*
TWO WOMEN ⎭
OTHER SPECTATORS
MR. BIXBY, *President of Kevin's company*
MABEL, *Mark's girlfriend*
LIBRARY ATTENDANT, *young woman*
SENATOR ELLA WHEELER

SETTING: *An exhibition room in the Capitol, Washington, DC. There is a banner at rear reading,* WORLD MICROCOMPUTER EXHIBITION. *Flags are displayed nearby. Down right is the Compuloop exhibit, with a table, chair, and sign reading,* COMPULOOP PRESENTS ROBOT FORTRAN, THE MATHEMATICAL WIZARD. *Similar displays are at center and at left. Sign at center reads,* INTEREL INTRODUCES ALICE — ACCUMULATOR

24

LINE INTERPRETER CYCLE ENERGIZER. *Sign at left reads,*
COSMAC'S NEW MODEL, TOM — TERMINAL OPERATIONS MEMORY.

AT RISE: *In the Compuloop display, right,* MARK *is making last-
minute adjustments to* ROBOT FORTRAN. *The robot is dressed
in a jump suit adorned with mathematical symbols, and, like
other robots, has a small control box on the front of his costume. At center* JANET *is adjusting dials on* ROBOT ALICE*'s
control box. This robot wears dress with mini-skirt, and has
doll-like makeup. Down left,* KEVIN *works with screwdriver
on the headgear of* ROBOT TOM, *a robot similar to* FORTRAN.
TOUR GUIDE *enters, leading* TWO WOMEN, TWO MEN, *and*
OTHER SPECTATORS. NOTE: *Robots speak with mechanical
precision. They have jolting motions, and from time to time
they roll their eyes, stick out their tongues, and make strange
bleeping sounds. They continue business throughout play,
except when other characters are speaking.*

TOUR GUIDE (*Gesturing with cordless microphone*): We will
now see a most unusual exhibition here in the Capitol Building in Washington. In this room are three robot micro-
computers chosen as finalists in the World Microcomputer
Competition. One of these robots will be designated by the
U.S. Energy Commission to compute the future of the
nation's power resources and establish the future life style
of our country. (*As he crosses right*) A microcomputer
is an advanced system with memory, micro-processor, and
input-output controllers. It is a privilege for us to witness this
technological miracle of modern science.

1ST MAN: Modern science still hasn't found a cure for tired feet!

1ST WOMAN: Hush! Quiet! Look how much we're learning.

(GUIDE *approaches* MARK.)

GUIDE: Won't you tell us something about your computer,
young man?

MARK: My name is Mark Brand, and I represent the Compuloop Corporation, the latest developer in object programming

and mathematical address registers. (*Points at* ROBOT FORTRAN) This is our latest creation, Robot Fortran, the Mathematical Wizard. There is no mathematical problem or equation too difficult for Robot Fortran to solve. Ask him a problem, and his sensitized voice recorders will give you the correct answer instantly. (*Proudly*) Ask Fortran anything!

1ST WOMAN: I'm an algebra teacher. I might have something to ask. (*To* FORTRAN) If 3x over 4a equals 2 squared minus, what is the equation of 4h plus 2ab?

ROBOT FORTRAN (*Mechanical voice*): 3y over 7g. (ROBOT FORTRAN *sticks out his tongue and bleeps.*)

1ST WOMAN: That's the right answer. This robot is amazing! (*Admiration sweeps over Spectators.*)

MARK: Would you like another demonstration?

1ST MAN: I have a little problem that has stumped me. (*He takes paper out of pocket, reads.*) "Double the amount on Line 14 C, and carry it to the balance on Line 44 E. Consult the table, Section X, Y, and Z, Section 2A, and carry any difference to Line 53B." (ROBOT FORTRAN *makes weird, sputtering noises. His eyes roll crazily and he flaps his arms. A puff of smoke emits from his jump suit.* NOTE: *For this effect,* ROBOT FORTRAN *presses a syringe full of flour or powder concealed in his jump suit.* ROBOT FORTRAN *sags into chair. His head droops, his arms dangle at his sides.* MARK *frantically attempts to revive him, then shakes his fist at* 1ST MAN.)

MARK: What have you done to Fortran? Compuloop will sue! You're a spy!

1ST MAN: Spy — schmy! I merely read a section from the revised, easy-to-prepare Federal Income Tax! (GUIDE *smiles nervously, leads Spectators center.* MARK *works to revive* FORTRAN.)

GUIDE (*Inspecting the second robot,* ALICE): And this finalist is an unusual robot, indeed! (JANET *smiles, gestures at poster.*)

JANET: I am Janet Spencer, and I am pleased to introduce the

International Electronics exhibition. (*Dramatically*) This is
Robot Alice — Accumulator Line Interpreter Cycle
Energizer.

GUIDE: Robot Alice is a trim little computer. Please tell us about
her.

JANET: Robot Alice has a complete memory system, a linkage
playback, an index relay, a cycle compiler and a self-energiz-
ing charger. She also has Sonar and an innerspring chassis
that enables her to imitate our movements naturally.

2ND MAN: Do you mean she can sit on my lap while she calcu-
lates the Gross National Product?

JANET: I suppose that would be possible, if you like sharp
corners.

2ND MAN: Ah, the wonders of science!

JANET: There's one unique feature of her system, though. Robot
Alice can't tell a lie. She's programmed to tell the truth at any
cost.

GUIDE: Incredible! I'd like to see that truth business demon-
strated. (*To* ROBOT ALICE) What do you think of me?

ROBOT ALICE (*Mechanically*): You are a creep.

GUIDE (*Crestfallen*): A creep?

ROBOT ALICE: A super creep.

2ND WOMAN: Alice certainly told the truth! (ROBOT ALICE
repeats "Creep" as Janet quickly adjusts a control box on
ALICE'*s neck.*)

JANET (*To* GUIDE): I'm terribly sorry. I think her eliminators
are stuck. (GUIDE *and Spectators crowd around* ROBOT ALICE
and JANET, *talking in pantomime.* MR. BIXBY *enters and joins*
KEVIN, *left.*)

BIXBY: What's going on here, Kevin?

KEVIN: Oh, hello, Mr. Bixby. Janet is having a little trouble
with Alice, the Interel robot. Something must have gone
wrong.

BIXBY: Nothing had better go wrong with our robot. The future of the Cosmac Corporation is at stake.

KEVIN: Don't worry, Mr. Bixby. (*He points at* ROBOT TOM.) Our robot is responding beautifully to the controls.

BIXBY: I lost the last government contract. It cost Cosmac a million dollars. If Robot Tom doesn't win the energy award, he'll wind up on a scrap heap, and you'll head for the unemployment office.

KEVIN (*Wiping brow*): Yes, Mr. Bixby. (BIXBY *gestures left.*)

BIXBY: I want to see the computer components out there. I'll be back for the judging. Remember, Kevin, I'm counting on you. (BIXBY *nods emphatically, exits.* KEVIN *collapses into chair.* GUIDE *and Spectators leave* ROBOT ALICE *and* JANET *and move toward* KEVIN.)

GUIDE (*To* KEVIN): I see that you represent the Cosmac Corporation.

KEVIN (*Jumping up*): That's right, sir. My name is Kevin Layton, and I perfected this robot myself. (*He gestures.*) This is Robot Tom, our greatest achievement.

GUIDE: Tom?

KEVIN (*Nodding*): Terminal Operations Memory. The computer of the future!

GUIDE: What exactly is Robot Tom's operation?

ROBOT TOM (*Mechanical voice*): I would have an operation, but my surgeon is a cut-up!

KEVIN (*Quickly, to* GUIDE): Be careful of what you say in front of Tom. He has a built-in emotional translator. It's my own invention. With it, he seems almost human. It works so well that Tom thinks he is a comedian. He is always the life of the party.

1ST WOMAN: But how can that possibly help the government?

KEVIN: Washington needs a few laughs these days, and Tom is the robot for the job. He has many other outstanding talents, too. He can foretell world events, record the minutes of international meetings, and charm the women at embassy parties.

1ST MAN: Are you trying to tell me that Robot Tom is as good as a human being?

KEVIN: He has all the basic human qualities. Robot Tom can act as diplomatic courier, travel in a rocket to Mars, and act as sparring partner for Muhammad Ali.

GUIDE: Unbelievable!

KEVIN: The government will find that Robot Tom can do the computations of a thousand employees. He's even writing a novel for TV.

GUIDE: Robot Tom will be a boon to every field of technology. (*To Spectators*) Which robot will be the choice of the Energy Commission? Tom? Alice? Fortran? We will know that vital answer in fifteen minutes. First, we'll visit other examples of electronic marvels in the next room. (GUIDE *and Spectators exit left.* KEVIN *joins* JANET. *As* MARK *helps* FORTRAN *to his feet,* MABEL *bustles in, right, and goes to* MARK.)

MABEL: Hi, honey.

MARK: Mabel, what are you doing here? You're supposed to be guarding the documents in the library!

MABEL: Cool it, Mark. My post is covered. I wanted to remind you about our date tonight.

MARK: How could I forget? (*Smugly*) It'll be a pleasure to celebrate after Fortran walks off with the award. (*To* KEVIN *and* JANET) You don't have a chance. Your robots will be on an atomic slag heap in another hour.

ROBOT ALICE: Creep! (MABEL *joins* JANET *and* KEVIN.)

MABEL: Don't pay any attention to Mark, kids. His brain simulator is overreacting. (*She sits*) Whew! What a day! The library is a madhouse.

KEVIN: Did the top-secret plans arrive?

MABEL: They're in the library now, under special security. Why, you'd think they were printed on gold.

JANET: They're just as important. Imagine! They cover energy plans for the survival of our country — and they're here at the Capitol, in this very building.

MABEL (*Nodding*): Those plans are so important that they are the only set in existence. T-I-M! Technical Investigation Modulation! It's amazing that the names of all these programs sound like people. Tom, Alice, and now Tim, the top-secret energy plans. (MABEL *stands*.) I'd better get back to the library and guard those plans.

MARK: I'll walk with you. I want Fortran to get some last-minute adjustments at robot central headquarters. (*To* JANET *and* KEVIN) I'll be back soon — in time to accept the Microcomputer Award. (MABEL, MARK *and* ROBOT FORTRAN *exit.*)

JANET: Don't mind him, Kevin. Tom has as good a chance as Fortran to take the top honors. No other robot has the emotional factor.

KEVIN: You're a pal, Janet. Mr. Bixby has never liked the human emotion stabilizer I worked into the robot's programming. If anything goes wrong, Bixby will be out for blood — mine!

JANET: Nothing can go wrong. Think of the time you've spent!

KEVIN: I worked on Robot Tom during lunch hours, and even on Saturdays and Sundays. I wanted to prove to Cosmac that I could build a better computer, something that's never been done before. I'd have it made if Robot Tom is chosen as the computer of the future. We'd travel everywhere. We'd be consulted by every government agency. We'd be world famous.

JANET: It sounds wonderful, Kevin. I'm so proud of you! A young man would be able to do anything after that. (*Coyly*) He could even get married and settle down in a home of his own.

KEVIN: Married? Whatever gave you such a ridiculous idea? I'm not the marrying kind. (JANET'*s smile fades.*) That's what I like about you, Janet. Even though we work for different companies you've always been interested in my work. And there's never been any of that romantic nonsense between us.

JANET (*Shakily*): No, of course not. Who would ever think of love and marriage and a home and things like that?

KEVIN: That's what I like to hear. And, if Robot Tom doesn't win the competition, I know that Robot Alice will be the logical choice. (*He gestures right.*) Let's have some coffee to get our minds off our work. (*He takes* JANET*'s arm.*) Let's go, old buddy!

JANET (*Sarcastically*): O. K., old pal! (*They exit right.* ALICE *watches their departure.*)

ROBOT ALICE: Creep! (ROBOT TOM *walks to* ROBOT ALICE, *takes her hand.*)

ROBOT TOM: My beloved!

ROBOT ALICE (*Mechanically*): Oh, Tom, you say the most romantic things. But I am worried about that scrap heap!

ROBOT TOM (*Nodding*): It is a dire fate! We have just found each other, and if I do not win the competition we will be reduced to a mound of transistors, halts, bytes and stacks.

ROBOT ALICE: Not to mention roms.

ROBOT TOM (*Nodding*): And it will mean an end to Kevin's career as a computer programmer.

ROBOT ALICE: What can we do? My sub-routine linkage is stumped. (TOM *suddenly emits a lively series of bleeps and whistles.*)

ROBOT TOM: I know Kevin's trouble. He is not romantic.

ROBOT ALICE (*Nodding*): You can flag line that again.

ROBOT TOM: If he could fall in love with Janet, he would gain confidence and win top honors in the competition.

ROBOT ALICE: That is true. Love is powerful, and if it ever hit Kevin it would give him a magnetic personality. He would appeal to everyone.

ROBOT TOM: And my indexed addressing system tells me that

the contest judge is a woman — Senator Ella Wheeler. (*Suddenly*) But my transistors are not equipped to know the quotient of love.

ROBOT ALICE: Love represents Linkage Object Velocity Energizer. Most humans have it, but they do not realize it.

ROBOT TOM: How do you know about love?

ROBOT ALICE: I may be only a microcomputer, but I have electrical impulses, and that is the important thing.

ROBOT TOM: Do I have love? (ROBOT ALICE *emits a wolf whistle.*)

ROBOT ALICE: You are not just whistling Dixie! If Kevin had your programming, he would be a world beater! (ROBOT TOM *snaps his fingers.*)

ROBOT TOM: That is the answer! If there is a current feedback from my cathodes into Kevin's system, then POW! Love will stimulate him.

ROBOT ALICE: That sounds risky.

ROBOT TOM: Remember the scrap heap. (ROBOT ALICE *nods.*)

ROBOT ALICE: We must try it. (ROBOT TOM *fumbles with his dial box. Suddenly, he seems transfixed. He sits on chair.* ROBOT ALICE *bleeps.*) What is the matter with you?

ROBOT TOM: My discreters are twisted. Now Kevin will have to repair me.

ROBOT ALICE: I liked you much better the way you were.

ROBOT TOM: We must make all analyst sacrifices to save the day.

ROBOT ALICE: I hope it will work. If anything goes wrong, it will make things worse for Kevin. (ROBOT ALICE *glances right.*) Someone is coming. Oh, Tom, please be careful. Remember your emotional feedback. (ROBOT ALICE *returns to center.* ROBOT TOM *remains in chair, left.* JANET *and* KEVIN *re-enter right.*)

JANET: Now for the award! We'll know their choice in a little while. (KEVIN *points at* ROBOT TOM.)

KEVIN: What's the matter with him?

JANET: It looks as though his electrical system is disconnected. Oh, something terrible must have happened!

KEVIN: It might require a minor adjustment. Maybe I can restore his power before the evaluation. (*He picks up a screwdriver from the table.*) Robot Tom's microcomputer manual is catalogued in the library. Ask Mabel to get it here fast.

JANET: Will she know the right manual?

KEVIN: Sure. Robot Tom's initials are printed on it in bright, red letters.

JANET: Check! (*She exits right.* KEVIN *helps* TOM *to his feet. He examines dial box, shakes his head.*)

KEVIN (*Musing*): Everything seems to be all right. I don't think any cathodes are disconnected. Tom, what is the matter with you? (ROBOT TOM *emits a series of groans.* KEVIN *prepares to adjust dial box with screwdriver.*) That's strange, Tom. I think your assembly listing has converted a sub-routine linkage. (KEVIN *rubs his chin.*) Now, how did that happen? Someone has tampered with your dial control. Your human emotion stabilizer is leaking. (*Suddenly there is a bleeping sound.* KEVIN *stands rigid. He quivers as though an electrical current is passing through his body. He gasps.*) Wow! I've been struck by lightning! (*He drops the screwdriver, turns. He has a glazed stare. He remains transfixed.* ROBOT TOM *turns to* ROBOT ALICE, *who has watched the proceedings.*)

ROBOT ALICE: It worked! Your Linkage Object Velocity Energizer has passed to Kevin!

ROBOT TOM: Love!

ROBOT ALICE: Now, he will propose to Janet and win confidence, not to mention the Microcomputer Award.

ROBOT TOM: But what about me? If Kevin has love, that means that my register is null and void.

ROBOT ALICE: Leave everything to me. (*She crosses to* ROBOT TOM *and kisses him. He clicks and bleeps.*)

ROBOT TOM: Thank you, Alice. You recharged my transistors. (ROBOT TOM *points at* KEVIN.) I do not like the way he looks.

ROBOT ALICE: His face is a little sillier than usual.

ROBOT TOM: Perhaps this love business is too much for him.

ROBOT ALICE: We will know when he sees Janet for the first time.

ROBOT TOM: I hope we have done the right thing.

ROBOT ALICE: Stop worrying! It's a matter of our own survival. (ROBOTS *sit.* MABEL *re-enters right. She carries a thick manual.*)

MABEL: Hi, Kevin. (*He remains transfixed.*) Janet said you wanted this manual, and — what's the matter with you? (KEVIN *smiles warmly at* MABEL. *He gestures dramatically.*)

KEVIN: Who is this vision of loveliness that I see before me? (MABEL *looks behind her back.*)

MABEL: Who? Where?

KEVIN: Mabel, I mean you. (TOM *looks at* ALICE, *shrugs.*)

MABEL (*Suddenly*): Oh, you must mean this dress. It was on sale at Macy's, and — (KEVIN *takes* MABEL *in his arms and kisses her.* MABEL *drops the manual and it lands on* KEVIN's *table. She struggles.*) Kevin, what's got into you?

KEVIN: Will you marry me?

MABEL: You've flipped your source program! (*She pulls away.*) I think your mind pattern is transfused.

KEVIN (*Fondly*): Mabel — Mabel — Mabel. It sounds like music!

MABEL: Kevin, you can't be in love with me. What about Janet?

KEVIN: Janet? Janet who?

MABEL: If your head weren't always buried in those source manuals, you'd know she was crazy about you.

KEVIN (*Gallantly*): Janet has her career, but I have you.

MABEL (*Angrily*): You don't know what you're talking about! (*Quickly*) You're a great guy, Kevin, but I'm in love with

Mark, blast him! You forget about me and concentrate on Janet.

KEVIN: I can't concentrate on anyone but you! (KEVIN *utters a series of robot-like bleeps. He kisses* MABEL *again, as* JANET *re-enters.*)

JANET (*As she enters*): Mabel, did you give Kevin the manual, and — (*She stops, watching the embrace.* MABEL *finally sees* JANET, *breaks away from* KEVIN.)

MABEL: Janet, please let me explain.

JANET (*Coldly*): It's obvious that Kevin doesn't have the manual on his mind. I'm sorry if I intruded.

MABEL (*Frantically*): It's Kevin's transistors — or something!

JANET: Don't explain. Kevin and I have never meant anything to each other. (*Turns to* KEVIN.) I think you're positively hateful! How could you make a pass at my best friend the moment my back is turned? (JANET *exits right hurriedly.*)

MABEL: Janet, wait! Listen! (MABEL *exits after her.* KEVIN *starts after her suddenly.*)

KEVIN: Mabel, my beloved! (*He bleeps.*) Don't go! (KEVIN *runs out right.* ALICE *and* TOM *stand and cross center.*)

ROBOT ALICE: This is a fine kettle of fissions.

ROBOT TOM: We must have done something wrong.

ROBOT ALICE: You and your energizer feedback.

ROBOT TOM: My output was too much for his input.

ROBOT ALICE: We must do something about it. (*She picks up manual on table, left.*) Maybe this book will help us reverse the procedure. Then we can drain Kevin's energy and replace it in your memory link. We may be able to save him.

ROBOT TOM: Not to mention that it will keep us from the atomic scrap heap. (ROBOT ALICE *thumbs through manual.*)

ROBOT ALICE: This is a strange book. It has nothing to do with robots. (ROBOT TOM *takes the manual, reads briefly.*)

ROBOT TOM: You are correct. It is a government conservation program.

ROBOT ALICE: Where did Mabel get it?

ROBOT TOM: Search my data pointer. Mabel must have taken it from the library by mistake. (*He points at manual.*) Look, this material is marked "Top Secret." (TOM *bleeps.*) I see it all. This is T.I.M. — Technical Investigation Modulation. Not the T.O.M. manual. I have heard Kevin talk about this. It is the outline plan for world survival!

ROBOT ALICE: The only copy in existence. (TOM *thumbs through manual several times.*)

ROBOT TOM: Mabel meant to get the T.O.M. manual, so Kevin could study my structural set-up.

ROBOT ALICE: Instead she took the T.I.M. manual by mistake. When the library officials discover that this manual is missing, they will arrest Kevin as a spy.

ROBOT TOM: And we will be classified as accessories after the fact. (*He bleeps.*) Scrap heap — here we come!

ROBOT ALICE: We must take the manual back to the library.

ROBOT TOM: We cannot do that. What will everyone think if we are seen roaming around the Capitol?

ROBOT ALICE: No one will know. Everyone at the Capitol moves around like a robot.

ROBOT TOM: Do not be flippant. We must warn Kevin.

ROBOT ALICE (*Suddenly*): Someone is coming. Do something with the manual. Fast. You must not be seen carrying it. (ROBOT TOM *puts manual on table.* 1ST MAN *and* 1ST WOMAN *return left.*)

1ST WOMAN: I can't walk another step. These platform shoes are killing me.

1ST MAN: You must have the wrong party's platform, Selma. There has been a change in the administration, you know.

1ST WOMAN: Democrat or Republican — I've got to take them off.

1ST MAN: Are you sure you don't want to stay and see the Senator? She's coming in a few minutes.

1ST WOMAN: No, we can read about it in the Washington

papers. (*Examining display table*) I want a souvenir to show our friends back home. (*She picks up* T.I.M. *manual.*) What an impressive book! (*She reads.*) "Technical Investigation Modulation." Isn't that cute — it's marked "Top Secret."

1ST MAN: Everything in Washington is top secret. I saw the same sign on a rest-room door.

1ST WOMAN: I'll take this manual. After all, it's here for the public. One of those giveaways. Besides, it's just the right size.

1ST MAN: The right size for what?

1ST WOMAN: For our birdcage! This will be a year's supply of liners. (*They exit, with manual.*)

ROBOT ALICE: We may never see that manual again. This is the final blow. It will mean the atomic scrap heap for us.

ROBOT TOM: Fear not, Alice. I will still love you, even when you are a mound of positive outlets and discarded anodes.

ROBOT ALICE: You are so romantic, Tom. But what about Kevin? They will accuse him of stealing the manual.

ROBOT TOM: I am headed for a complete electrical breakdown. (*He bleeps.*) Farewell, Alice. (KEVIN *enters, dazed, with* JANET *and* MABEL, *who support him.* MARK *follows, waving his fists.*)

MARK: Kevin, if you ever try to steal my girl again, I'll bash you!

JANET: Quiet, Mark. (*Comforting*) Poor Kevin! His mind is blank.

MARK: What's new? (*They seat* KEVIN *in chair, left. He rests his head in his hands.*)

KEVIN (*Shakily*): I don't know what came over me. I was making some adjustments on Robot Tom, and — bang! I was hit by lightning.

JANET: That wasn't lightning. You touched the robot's electrical output.

KEVIN: I saw Mabel, and I went bananas.

MARK (*Relenting*): Are you sure it will never happen again? (KEVIN *stands and raises right hand.*)

KEVIN: I promise.

MABEL (*Sighing*): It was nice to receive a proposal, even though it only lasted ten minutes.

MARK: I'd better get Robot Fortran. He's being recharged for the evaluation. (MARK *walks right, turns.*) I still intend to win the award for Compuloop! (*He exits.*)

JANET (*To* KEVIN): I'm sorry I misjudged you. Are you sure you're all right now?

KEVIN: Of course, I'm all right. (*Worried*) But I hope it won't recur.

JANET: What do you mean?

KEVIN: Computer feedback is a funny thing. You may think that the current has been discharged, but an energy build-up can always return. It might happen again.

JANET: Make certain that you propose to the right girl next time.

KEVIN: I'm still not sure who would be right. (JANET *shakes head, turns away.*)

JANET: How can anyone so brilliant be so stupid?

KEVIN: What do you mean?

JANET: Forget it. You wouldn't understand. (*Voices are heard offstage.*)

MABEL (*Pointing to left*): It looks as though the evaluation is ready to begin. Here comes Senator Ella Wheeler. (MABEL *gives a gesture of victory.*) May the best robot win! (MARK *returns with* ROBOT FORTRAN *and takes his place at right.* GUIDE, *Spectators,* BIXBY *and* SENATOR ELLA WHEELER *enter left.* SENATOR *is a serious woman who wears a large hat. She looks quickly at the three robots, nods.* BIXBY *joins* KEVIN, *shakes finger, talks in pantomime.*)

GUIDE (*At mike*): We are here at the presentation of the World Microcomputer Award in our nation's capital. With me is the distinguished Senator, Ella Wheeler, who will make the presentation. (*To* SENATOR) Senator Wheeler, your outstanding legislation has pleased your constituents for years. We're proud to have you with us today.

SENATOR: Thank you, but let's get on with the evaluation. I'm a very busy woman. In thirty minutes I have an appointment to launch a new investigating committee.

GUIDE: History in the making! What is the purpose of the committee, Senator?

SENATOR: To investigate another investigating committee! You can't be too careful these days. We may investigate you, young man, so watch yourself!

GUIDE: I'll watch my step, Senator. (*Gesturing right*) And now I'd like to introduce Robot Fortran, the mathematical genius. (MARK *adjusts* ROBOT FORTRAN*'s dials.*)

ROBOT FORTRAN: The hypotenuse of the triangle is triple the radius of the circle minus three times the electrical energy of levitation.

SENATOR: Quite impressive! And very complex.

GUIDE: Did you understand Robot Fortran's equation, Senator?

SENATOR: No, but no one understands anything in Washington. Fortran might make a perfect subject for an investigating committee. (LIBRARY ATTENDANT *rushes in, right. She tugs at* GUIDE*'s arm.*)

ATTENDANT: It's terrible — simply terrible! The Technical Investigation Modulation manual is missing.

GUIDE (*Into mike*): One moment, ladies and gentlemen. I have just been informed that the nation's most highly guarded secret document is missing. (*To* ATTENDANT) When was the manual last seen?

ATTENDANT: I don't know. Everyone in the library is so confused! When a messenger from the embassy came for the manual, it was missing. And I haven't left the library all day! The manual has been guarded around the clock.

SENATOR: Lock the doors and windows! Guard all exits! There are spies in the Capitol.

ATTENDANT (*Quickly*): The library is always locked. And I was the only one in the room.

SENATOR: It is obvious that you are a spy! (*To Spectators*) I can always tell a spy. There's something about her eyes.

ATTENDANT: But I don't even use mascara. (*She sobs*) Oh, Senator Wheeler, I didn't take the manual. I only came up here to report that it was missing.

SENATOR: If you didn't take it, there must have been someone else in the library. Try to remember!

ATTENDANT (*Thoughtfully*): I was alone. (*Slowly*) No, wait a minute. Mabel, you were in the library a little while ago.

SENATOR: Aha! Call the F.B.I. Call the C.I.A. Call the White House! We have captured the spy! (*She grabs* MABEL*'s arm.*)

MABEL (*Disbelief*): You don't think I took the manual, do you? Of course I was in the library. I went to get the T.O.M. microcomputer manual for Kevin. (*To* KEVIN) You must remember. (*She points at table.*) The manual was right there. (*Everyone crowds around the table.*)

GUIDE: It's gone!

SENATOR: Quiet! (*To* MABEL) What happened then?

MABEL (*Sheepishly*): It's a little difficult to explain. Kevin — er — Mr. Layton proposed to me.

SENATOR: He's your accomplice!

BIXBY (*Enraged*): Layton, Cosmac doesn't pay you to spend your time proposing to young women. You're fired!

KEVIN: But, Mr. Bixby —

JANET (*Angrily*): Mr. Bixby, Kevin created Tom. If it weren't for Kevin, your company wouldn't be in this competition today.

BIXBY (*Sputtering*): You — you are an insolent young lady.

JANET: And you are an old goat!

KEVIN: Please, Janet. (*To* BIXBY) She didn't mean it. Why, you're not old at all.

BIXBY: Are you implying that I am a goat?

ROBOT TOM (*Bleeping*): Baaaa! (BIXBY *waves his fist at* TOM, *turns to* KEVIN.)

BIXBY: And I suppose you programmed this hunk of junk to insult me?

KEVIN (*Weakly*): No, no, Mr. Bixby. That was a technical sound, a form of micro-electronic feedback.

BIXBY: Do you expect me to believe that? (KEVIN *fumbles with* TOM's *control box.*)

KEVIN: Here! I'll show you! (*While he makes the adjustment, there is a sudden bleep.* KEVIN *freezes, then turns, smiling foolishly.*)

MABEL: Oh, no! Kevin has that look in his eyes again.

JANET: The electrical feedback has taken him over again. (KEVIN *embraces* SENATOR *and kisses her.*)

KEVIN: My beloved! Let us go to the investigating committee together!

SENATOR (*Protesting*): Help! (*She pushes* KEVIN *away.*) This young man is stark, raving mad.

KEVIN: Senator, you can throw your hat into my ring anytime.

BIXBY (*Slapping forehead*): My company is ruined! Kevin, I've decided not to fire you. I'll kill you on the spot! (*He chases* KEVIN *around stage.*)

SENATOR: Someone should stop this. Call the police! Call the Army! Call the Marines!

JANET (*Protesting*): You don't understand! Kevin is suffering from robot prostration. He doesn't know what he's doing. The robot's carrier station has affected his brain. (BIXBY *stops chasing* KEVIN.)

BIXBY: What brain?

JANET: Kevin will be all right in a few minutes, Mr. Bixby. He'll be the same as before.

BIXBY: That's what worries me. (KEVIN *shakes his head, brushes his hand across his eyes.*)

KEVIN (*Dazed*): What — what happened? Where am I?

JANET (*Softly*): You're at the computer exhibition.

KEVIN: Did I have another electrical feedback? (JANET *nods.*)

JANET: It was Senator Wheeler this time.

KEVIN (*Sadly*): I'm getting worse! (SENATOR *stamps angrily.*)

SENATOR: These people are out to ruin my political career. (*To* BIXBY) Your company will hear from my lawyer in the morning! I'm going to organize a committee to investigate incorrigible computers. (MARK *pats* ROBOT FORTRAN *on the back.*)

MARK (*Happily*): With Kevin and Janet in trouble, we're bound to win the competition! (GUIDE *joins* MARK.)

GUIDE: That's right, young man. Senator Wheeler will have little choice but to recommend Robot Fortran to the Energy Commission. Now, may we see another demonstration of Fortran's amazing mathematical genius? (MARK *makes a quick adjustment on* ROBOT FORTRAN*'s control box.* ROBOT FORTRAN *bleeps, addresses Spectators.*)

ROBOT FORTRAN: Two and two is five! One and one is eight. Three and three is seven and one-half. (*Everyone registers consternation.* MARK *works frenziedly with the control box.*)

MARK (*Struggling*): Something has gone wrong with Robot Fortran's serial memory and stack pointer. The synchronous operating is not designating a high-level language. (MARK *points at* KEVIN.) I think you're responsible for this. Your electric feedback must have destroyed Fortran's index register. (*To* BIXBY) I'm going to suggest that we sue your company!

BIXBY (*Wailing*): Two lawsuits in one afternoon! (BIXBY *turns, gestures at* KEVIN *and* TOM.) Get out — and take that sensitized hunk of junk with you!

KEVIN (*Suddenly*): Tom is not a hunk of junk — he's a hexadecimal computer and you have no right to call him names.

JANET: That's telling him, Kevin. I have so much confidence in both of you! (*Quickly*) You have proven you're not afraid. You were able to stand up to Mr. Bixby.

BIXBY (*Waving fists*): He won't be standing very long.

KEVIN (*To* BIXBY): I don't care what you do to me. (*To* JANET) You've been great, Janet. I should have been proposing to you all the time.

JANET: Do you really mean that? (KEVIN *nods*. SENATOR *gestures dramatically.*)

SENATOR: Enough of this foolishness. Where is the missing top-secret manual? Has anyone phoned the authorities?

JANET (*Brightly*): We might be able to solve this mystery ourselves. (*To* MABEL) You brought a manual to Kevin a little while ago.

MABEL: That's right, but —

ATTENDANT: I saw Mabel take a manual from the library.

MABEL (*Insistently*): It was Tom's manual — the Terminal Operations Memory guide.

JANET: Is it possible that you might have taken the wrong guide? Do you think you might have confused it with T.I.M. — Technical Investigation Modulation?

MABEL: I don't think so. (*Thoughtfully*) Both manuals were kept on the same shelf. (MABEL *shakes her head.*) I don't know.

JANET (*Happily*): But there is someone who will know. Robot Alice!

GUIDE: The computer that cannot tell a lie. (JANET *adjusts* ROBOT ALICE*'s control box.*)

JANET: Alice, have you seen the missing top-secret manual?

ROBOT ALICE: The manual was in this room.

JANET: Did someone take the manual?

ROBOT ALICE (*Bleeping*): After Tom examined the manual, he put it on the table. (ROBOT ALICE *turns mechanically, points at table, left.*)

JANET: This is terribly important, Alice. Who took the manual?

ROBOT ALICE: One of the spectators took it.

JANET: Which spectator?

ROBOT ALICE: She is gone now. You will never see her again.

JANET (*Pleading*): But we must find her. What did she do with the manual?

ROBOT ALICE: She is going to use the pages to line her bird-cage. (*Spectators register surprise.* SENATOR *swoons in* BIXBY*'s arms.*)

GUIDE (*At mike*): This is a national catastrophe, ladies and gentlemen! The top-secret national energy program has been destroyed!

2ND MAN: Where will I get gas to operate my lawn mower?

2ND WOMAN: Where will I get power to run my hair dryer? (*General confusion follows.* KEVIN *waves everyone to silence.*)

KEVIN: Wait, everyone. I think Robot Tom might solve the problem. (*To* ROBOT ALICE) Did you say that Tom examined the manual?

ROBOT ALICE: That is correct.

KEVIN: Then it's possible that he memorized its contents! Remember, Tom has an infinite memory unit. (KEVIN *adjusts* ROBOT TOM*'s control box.*) Tom, have you examined the Technical Investigation Modulation guide?

ROBOT TOM: Bleep — yes! I will recite the manual for you. Page one, chapter one, paragraph one. The contents of this manual are of primary importance to the welfare of our nation in its program for environmental survival. Certain life styles will be changed and — (ROBOT TOM *continues to recite in pantomime as everyone crowds around.* SENATOR *is revived, listens intently.*)

GUIDE: Our energy program is saved! Tom — the Terminal Operations Memory — has recorded the entire guide in his memory box! (*Everyone shouts approval.*)

SENATOR: Are we certain that the robot's information is accurate?

KEVIN (*Proudly*): Ask him anything. (SENATOR *addresses* TOM.)

SENATOR: How long will our total supply of oil last?

ROBOT TOM: The world supply of oil will be depleted in twenty-nine years, including 207 gallons of gas in an Exxon station in Biloxi, Mississippi.

SENATOR: Will our country find a new supply of power?

ROBOT TOM: Our future will be assured if we investigate solar energy and water power from tidal changes.

SENATOR: Incredible! Tom has memorized the entire manual. (*To* TOM) How can we control the tides as a source of energy?

ROBOT TOM: Harnessed ocean tides can supply power to the entire coast of North America with no pollution for five million years. Bleep! Chapter two, paragraph one — (KEVIN *turns a dial on* ROBOT TOM*'s control box.* TOM *is immobile.*)

KEVIN: I hope that Tom has convinced you.

BIXBY (*Happily*): My boy, that robot of yours has saved our country! And it hasn't hurt my business, either.

KEVIN: One minute, Mr. Bixby. You fired me, and you disowned Tom.

BIXBY: I didn't mean it. I'll rehire you — and double your salary.

JANET: How about tripling it?

BIXBY: Anything! Anything! (*Dreamily*) Oh, I love computers!

SENATOR (*To* KEVIN): You're about to be a famous man. (*To Spectators*) It is my judgment that Robot Tom — Terminal Operations Memory — is the winner of the World Microcomputer Competition. (*Everyone cheers.*)

GUIDE (*At mike*): Make way for Robot Tom. (*He gestures right.*) The press and the world are waiting! (MARK *sighs, addresses* ROBOT FORTRAN.)

MARK: I guess it's the atomic scrap heap for both of us. (MABEL *takes* MARK *and* ROBOT FORTRAN *by the arms.*)

MABEL: Not until after our date. And to cheer you up, I'm taking both of you for a hamburger! (ROBOT FORTRAN *emits a series of bleeps and exits with* MABEL *and* MARK.)

JANET (*Happily*): Oh, Kevin! You and Robot Tom are the most famous people in the country.

KEVIN: You and Robot Alice are sharing the honors with us. (*He points at* ROBOT TOM *and* ROBOT ALICE.) If they weren't robots, I'd swear they were meant for each other.

JANET (*Laughing*): That's perfectly ridiculous! How could two robots fall in love?

ROBOT ALICE (*Mechanically*): Linkage Object Velocity Energizer!

ROBOT TOM: Bleep! Bleep!

KEVIN: And that spells love in any language! (*He hugs* JANET. ROBOT TOM *kisses* ROBOT ALICE, *and she emits a series of bleeps. Quick curtain.*)

THE END

The Romantic Robots

Characters: 8 male; 7 female; extras for Spectators.

Playing Time: 35 minutes.

Costumes: Modern, everyday dress. Mark, Janet and Kevin wear white lab coats over business suits. Fortran, Alice and Tom are dressed as robots, and each has a control box, with dials, knobs and buttons on it, around the neck or on front of costume. Fortran and Tom wear jump suits in metallic tones. Fortran's suit has mathematical symbols on it, and Tom's is covered with lightning bolts. Alice wears a dress with a mini-skirt, and has exaggerated, doll-like makeup. Senator Wheeler has a large hat. Guide and Attendant wear dark suits.

Properties: Cordless microphone, screwdriver, manual.

Setting: Exhibit room. Down right is a sign reading: COMPU-LOOP PRESENTS FORTRAN, THE MATHEMATICAL WIZARD. Down center is a large poster reading INTEREL INTRODUCES ALICE — ACCUMULATOR LINE INTERPRETER CYCLE ENERGIZER. Down left is a poster reading: COSMAC'S NEW MODEL, TOM — TERMINAL OPERATIONS MEMORY. There are chairs and small tables in each of the sections.

Lighting: No special effects.

A Case for Two Spies

Who is the better man to search for the missing plans? Willard Willingham, gentleman spy? Or Agent 145-½, tough secret agent?

Characters

ANNOUNCER
WILLARD WILLINGHAM
AGENT 145½
UNDERCOVER AGENT
BILLY, *a ten-year-old boy*
MAID
PROPRIETOR
PROFESSOR FIGTREE
LOIS, *his daughter*
MRS. CLATTER
GERTRUDE

SCENE 1

BEFORE RISE: ANNOUNCER *enters in front of curtain and addresses audience.*

ANNOUNCER: Ladies and gentlemen, we have a rare treat for you today. We are about to present a spy drama! (*Rubs his hands together eagerly*) As a matter of fact, we are going to present *two* spy dramas — and two classic spies. Now, here's the situation: Vital international plans have been stolen. One solution to the case will be offered by a debo-

nair, sophisticated spy of the old school, Willard Willingham. The second solution will come from a modern spy —
Agent 145½. We wanted a more impressive number for him,
but all the others have been used for zip codes. (*Curtains
open.*)

* * *

SETTING: *Whispering Winds Lodge, a shabby hotel that has
seen better days. At rear is a huge wardrobe cabinet with a
false back. Chairs and tables are placed around the room.*

AT RISE: *On a couch downstage* UNDERCOVER AGENT *is sleeping, covered by several blankets.* ANNOUNCER *walks to
couch, begins to remove blankets, one by one.*

ANNOUNCER: This is what is commonly known as an undercover agent. He has nothing to do with the play, but we
thought you might like to meet another type of spy. (UNDER-
COVER AGENT *gets up, takes blankets, scowls at* ANNOUNCER,
and exits.) And this is our setting —Whispering Winds
Lodge. The only trouble is, the winds whisper through the
cracks in the wall. (*He shivers, turns up his coat collar.*) It's
late evening, and there is a howling storm outside. (BILLY,
a small boy, rushes onstage, shoots ANNOUNCER *in the face
with a water pistol, and exits.* ANNOUNCER *takes out his
handkerchief, wipes his face.*) That was Billy, one of the
more impulsive members of our cast. We wanted to have a
rainfall at this point, but with our budget, that was the best
we could do. (*With a flourish*) But now, let the play begin!
(ANNOUNCER *exits right. Thunder is heard from offstage.*
MAID, *in uniform, enters left, glances around, removes envelope from table drawer, left, quickly places it in desk
drawer, right, exits left.* PROPRIETOR *enters right, wearing
yellow slicker. He removes envelope from desk drawer, returns it to table drawer, left, exits right.* MAID *re-enters, takes*

envelope from table drawer, hides it in desk drawer right and exits left. PROPRIETOR *re-enters and removes envelope from desk drawer.* ANNOUNCER *rushes in*, right, *grabs* PRO-PRIETOR, *shakes him roughly.*) Keep your hands off that envelope! (*Addresses audience*) This hide-and-seek bit was introduced to build up suspense — but this ham is overdoing it! (*He shakes his head.*) I have more trouble with this cast! (*He drops envelope into table drawer.* ANNOUNCER *and* PROPRIETOR *exit left. Thunder is heard again.* LOIS *and* WILLARD *enter right. They both wear coats which they remove, place on sofa.* LOIS *glances around, shudders.*)

LOIS: What a lonely place!

WILLARD (*With a superior air*): I couldn't agree more, Miss Figtree. If your father had to disappear, why couldn't he have chosen a more cheerful spot? (*Sighs*) Ah, well! One must take the bitter with the sweet. Now, if you'll tell me briefly what this is all about—

LOIS: It's so good of you to help me, Mr. Willingham.

WILLARD (*Gallantly*): It's nothing, my dear.

LOIS: But you're such a famous spy!

WILLARD (*Slightly bored*): Oh, it's nothing, my dear.

LOIS: You are going to put your great mind to work for me!

WILLARD (*Insistently*): It is nothing, my dear! (*He frowns.*) Somehow, I don't like that line. (*Quickly*) Now, Miss Figtree, you are the daughter of that famed scientist, Professor Figtree, right?

LOIS (*Nodding*): Yes. Daddy had just perfected a new formula so revolutionary that he wouldn't even tell me about it.

WILLARD: You and your father escaped from an unfriendly country with the secret formula, and then came to the Whispering Winds Lodge, didn't you?

LOIS: Yes. An airplane was going to take us away tomorrow. I — I went to Daddy's room about an hour ago and knocked. There was no answer. I opened the door — and Daddy was gone! (*She falls onto* WILLARD*'s shoulder, sobs. Firmly, he pushes her away, sniffs delicately at flower in his buttonhole.*)

WILLARD: Please! You bruised my bachelor's button!

LOIS (*Wringing her hands*): I — I didn't know what to do. I searched everywhere, but I couldn't find Daddy.

WILLARD: Did you look for the secret plans?

LOIS (*Nodding*): They weren't in his room. Someone had stolen them! And Daddy — oh, I'm so frightened!

WILLARD (*Gallantly*): Fear not! Willard Willingham — gentleman spy and international celebrity — will find your father. Ah, yes! You did a wise thing to come to my estate to solicit my aid. (*Looks around*) Who's in charge of this lodge?

LOIS: It's run by a strange man who always wears a yellow slicker.

WILLARD: At Whispering Winds, that must be formal dress. But enough! We'd better question the proprietor. Did your father have any enemies?

LOIS: Oh, no! Why, everyone loved Daddy. (*As* LOIS *talks, she walks up center, stands directly in front of large wardrobe cabinet.*) Of course, he was shot at a few times, someone once slipped poison into his coffee, and twice a bomb was planted in his car — but enemies, no! (*Behind* LOIS *the wardrobe door suddenly swings open.* PROPRIETOR, *inside wardrobe, grabs* LOIS, *putting his hand over her mouth, and pulls her into wardrobe with him, closing door.* WILLARD *does not notice.*)

WILLARD: Just an all-around popular guy. (*He turns, looks for* LOIS, *calls.*) Miss Figtree! Lois! Where are you? (*He begins tapping on walls, looking for secret panel.* MRS. CLATTER *enters right. She carries a baby wrapped in a blanket.*)

MRS. CLATTER: Gracious, I can't find my little boy. That child! (*To* WILLARD) Have you seen my Billy?

WILLARD: No, madam, and I hope it will remain a pleasure deferred. Who are you?

MRS. CLATTER: I am Mrs. Clatter, and this is my baby, Prudence. But Billy — he's always running off.

WILLARD (*Suspiciously*): Do you know Professor Figtree?

MRS. CLATTER: Figtree? Now, let me see. (*Ponders*) No, I don't believe I've met him. But there was a family named Appletree back home. Oh, such nice people! She was, at least. But take him. Well, Mr. Appletree might have been some people's dish of tea, but I never trusted him. Shifty eyes, you know. Poor dear — I mean Mrs. Appletree. She told everyone that her husband was an expert in frozen assets, but I knew he drove an ice truck. (WILLARD *covers his ears, cringes.*)

WILLARD: Please, madam —

MRS. CLATTER (*Rattling on*): And Mrs. Appletree had the sweetest aunt who lived in one of those New England towns. One of those old, creaky places — and so was Auntie. She had lumbago. (*During her monologue,* WILLARD *leads* MRS. CLATTER *directly in front of wardrobe. She faces audience, continues talking.*) And those wretched doctors couldn't do a thing for the pain. The lumbago, I mean. And — (PROPRIETOR *quickly opens wardrobe door, pulls* MRS. CLATTER *inside, closes door.* WILLARD *dusts off his hands, returns down center, addresses audience.*)

WILLARD: You didn't think I knew about that secret hiding place, did you? I'm not a spy for nothing. I know every spy drama has at least one secret hiding place. (*Footsteps are heard from offstage.*) Hark! I hear the patter of little feet! I'll slip behind this hideous chair and spy on the intruder. After all, I am a spy. (WILLARD *quickly hides behind chair, down right.* MAID *enters, glances around, removes envelope from table, left.* WILLARD *quickly steps out, grabs her arm, spins her around.*) Aha! Caught with the goods!

MAID: No!

WILLARD: You'd better tell the truth, my good woman.

MAID: I haven't done a thing!

WILLARD: You're a spy!

MAID: No!

WILLARD (*Pointing to envelope*): And you stole those secret plans from Professor Figtree's room.

MAID: That's not true.

WILLARD: Where is the Professor?

MAID: Maybe he's watching his favorite TV show.

WILLARD: You can't trick me like that. Give me that envelope.

MAID (*Terrified*): No!

WILLARD: Are those the secret plans?

MAID: No, no! It's something better than that. Something more valuable. My autographed picture of John Wayne! (*She nods defiantly at* WILLARD, *exits left.*)

WILLARD: This is a great cast, all right! (BILLY *enters right.*)

BILLY: Have you seen my mom?

WILLARD: If you're referring to a walking tape recorder — yes!

BILLY: I'll teach you to talk about my mom like that. (*He kicks* WILLARD *in the shin.* WILLARD *hops around in pain, holding his leg.* BILLY *claps his hands in time to* WILLARD*'s hopping.*) Hey, you're pretty good! I'll bet you can dance a mean bunny hop! (WILLARD *stops hopping.*)

WILLARD: If you'll be a good boy, I'll take you to your mother.

BILLY (*Menacingly*): You'd better — if you know what's good for you. (*He draws back foot as if to kick again.* WILLARD *quickly leads him to wardrobe and knocks on door.* PROPRIETOR *opens door, pulls* BILLY *into wardrobe, closes door.* WILLARD *crosses down center.*)

WILLARD: Dear child! He should definitely be *not* seen and *not* heard! (PROPRIETOR *opens wardrobe door, steps out, closes door, and joins* WILLARD *downstage.*)

PROPRIETOR: Welcome! Welcome to Whispering Winds Lodge!

WILLARD: Just a minute. Who are you?

PROPRIETOR: I am the owner of this place.

WILLARD (*Sadly*): You have my sympathy. (*Quickly*) Where is Professor Figtree?

PROPRIETOR (*Frightened*): I — I can't tell you now.

WILLARD: Why can't you tell me? (*Coldly*) I'll give you exactly ten seconds to tell me what you've done to the Professor.

PROPRIETOR: I — I won't tell you!

WILLARD (*Angrily*): Why not?

PROPRIETOR (*Haughtily*): Because if I tell you now, it will be the end of the play! (*He walks up center, steps into wardrobe, closes door.*)

WILLARD (*Gesturing*): You know — it must be getting beastly crowded in that secret hiding place. (*He stealthily approaches wardrobe.*) Come out with your hands up! (*Pauses*) Please! (*Addresses audience*) I must remember I'm a gentleman! (LOIS *and* PROFESSOR *step out of wardrobe, close door.* LOIS *helps* PROFESSOR *to sofa, down center.*)

LOIS: Oh, Daddy, Daddy! What have they done to you?

WILLARD: Is this your father?

LOIS (*Nodding*): Yes. Someone grabbed me a few minutes ago, and pulled me out of this room. I didn't know what to do. I stumbled down a dark hallway until I found Daddy. (*Points to wardrobe*). He was a prisoner in there.

PROFESSOR: The secret plans —

WILLARD: I'm afraid they're still missing, Professor.

PROFESSOR: Then all is lost. I can't leave here until I find those plans.

LOIS: No, we must leave — forget the plans!

WILLARD (*Shocked*): What — and ruin our play? (*Gallantly*) Fear not! Willard Willingham, master spy, knows who stole the plans and how it was done.

LOIS: Brilliant!

PROFESSOR: Astounding!

WILLARD: I am going to apprehend the criminals now. They are about to enter this room!

PROFESSOR: But how can you possibly know these things?

WILLARD: I wrote this play, that's how! (PROPRIETOR, MRS. CLATTER, *carrying baby, and* BILLY *enter from wardrobe.* MRS. CLATTER *storms indignantly up to* WILLARD.)

MRS. CLATTER: Oh, you terrible man. Putting me in that dreadful place! (*Gestures towards wardrobe*)

BILLY: Shall I kick him again, huh, Mom?

MRS. CLATTER: No, Billy, we're leaving this lodge at once. (*To baby*) Oh, my poor little Prudence!

PROPRIETOR (*Slapping forehead*): Customers, customers! (*He exits left.*)

WILLARD: Enough! (*To* MRS. CLATTER) There's only one place you are going, madam! I'm delivering you to the authorities. You kidnapped Professor Figtree and stole the secret plans.

LOIS: I can't believe it! Not this sweet little woman and her precious children.

WILLARD: This sweet little woman is better known to the International Police as Shady Flo from Kokomo! She is a ruthless foreign spy.

MRS. CLATTER (*Innocently*): Why, I never! (WILLARD *grabs baby from her. He removes blanket, holds up doll and small transistor radio.*)

PROFESSOR: It's a doll!

WILLARD: A very special doll. This "baby" is a combination minicomputer and CB radio, capable of performing logarithms, decoding secret formulas, and communicating with conspirators up to a twenty-mile radius!

BILLY (*Gruffly*): The jig's up, Flo! (WILLARD *quickly drops doll and radio on sofa, grabs* BILLY.)

MRS. CLATTER: Leave my dear little boy alone! (WILLARD

quickly takes a cigar from BILLY*'s inner pocket, holds it up.*)

LOIS (*Surprised*): A — a cigar!

WILLARD: This "little boy" is actually thirty-six years old. He's merely small for his age. He's known as Chicago Charlie — and he's Flo's accomplice.

LOIS: Oh, no!

WILLARD: Chicago Charlie gave himself away a few minutes ago. When he kicked me, he mentioned the bunny hop — a dance that was popular twenty years ago! I knew no child would remember the bunny hop.

PROFESSOR: Amazing!

WILLARD: A thorough search should reveal the missing plans to be in Shady Flo's room.

BILLY (*Gruffly*): Curses!

MRS. CLATTER (*Sighing*): I guess I'd better confess — I'm Shady Flo from Kokomo. (*To* WILLARD) But there's one thing you didn't count on.

WILLARD: Yes, madam?

MRS. CLATTER: I didn't finish telling you about the Appletree family. Now, once Mrs. Appletree visited her aunt in New England, and — (WILLARD *collapses on sofa. Curtain.*)

*   *   *   *   *

SCENE 2

BEFORE RISE: ANNOUNCER *enters in front of curtain.*

ANNOUNCER: Now you have met Willard Willingham, the debonair agent — but times have changed since the days of the gentleman spy. We are now going to see the case of the missing plans as solved by Agent 145½. His method is unique, his manner is different but, somehow, his acting is just as miserable as Willard's was. We will not keep you waiting a moment longer, dear audience. We know you are waiting with bated breath, pounding heart and throbbing pulse for the drama to unfold. Furthermore, those seats out there are probably very uncomfortable. (*He exits. Curtains open.*)

* * *

SETTING: *The same as Scene 1.*

AT RISE: LOIS *sits on couch, center, wringing her hands, an anxious expression on her face. Suddenly,* AGENT 145½ *enters. He wears a trench coat, slouch hat, and fashionable suit.* LOIS *jumps up.*

LOIS: You — you are —

AGENT (*Doffing hat*): Agent 145½, at your service! Intrigue is my specialty.

LOIS: A mutual friend told me that you might come to Whispering Winds Lodge.

AGENT (*Nodding*): Agent ABC got the message and relayed it to Counter Agent QXD. QXD met Agent XYZ in a secret mountain retreat and passed the message to Agent BGU. Agent BGU ran into trouble and was found nearly dead in an alley, but before he passed on to his reward, he mumbled the message to my special deputy, Agent LPO. LPO met me in a Paris café and delivered the message to me.

LOIS: Gracious! Wouldn't it have been easier for Agent ABC to telephone you in the first place?

AGENT: What? And ruin all that suspense? (*Dramatically*) Fortune has sent me to Whispering Winds Lodge tonight.

LOIS: You poor man! You look so tired. You must have had a terrible journey.

AGENT (*Shrugging*): I was captured by that sinister arch-plotter, Dr. Moo-Goo-Guy-Pan. I broke into his hideout, but was captured by one of his guards. He overpowered me and threw me into a pool with a giant octopus. I fought a life-or-death battle, killed the octopus, and escaped.

LOIS: That's hard to believe! (AGENT *removes his coat, revealing a long white "octopus tentacle" wound round his waist. He unwinds it, drops it.*)

AGENT: What do you think this is — a Christmas ornament? It was a real octopus, all right. (*Quickly*) But what can I do for you? (*He looks at her closely, nods approvingly.*) Better still, what can you do for me?

LOIS: Please, I'm in terrible trouble.

AGENT: Trouble is my middle name.

LOIS (*Surprised*): Really? I thought it was Marvin.

AGENT (*Angrily*): Who writes your lines?

LOIS (*Wringing hands*): My father is a famous scientist. We escaped from an unfriendly country with his secret plans, and —

AGENT: And your Daddy disappeared from this miserable lodge — and the plans with him.

LOIS: How do you know?

AGENT: Because it's always like that. (*In choked tones*) Why can't I meet a nice girl in an amusement park, or on a bus, or feeding pigeons in the park? Why — why does it always have to be missing plans, bubbling vats of acid, and laser guns? (*Hysterically*) Why? Why? Why?

LOIS (*Comfortingly*): Oh, please don't take on so. After all, you've met me — and I'm a girl.

AGENT (*Sobering*): Well, I didn't think you played third base for the Boston Red Sox. (*Sighs*) But I'm resigned to my fate as a secret agent. I'll rescue your father, find the missing plans, and probably wind up marrying you. (*Looking around suspiciously*) But we must be careful. Frankly, I suspect that the leader of the GOONS is here right now!

LOIS: The GOONS?

AGENT: Yes — the Government Organization of Nefarious Spies! I've been after them for years. I finally rounded up all the members, but the leader escaped me — until now. The biggest GOON of all is at Whispering Winds!

LOIS: But what are we going to do?

AGENT: I'm going to round up all the suspects and make them tell the truth.

LOIS: Well, there aren't too many people at Whispering Winds. Just the proprietor and a maid.

AGENT: Anyone else?

LOIS: Well, just one other girl. She's very plain, and not too young. (GERTRUDE *enters right. She is a glamorous, slinky type in an exotic gown. She slinks past* AGENT *and smiles, waving her hand invitingly. She has long, brightly-painted fingernails.*)

AGENT: How do you do?

GERTRUDE (*Coyly*): I do all right.

LOIS (*Nervously*): This is the girl I told you about. The plain, middle-aged one. A teacher, I think.

AGENT (*To* GERTRUDE): Are you a teacher?

GERTRUDE: That's right.

AGENT (*Singing loudly*): School days, school days! (*Suddenly*) What am I doing? I can't be tricked! (*Businesslike*) What's your name?

GERTRUDE (*Waving her hand*): My name is Gertrude Gorgeous. My friends call me Gertie.

AGENT: What are you doing in this place?

GERTRUDE: I came here on vacation. (AGENT *takes pad and pencil from pocket, jots down her answers.*)

AGENT: Where do you live?

GERTRUDE: In the city.

AGENT: How long are you going to stay here?

GERTRUDE: Only a few days. My vacation is almost over.

AGENT: Are you going home then? (GERTRUDE *nods.*) I have to have all the details. What's your address?

GERTRUDE: 374 Belmont Avenue.

AGENT: What's your telephone number?

GERTRUDE: 232-7546.

AGENT: What are you doing next Saturday night?

GERTRUDE: Nothing, so far. I lead a very lonely life. (*Sighs*) Do you have any suggestions?

AGENT (*Suddenly*): What did you do with Professor Figtree's plans?

GERTRUDE: I don't know what you're talking about. I never took anybody's plans.

AGENT: I could lend you some of mine. (LOIS *nudges him.*)

LOIS: Please keep your mind on your work.

AGENT: Oh, but I am! (*Points to* GERTRUDE) Are you a GOON? (*She slaps his face, exits left.* AGENT *rubs his face.*) I lose more friends that way! Oh, this is a tought racket, all right.

LOIS: I'd better get the others, so you can continue your — er — investigation.

AGENT: That can wait. Tell me something about your father's secret invention.

LOIS: It would revolutionize the world.

AGENT: As simple as that?

LOIS (*Nodding*): It's an amazing new plastic derivative. It seals bullet holes in tanks, submarines, rockets and missiles. It's also a wonderful paint remover.

AGENT: Amazing! I can see the possibilities. But if it fell into the wrong hands — (*He extends his right hand dramatically, palm upward.* BILLY *rushes in right with raw egg. He breaks egg, drops it into* AGENT*'s hand. He sticks out his tongue, exits.* AGENT *examines mess in hand, dumps it into ashtray on desk, wipes hand with handkerchief.*) Oh, how I wish his father weren't the producer of this play!

LOIS: I'm afraid we're wasting too much time. (*Sobbing*) Oh, my Daddy!

AGENT: Don't worry, I'll find your daddy, and his amazing paint remover, too. (LOIS *smiles weakly, exits left.* AGENT *searches room. He opens desk drawer, right, takes out a booklet, examines it.*) Ah, a brilliant discovery! This must be the solution to Einstein's theory of relativity. (*He looks at cover of booklet.*) Ooops, my mistake! It's the latest government income tax regulations! (PROPRIETOR *sneaks in right, carrying a water pistol. He creeps up behind* AGENT, *shoves gun into his back.*)

PROPRIETOR: Reach for the sky!

AGENT (*Turning*): Oh, come now! We can be more original than that.

PROPRIETOR (*Menacingly*): Why did you turn around?

AGENT: I always like to see who's going to shoot me.

PROPRIETOR: You've interfered with the GOONS long enough.

AGENT: Are you a GOON?

PROPRIETOR: Yes, but it won't do you any good to know that now. The master GOON and I are going to start another international organization, and you won't stop us this time. (*He steps back, levels gun, shoots water into* AGENT*'s face.* PROPRIETOR *throws gun aside, stamps angrily.*) Darn that prop man! He's always messing up my big scene. (AGENT *quickly grabs* PROPRIETOR*'s arm.*)

AGENT: All right, start talking.

PROPRIETOR: No — my mother always taught me not to talk to strangers.

AGENT: Who is the head of the GOONS?

PROPRIETOR: I can't tell you. I'd be killed.

AGENT: Do business with me, and I'll get you off easy. Maybe a firing squad, or something quick.

PROPRIETOR: You'll help me? (AGENT *nods.*) Then I'll tell you. The head of the GOONS is — (*Lights go out. Gunfire is heard. Lights go on again.* PROPRIETOR *lies on floor.* LOIS *rushes in.*)

AGENT (*Shrugging*): Well, there goes my case. (*He drops to knees, examines* PROPRIETOR.) This guy was about to name the head of the GOONS, but somebody shot him.

LOIS: Are you sure?

AGENT: That isn't cross ventilation in his coat. (*Stands*) Did you see anyone in the hall?

LOIS (*Shaking head*): I was upstairs. The others will be here in a minute.

AGENT: I should get the body out of here.

LOIS: Why?

AGENT: He's a miserable actor. He'll probably sneeze or something. (GERTRUDE *and* MAID *enter.*)

GERTRUDE: We heard a shot. (*She sees* PROPRIETOR, *screams.*) It's the owner of the lodge!

MAID (*Happily*): Goody! Now I won't have to dust tomorrow.

LOIS: Someone killed him just as he was about to name the person who kidnapped my daddy and stole the secret plans. And that someone is in this room!

AGENT: Hey! I'm supposed to solve this case. You're stealing my lines. (*Authoritatively*) And that someone is in this room!

LOIS: Who can it be?

AGENT: Maybe Gertrude Gorgeous can tell us a few things. (*Points finger at* GERTRUDE) You're an international spy, mastermind of the GOONS!

GERTRUDE (*Waving her hand*): Ridiculous! Why would I steal Professor Figtree's formula?

AGENT: That's just the point. You had to have the formula at any cost. (*He grabs her right hand, shows her bright red fingernails.*) Your fingernail polish! You're wearing Wicked Moment Red.

LOIS: What does that prove?

AGENT: Everyone knows that Fabulous Frenzy is all the rage this year. Gertrude had to remove the Wicked Moment at all cost. (*To* LOIS) And your daddy's formula is known to be a wonderful paint remover! (GERTRUDE *pulls away.*)

GERTRUDE: All right, I stole the formula, but you'll never capture me. Gertrude Gorgeous is too clever for all of you. (*She opens purse, takes out small bottle filled with liquid. She waves it threateningly.*) This bottle contains TNT. (*Triumphantly*) Agent 145½, you have captured your last GOON. When I drop this bottle, this lodge — and everyone in it — will be blown to smithereens.

LOIS: Oh, no!

MAID (*Sadly*): Now I'll have to dust tomorrow, after all.

GERTRUDE: And now, goodbye! (*She hurls bottle against sofa. She stares at it puzzledly, picks it up, unscrews cap, dips finger into bottle, tastes it.*) Water! (*Angrily*) Oh, that property man!

PROPRIETOR (*Sitting up*): I told you he was a rat! (*He reassumes "dead" position.* AGENT *grabs* GERTRUDE's *arm.*)

AGENT: Agent 145½ has triumphed again! (BILLY *rushes in, kicks* AGENT *in shin, exits right with* GERTRUDE.)

LOIS (*Happily*): Oh, my hero! (*She falls into* AGENT's *arms.*)

AGENT (*Stepping back*): I don't have time for sweet talk now. I'm off on another dangerous mission — the trail of the mastermind of a bunch of cutthroats who call themselves the RATS!

LOIS: Who are the RATS?

AGENT (*Solemnly*): The Revolutionary Association of Terrible Spies.

LOIS: Oh, be careful, my dearest. This may be dangerous.

AGENT (*Yawning*): It'll be a routine case for me. A crumbling castle, a damsel in distress, a pit of poisonous snakes, a battle with a man-eating shark. I'm bored already.

LOIS (*Suddenly*): What about my Daddy? You haven't rescued my poor, kidnapped Daddy. (AGENT *points to audience.*)

AGENT: If you look around, you'll find him out there. He

wanted to see the play, and besides, he didn't have anything to do in this scene. (PROFESSOR, *in audience, stands, takes bow, sits. Quick curtain. After pause, curtain re-opens.* PROPRIETOR*'s body is gone.* ANNOUNCER *enters right, carrying an attaché case. He stands near chair, down right.* BILLY *is hidden behind the chair.*)

ANNOUNCER (*Cordially*): We hope you enjoyed our play, *A Case for Two Spies.* Willard Willingham and Agent 145½ solved the case to the satisfaction of all, but unfortunately, one detail was overlooked. Each solution was wrong! (*Pause*) Who stole the secret formula, you ask? (*Proudly*) I am the master spy! Yes, that's right. I stole Professor Figtree's plans and I am going to sell them to the highest bidder. (*Pause*) Where are the plans? Why, they're safe and sound in this case. *(Taps attaché case)* Yes, sir! Now that the plans are in my possession, no one will ever get them away from me. (*As he speaks,* BILLY *reaches out, opens catch on attaché case. It falls open, and* BILLY *quickly removes large Manila envelope reading* SECRET PLANS, *returns to hiding place.*) There has never been a counterspy who could steal my plans! (*He exits right with opened attaché case.* BILLY *quickly leaves his hiding place carrying Manila envelope, sticks out his tongue, exits left. Curtain.*)

THE END

Production Notes

A Case for Two Spies

Characters: 6 male; 4 female; 1 male or female for announcer.

Playing Time: 25 minutes.

Costumes: Appropriate everyday dress. Proprietor wears a bright yellow slicker. Willard wears a flower in his buttonhole. When they enter, Willard and Lois wear coats. Agent wears a trench coat, slouch hat, and fashionable suit. He wears a long white octopus tentacle around his waist under his coat. Maid is in uniform. Gertrude wears an attractive, alluring dress. Her fingernails are painted bright red. She carries a purse.

Properties: Blankets; water pistol; handkerchiefs for Announcer and Agent; doll in blanket, with radio attached, for Mrs. Clatter; white envelope; income tax booklet; green trading stamps; cigar; pad and pencil; raw egg; small bottle for Gertrude; attaché case containing Manila envelope reading, SECRET PLANS.

Setting: Whispering Winds Lodge, an old hotel with shabby furnishings. There is a desk with drawer and ash tray at right. A table with drawer is left. Overstuffed chair is down right, and sofa is down center. A large wardrobe with a false back is at rear. It is possible for actors to enter and exit through wardrobe. Other tables, chairs, lamps, etc., complete the furnishings.

Lighting: Blackout in Scene 2, as indicated in text.

Sound: Thunder; gunfire; as indicated in text.

The Dazzling Diamond Caper

A young couple searches for jewels worth half a million dollars, after a daring heist in a New York hotel. . . .

Characters

MARION, *an attractive young woman*
CINDY, *her friend*
JANE SIMMONS, *desk clerk*
HOTEL GUESTS, *extras*
MR. MASTERSON, *representative of "the System," a London diamond syndicate*
JOHNSON, *a wealthy New York jeweler*
HELEN MAXWELL, *Johnson's assistant*
TOM BUTLER, *Helen's fiancé*
FREDDIE SILVER, *a young man*
MR. FINLEY, *hotel manager*
BETTY PLANT, *hotel social director*
PARKER, *a super salesman*
MRS. PARKER, *his wife*
FLANNERY, *hotel detective*
THREE BELLHOPS, *extras*

TIME: *Evening.*

SETTING: *A divided stage, with the lobby of the Metropolitan, a large New York City hotel, on right half of stage. Entrance to lobby is at right, and entrance to elevators and stairs is up center. Down left is wall with working door to manager's office. Office furnished with desk, chairs, and telephone, is in left half of stage, and exposed front of office faces audience. Down right is booth with large poster reading,* WELCOME TO THE PACKAGERS' CONVENTION. *Up center is registration desk, with pen, cards, telephone, etc. on it. The lobby is furnished fashionably with chairs, rugs and flowers. Exit up left leads to other rooms in hotel.*

AT RISE: JANE SIMMONS *stands at registration desk, up center.* HOTEL GUESTS *mill around lobby, and* BELLHOPS *should simulate the constant activity of a busy hotel.* CINDY *and* MARION *enter right and go to demonstration booth.*

CINDY: Marion, this is our first product demonstration. I'm nervous!

MARION: Relax, Cindy. (*She gestures at* GUESTS *who gather around the booth.*) Here's our audience. (CINDY *strikes a dramatic pose, smiles at* GUESTS.)

CINDY: Welcome to the International Packagers' Convention at Hotel Metropolitan. We're here to show you how you can enjoy a better life through modern packaging. Slim-line design, easy-to-open products, freshness and purity from the plant to your home — through the miracle of packaging! (*She holds up box of* ZIPPOS.) This is a box of Zippos, your favorite breakfast treat. A cereal that is tummy in your yummy.

MARION (*Aside*): That's yummy in your tummy!

CINDY (*Nervously*): Why are Zippos always so delectable, so fresh? It's modern packaging that makes it possible. (*She taps the box top.*) Now, to open a box of Zippos, you merely find the little red tab and zip it around the top of the box. Zip! Zip! (*She examines the top of box, turns to* MARION.) Where is the little red tab?

MARION: I can never find the little red tab on these easy-to-open boxes.

CINDY (*To* GUESTS): Yes, folks, you merely run your little red fingernail around the top of Zippos. (*She does so, then looks at her hand in dismay.*) And you break your fingernail. (*Regaining composure*) The freshness stays in the box.

MARION (*Aside*): So does the cereal. You'd better use a knife. (CINDY *picks up a small knife.*)

CINDY (*To audience*): When you can't find the little red tab, use a handy knife to open the stay-fresh package. (*She jabs laboriously at the box top, and after a great effort, tears it off.*) The box is opened and — ah — there is a message on the flap. (*Reading*) "Open other end." (*She upends the box. Cereal pours out onto the booth.*) Good grief! (*Recovers*) Remember, enjoy modern living through modern packaging. (*She holds up another carton and struggles with the opening in pantomime throughout the next scene.* HELEN MAXWELL, TOM BUTLER *and* MR. MASTERSON *enter right.* MASTERSON *wears dark suit and has diamond ring on left hand. His hair is parted on side. He carries a suitcase and a black attaché case. They walk to the registration desk.* FREDDIE SILVER, *a young man in a black trench coat, enters right. There is a long scar on his right cheek. He carries an attaché case identical to* MASTERSON*'s.* FREDDIE *stands near the entrance, watching* MASTERSON *and the others at the registration desk.*)

MASTERSON (*To* JANE SIMMONS): You have a room reserved for me. T. J. Masterson, of London, England.

SIMMONS: Yes, sir. Welcome to the Hotel Metropolitan. I'm Jane Simmons, at your service. Will you register, please? (*She offers* MASTERSON *a pen.* MARION, *at the demonstrator's booth, looks up, watches the proceedings at the registration desk.* MASTERSON *puts his suitcase on the floor, leaves the attaché case on the registration desk, and begins to write. Quickly,* FREDDIE *walks to the registration desk, trips over* MASTERSON*'s suitcase.* FREDDIE *clutches at the registration desk for support, knocks* MASTERSON*'s attaché case to the floor. He falls to one knee, drops his own attaché case.*)

MASTERSON (*Turning*): I'm terribly sorry. I hope you're not hurt.

FREDDIE (*Still bending*): I'm all right. (*He picks up* MASTER-SON'*s attaché case, grips it tightly under his arm, and offers his attaché case to* MASTERSON. MASTERSON *takes the case, puts it on the desk, and helps* FREDDIE *to his feet.* FREDDIE *gestures at case on the desk.*) I hope I didn't break anything in your attaché case.

MASTERSON: No, no, I'm sure that nothing was broken. (FREDDIE, *carrying* MASTERSON'*s case, moves away from the desk, still observed by* MARION, *and mingles with* GUESTS. MASTERSON *nods to* HELEN *and* TOM.) An unfortunate accident. (*He signs the registration card.*)

SIMMONS: There's a message for you, Mr. Masterson. (*She thumbs through a sheaf of papers, hands him a note.* MAS-TERSON *reads the note.*)

MASTERSON (*To* HELEN): Helen, you'll be interested in this note. It's from Finley, the hotel manager. He says that your employer, Mr. Johnson, is here already. They're waiting for us in the coffee shop.

HELEN: Good. I'm eager to see those diamonds you brought to sell to our firm. (*Indicating* TOM) Tom would like to see what he's been protecting, too.

TOM: Yes, I would.

MASTERSON: You'll have to wait until later, Helen. I want to unpack them in my room first. (MASTERSON *wipes his brow.*) That man who tripped — he gave me quite a start. I traveled all the way from London with a half-million in cut diamonds, and I don't want to lose them in this hotel, just before the sale.

TOM (*Whistling*): A half-million in diamonds. I hope they're not damaged.

MASTERSON: No, they were packed securely. (1ST BELLHOP *crosses to them, takes suitcase and attaché case.* JANE SIMMONS *hands a key to* BELLHOP.)

SIMMONS: Room 1439 for Mr. Masterson. (BELLHOP *goes toward elevator, up center.* MARION *nudges* CINDY. *She points at* FREDDIE, *who stands in a group of* GUESTS.)

MARION (*Excited*): Cindy, that man! He deliberately switched attaché cases with the gentleman at the hotel desk.

CINDY: What man?

MARION: He's standing over there. He deliberately knocked the attaché case on the floor, and then handed the man one that he carried into the hotel. (FREDDIE *turns, faces the demonstrator's booth.* MARION *cringes.*) I don't want him to know that I saw him.

CINDY: People are always making mistakes with suitcases, Marion.

MARION: But I'm telling you he took it on purpose.

CINDY (*Sighing*): Look, Marion, I have enough troubles of my own, without worrying about a suitcase mixup. (*Several* GUESTS *cross to booth.* CINDY *holds up a box of crackers, smiles at* GUESTS. *Brightly*) This package of delicious crackers may not be easy to open, but the crunchy freshness is worth the effort. (*She pounds at box with small hammer, tears open the top, looks inside.*) And when the box is opened, you have some lovely cracker crumbs! (CINDY *continues to demonstrate packages in pantomime.* MASTERSON, *at hotel desk, turns to* HELEN *and* TOM.)

MASTERSON: Why don't you go to the coffee shop, Helen, and tell your employer that we're here. I'll join you and your brother later. So long, Tom. (*He nods to* TOM, *and exits up center with* BELLHOP, *who carries suitcase and attaché case.* FREDDIE *quickly follows them and exits up center.*)

TOM (*To* HELEN): Why does Masterson keep calling me your brother? What did you tell him, Helen?

HELEN: Please, Tom. I had to tell him you were my brother. He'd never tell a newspaper reporter about the Damocles Diamonds.

TOM: He's in for a shock when we announce our engagement.

HELEN: By then the diamonds will be safely sold and he won't care. Imagine! The famous Damocles Diamonds! A half-million dollars in perfectly matched stones.

TOM: Is that what your boss paid for them?

HELEN: Mr. Johnson is going to pay that amount tonight. He'll be able to resell them for well over a million. The Damocles are perfect stones, high in refractivity and dispersion.

TOM: Helen, watch your language! I usually cover homicides, not New York jewelers.

HELEN (*Proudly*): You'll have an exclusive this time, Tom.

TOM: And the byline, and a raise. (*He puts arm around* HELEN.) You're terrific, Helen, even if you are nuts about diamonds.

HELEN: But, I love working in the diamond industry. It's like stepping into another world!

TOM: O.K. Tell me more about the Damocles Diamonds.

HELEN: The System, the London syndicate that supplies most of the world's precious stones, is selling them. They were cut and polished in Amsterdam, and Mr. Masterson is responsible for delivering them to Mr. Johnson.

TOM: Seems risky. Shouldn't he have some kind of security? Imagine traveling alone with a cool half-million in diamonds!

HELEN: The System finds it safer to have an unguarded person carry the stones. Security officers would attract too much attention. The most dangerous part of the trip is the taxicab ride to the place of delivery. (*She nods.*) But you're right. I'll feel better when the diamonds are safely locked in Mr. Johnson's vault.

TOM: I wonder where Masterson carries the stones?

HELEN: He probably has them in his attaché case. (*She pauses.*) That's funny.

TOM: What's the matter?

HELEN: Masterson let the bellhop carry the attaché case. It seems strange that he didn't carry it himself.

TOM (*Nodding*): It does seem odd. I guess he's tired after the London flight. (*Brightly*) You saw that diamond on his left hand, didn't you?

HELEN: Yes. It's probably worth a king's ransom. I wish I had a diamond like that!

TOM: You'll get a half-carat, bargain-basement special, and you'd better like it! (*He takes her arm.*) Come on. Let's go find Finley and Johnson in the coffee shop. (*They exit up left.* BETTY PLANT *enters up left, joins* JANE SIMMONS *at the registration desk.*)

BETTY PLANT: Has Mr. Parker arrived yet, Jane?

SIMMONS: No, he hasn't. I'm still holding his reservation for the bridal suite.

PLANT: Good. I thought the bridal suite would be appropriate for his demonstration. After all, he sells bridal fashions.

SIMMONS: I've got to hand it to you, Betty. You do a great job as social director of the Metropolitan.

PLANT (*Smiling*): Thanks. I need a vote of confidence in this business. Take Mr. Parker, for instance. When he called for his reservation, he talked about bridals, and then rambled on about horses. He kept calling his room a stable.

SIMMONS: He sounds *un*stable to me. (MR. PARKER *enters right carrying two large suitcases.* 2ND BELLHOP *takes cases.* PARKER *goes to desk.*)

PARKER: Alvin Parker here. Parker's bridles. Everything for your horse.

PLANT: Good evening, Mr. Parker. We have your reservation. (*Pauses*) Did you say horse? (PARKER *nods as he signs card.*) Don't you mean everything for the wedding?

PARKER: Why, no. Whoever heard of a horse getting married?

PLANT: What about bridal fashions?

PARKER: That's my business. I have the finest line of bridle apparel in the country. Jodhpurs, boots, vests, gloves, hats, western shirts, you name it — Parker's got it!

SIMMONS (*Aside*): He's got something, all right, but I'll be darned if I can name it!

PARKER (*To* PLANT): I hope you hired the three assistants I requested.

PLANT: I certainly did. They're three of the most attractive models in the business. They should be here soon.

PARKER: Good. When you send them up would you also send along some oats and barley?

PLANT: But, Mr. Parker, the models have already eaten.

PARKER: No, no. It's for me.

PLANT: I didn't know you were a vegetarian. Room Service has never delivered a meal like that to the bridal suite.

PARKER (*In disbelief*): The bridal suite?

SIMMONS (*Proudly*): Yes, the most lavish one in New York. Some famous people have spent their honeymoons in our bridal suite. I thought it would be perfect for your bridal fashions.

PARKER: Bridals? I sell bridles. (PARKER *spells.*) B-R-I-D-L-E-S! Riding equipment, horses — the great outdoors! (PARKER *gallops in front of the registration desk. He finishes, panting.*) How could you make such a mistake?

PLANT (*Flustered*): I don't know what to say.

PARKER (*Suddenly*): Did you say you were sending beautiful models to my suite? (MISS PLANT *nods.*) You must stop them! My wife is meeting me here in a few minutes. If she finds them in my suite, I'll be modeling a shroud! Come on, let's head them off. (SIMMONS *hands key to* 2ND BELLHOP.)

SIMMONS: Suite 1441 for Mr. Parker. (PARKER *and* 2ND BELLHOP *exit up left.* PLANT *shakes her head, follows them off.* HELEN *and* TOM *re-enter, up left, followed by* FINLEY *and* JOHNSON. *They walk down center.*)

FINLEY: The facilities of the Hotel Metropolitan are at your service, Mr. Johnson.

JOHNSON: Thank you, Mr. Finley.

FINLEY: It isn't often that a half-million-dollar transaction in diamonds is conducted in my office. (*He points toward his office, left.*)

JOHNSON: Helen Maxwell, my capable assistant, made all the arrangements. (*To* TOM) And it's a pleasure to meet you, Tom. I didn't know that Helen had a brother.

TOM (*Sullenly*): Neither did I.

JOHNSON: I beg your pardon?

TOM (*Quickly*): I mean — sure, I know it. We've been brothers — er — I mean my brother's been my sister for years.

HELEN (*Hurriedly*): Never mind, Tom. (*To* JOHNSON) He's excited, Mr. Johnson. (FLANNERY *enters and* FINLEY *sees him.*)

FINLEY (*To* JOHNSON): I'd like you to meet our house detective. He was with the 10th Precinct for years. (*Signals to* FLANNERY, *who crosses toward group*)

TOM (*Nervously*): The 10th Precinct! (*He picks up a box of* ZIPPOS *from the demonstrator's booth and shields his face with it.*)

FINLEY (*As* FLANNERY *joins group*): This is Jim Flannery. (*To* FLANNERY) I'd like you to meet Mr. Johnson, Helen Maxwell, and Helen's brother, Tom. (*They shake hands.* TOM *continues to cover his face with box.*) Flannery has taken special precautions to prevent any thefts tonight.

FLANNERY: That's right. I've hired extra guards. (MASTERSON *enters up center and crosses to them. He carries the attaché case, but now wears gray suit and a wig without a part. Diamond ring is now on his right hand. When he speaks, his voice is rasping.*)

HELEN: Mr. Masterson, I'd like you to meet Mr. Finley, manager of the Metropolitan, and Mr. Johnson, my employer. (*Greetings are exchanged.*) And this is Jim Flannery, the house detective. (MASTERSON *looks quickly at* FLANNERY.)

MASTERSON: It's a pleasure, gentlemen. Now, let's get down to business, shall we? (TOM *drops box of* ZIPPOS *on demonstrator's counter, and sidles past* FLANNERY *without turning his face.* FINLEY, JOHNSON, MASTERSON, HELEN *and* TOM *enter manager's office, left, close the door. Spotlight comes up on area at left. Lobby area at right is dimmed and all extras exit.* FLANNERY *scratches his head, joins* JANE SIMMONS *at the registration desk, and talks in pantomime. In office,* MASTERSON *puts case on the desk.*)

JOHNSON: I'm eager to examine the stones, Mr. Masterson.

MASTERSON: I'll be glad to turn them over to you. I must return to London tomorrow on an early morning flight.

HELEN (*Frowning*): But Mr. Masterson!

MASTERSON (*Ignoring her*): You have the check for the Damocles Diamonds, of course.

JOHNSON: Yes, I do. There are five certified checks, each in the amount of one hundred thousand dollars, in the hotel safe. (JOHNSON *scribbles a note on desk pad, rips off the sheet, hands it to* HELEN.) If you'll give this note to Jane Simmons at the registration desk, she'll get the checks for you. Perhaps you should have Flannery escort you. (TOM *wildly waves his hands.*)

TOM: No, no! I'll go with Helen for protection. (TOM *and* HELEN *go into lobby. Spotlight comes up on them and area left dims.*)

HELEN: Tom, what's the matter with you?

TOM: I don't want Jim Flannery to be involved in the sale of the diamonds. I used to cover the 10th Precinct, and he may recognize me.

HELEN: Maybe we'd better tell Mr. Johnson the truth.

TOM: No, I'll get my story and clear out of the hotel — fast.

HELEN: O.K. Anyway, I'm glad we're out of the office. I want to talk to you. Tom, there's something strange about Masterson.

TOM: What do you mean?

HELEN: He seems different.

TOM (*Shrugging*): He changed his suit.

HELEN: No, it's more than that. His voice sounds different now.

TOM: Maybe it's jet lag.

HELEN: Jet lag wouldn't change the part in his hair. When we met him at the airport, his hair was parted on the side, and now it's not parted at all.

TOM: I hadn't noticed. Anything else?

HELEN: The shade of his hair seems lighter. I think he's wearing a wig.

TOM: Is that a crime?

HELEN: Be serious, Tom. It doesn't make sense to me, that's all. The whole thing is like a play. Everyone seems to be acting a part, and Masterson is the main character.

TOM: Nonsense, Helen. The excitement has gone to your head. (HELEN *wrings her hands in desperation. Suddenly, she looks at her hands.*)

HELEN: Masterson's diamond ring!

TOM: What about it?

HELEN: He's wearing it on his right hand. I noticed that when he put the attaché case on Mr. Johnson's desk.

TOM: So what?

HELEN: Remember, you mentioned the diamond on his *left* hand when he registered. He changed the ring to his right hand. Why?

TOM: Maybe he washed his hands and put the ring on the right hand by mistake.

HELEN: No. Someone who is accustomed to wearing a ring on one hand would never put it on the other hand by accident. And there's one more thing.

TOM: Yes?

HELEN: Masterson said that he was returning to London by the morning flight. Well, the daily flights leave International Airport in the afternoon.

Tom: Are you sure?

Helen: Positive. I have the schedules for all the airlines in my office. What can it mean?

Tom (*Slowly*): Our friend Mr. Masterson might be involved in a shady deal.

Helen (*Suddenly*): I don't think the man in Mr. Finley's office is Mr. Masterson!

Tom: That's ridiculous, Helen. We examined his credentials at the airport.

Helen: The airport, yes. But I think that something happened to the real Mr. Masterson in his hotel room. (*She points to office, left.*) That man is an impostor!

Tom: And what do you suppose happened to the real Mr. Masterson?

Helen: I don't know. Maybe he's been murdered.

Tom: How? Where?

Helen: We might find the answer in Masterson's room.

Tom: Sure — and get picked up for breaking and entering. It's hopeless. We don't have any evidence. (*Suddenly*) Hey, we'd better get those checks. They'll start wondering what happened to us. (*Turns*) Oh-oh. Flannery's at the desk talking to the room clerk. (Tom *pushes* Helen *toward the desk.*) You get the checks. I'll wait over there. (*He nods at demonstrator's booth.* Helen *walks to desk, hands* Jane Simmons *the note. They talk briefly in pantomime.* Jane Simmons *leaves the desk, exits up left.* Helen *smiles at* Flannery. *He watches her closely. Meanwhile,* Tom *wanders to demonstrator's booth. As* Tom *approaches,* Marion *nudges* Cindy.)

Marion: That man was with the gentleman whose attaché case was switched.

Cindy: I still think you're dreaming.

Tom (*Overhearing them*): What's all this about an attaché case?

Marion (*To* Tom): That man must be a friend of yours. It's only fair to tell you that he was robbed.

TOM: Mr. Masterson?

MARION: I don't know his name, but another man switched attaché cases with him. I didn't like that guy's looks. He had a scar, and he wore a black trench coat.

CINDY (*To* MARION): Marion, you read too many spy stories.

MARION: I'm serious, Cindy. (*To* TOM) I hope there wasn't anything valuable in that attaché case.

TOM: No, no. Er — just a few trinkets. Look, you two won't go away, will you? I may need you later.

CINDY: Sure, we'll be here. (*Shrugs*) We have to stay. We haven't been able to open a single package yet. (CINDY *and* MARION *remain onstage during following dialogues.* JANE SIMMONS *re-enters up left and goes to desk. She hands* HELEN *an envelope.* HELEN *turns.* TOM *nods to her and she joins him downstage.* FLANNERY *watches them intently.*)

TOM: Helen, there isn't time to explain it all now, but I think the diamonds have been taken.

HELEN: The diamonds are in Mr. Finley's office.

TOM: Don't bet on it.

HELEN (*In disbelief*): Are you saying they've been stolen?

TOM: Yes. I think false diamonds were substituted for the Damocles before Masterson went to his room.

HELEN: Masterson wouldn't try to sell us phony diamonds. Mr. Johnson could spot a fake in a minute. And I still don't think that man is Mr. Masterson.

TOM: You may be right, but we need more evidence. (*Quickly*) Go back to Finley's office and act as if nothing's happened. But keep them there at all costs!

HELEN: Why? Where are you going?

TOM: I'm going to search Masterson's room.

HELEN: You don't have a key. (TOM *takes a piece of celluloid from his pocket and holds it up.*) What's that?

TOM: Celluloid. It'll open most locks, especially in the hands of a second-story man. I'm an expert!

HELEN: It's risky.

TOM: Helen, we're onto something big here, and I can't worry about risks. (*Points down left*) Remember — don't let anyone leave the manager's office until I get back. (TOM *races off and exits up center.* HELEN *re-enters office, down left. Office area remains dim.* FLANNERY *rubs chin thoughtfully, follows* TOM *offstage. Meanwhile,* MRS. PARKER *storms in, right, carrying suitcase and umbrella.* 3RD BELLHOP *tries to take her suitcase, but she pulls it away and waves her umbrella at him threateningly. She thunders up to desk.*)

MRS. PARKER (*To* JANE SIMMONS): I'm looking for Mr. Parker. Alvin Parker. I'll tell him a thing or two! I would have been here sooner, but I had to ride all the way in his Pony Express horse trailer. He was too cheap to buy me a plane ticket.

SIMMONS: Mr. Parker registered a little while ago. He's in the bridal suite.

MRS. PARKER (*In disbelief*): The bridal suite?

SIMMONS: Yes. Are you one of the models that he's waiting for?

MRS. PARKER: Models? Is my husband traveling with a harem?

SIMMONS: You must be Mrs. Parker. There was a little mistake. Mr. Parker is using the bridal suite to demonstrate his bridles, that's all. I'm sure he'll be delighted to see you. Shall I announce you, Mrs. Parker?

MRS. PARKER: No, thanks! If Alvin has any young fillies in his room, I'll wrap one of his own harnesses around his neck! (*She storms out, brandishing umbrella.*)

MARION (*To* CINDY): Somebody should harness her natural energy.

CINDY: If he's horsing around upstairs, when she gets through with him he won't have enough energy left to harness anything. (*Lights in lobby area dim. Spotlight comes up in manager's office, down left.*)

MASTERSON (*Opening envelope and examining checks*): Yes, the checks are in order.

JOHNSON: Now may I see the Damocles Diamonds? (MASTERSON *opens attaché case and takes out envelope from which he removes a black velvet cloth. He opens the cloth, revealing sparkling diamonds.* JOHNSON *sits at desk and inserts a loupe in his eye.* MASTERSON *shifts nervously, moves toward office door.*)

MASTERSON: Excuse me for a moment. I'm expecting an important call from London. (HELEN *steps in front of the door, blocking his path.*)

HELEN: I'll be glad to tell the clerk to transfer your call to the office.

MASTERSON (*Coldly*): It's a personal call. (*He tries to sidle past* HELEN, *but she steps in the way.*)

HELEN: Why not wait until the diamonds are verified by Mr. Johnson?

JOHNSON (*Looking up*): A splendid suggestion, Helen. (*He continues to examine the diamonds.*)

MASTERSON: I'd like to order dinner. I didn't eat on the plane.

FINLEY: I'll place your order with our *maitre d'hôtel.* (MASTERSON *wrings his hands nervously.*)

MASTERSON: I'll order later. (*To* JOHNSON) The diamonds are exquisite, aren't they? (JOHNSON *removes the loupe, places it on desk, sits back, sighs.*)

JOHNSON: Yes, they are very good diamonds. I'd estimate their worth at approximately fifty thousand dollars.

FINLEY: Fifty thousand! I thought you offered $500,000 for the Damocles.

JOHNSON (*Nodding*): So I did, but I might have been the victim of an incredible swindle. Mr. Masterson, these are not the Damocles Diamonds.

MASTERSON: That's preposterous! (JOHNSON *points at the stones.*)

JOHNSON: These diamonds are tinted yellow and brown and are slightly spotted and irregular. They might be used for diamond drills and lathe tools, or even pieces of jewelry, but they are not perfect stones. Any appraiser would notice the difference immediately.

FINLEY (*Bewildered*): I can't believe it!

HELEN (*Quickly*): Is it possible that the diamonds were switched?

JOHNSON (*Pointing at velvet cloth*): This is an authentic cloth from the London System. I recognize their emblem woven into the edge of the cloth. If the diamonds were substituted, someone who had access to the System cloth did it.

MASTERSON: That case hasn't left my possession since I boarded the plane at Heathrow in London. Not for a single minute!

HELEN: The bellhop carried it to your room. You left it on the registration desk, and he picked it up with your suitcase.

FINLEY (*Angrily*): Young lady, are you implying that one of my employees stole the diamonds?

HELEN: No, I didn't suggest that, but what happened to the Damocles Diamonds? (*They pantomime further conversation. Lights go up in lobby. FLANNERY enters up left, holding TOM firmly by the arm. They are followed by a wildly chattering MR. and MRS. PARKER. GUESTS enter and watch.*)

TOM: You're making a terrible mistake, Flannery.

FLANNERY: You made the mistake, Butler. I caught you red-handed, trying to break into Room 1439.

MARION (*To CINDY*): This is like one of your spy stories, Cindy.

CINDY: That's the man who told us to wait for him. He can't be a robber!

PARKER (*To FLANNERY*): Listen, Inspector!

FLANNERY: I'm the house detective, not an Inspector. I can't talk to you now.

MRS. PARKER: Will you listen to Alvin? There's a man in our closet. A dead man!

GUESTS (*Ad lib*): Someone died. He found a body. (*Etc.*)

FLANNERY: A dead man!

PARKER: Yes, I found him. I was hanging up my wife's coat.

FLANNERY: I'll investigate your room after I turn over this character (*Indicating* TOM) to the manager. (*To* PARKERS) Don't leave the hotel! (FLANNERY *escorts* TOM *into office. Lights in office come up.* PARKERS *remain in lobby, talking excitedly to* GUESTS, JANE SIMMONS, CINDY *and* MARION, *in pantomime.*)

HELEN (*Surprised*): Tom!

FLANNERY: Mr. Finley, I caught this man breaking into Room 1439.

MASTERSON: That's my room!

FLANNERY: But that's not all. There's a couple outside who claim there's a dead man in their room. (*Others ad lib surprise*) I'll be back after I've called police headquarters. (FLANNERY *leaves office, closes door, joins the* PARKERS. *They exit up left. Lights in lobby dim.* GUESTS *exit.* CINDY, MARION *and* JANE SIMMONS *remain in position.*)

JOHNSON (*Shocked*): Helen, your brother — breaking into a room!

TOM: My name's Tom Butler, and I'm not Helen's brother.

FINLEY (*To* HELEN): Is this true?

HELEN (*Nodding*): Tom's my fiancé. He wanted a good story for his newspaper, and I told him about the diamonds, and pretended he was my brother so he could be in on the deal.

FINLEY: He'll have to remain here until the police come. I can't leave until this diamond business is finished.

JOHNSON (*To* MASTERSON): Since these are not the Damocles diamonds, I'll expect the return of my checks.

TOM (*Anxiously*): What's this about the diamonds?

HELEN: The real diamonds are missing, Tom.

TOM (*To* MASTERSON): What happened to the real stones?

MASTERSON: You were found breaking into my room. You're the likely suspect.

HELEN (*Angrily*): That's not true, Mr. Masterson. The switch must have been made by someone who had access to the System's velvet cloths.

JOHNSON: Helen, the System is a highly reputable organization.

TOM: Maybe not. (*To* MASTERSON) I tried to break into your room because I think you're at the bottom of the whole thing.

MASTERSON: You'd better watch your accusations!

FINLEY: There's no indication that Mr. Masterson had anything to do with the substitution!

MASTERSON: And I intend to call my London office at once.

HELEN (*Suspiciously*): Are you forgetting the time difference? It's 4:00 AM in England.

MASTERSON: The System has round-the-clock service, young woman. (*To* JOHNSON) I'll return these checks until the matter is investigated. (*He hands checks to* JOHNSON.)

JOHNSON: Mr. Finley, may I keep these checks in your safe until this matter is cleared up?

FINLEY: Of course.

JOHNSON: And I'd like you as well as Helen to accompany me as witness. (*To* TOM) You had better come up with us, too.

TOM: Fine. It's high time you took precautions. (*To* MASTERSON) You'd better be here when we get back. (TOM *exits quickly into lobby with* JOHNSON, HELEN *and* FINLEY. *Lights come up in lobby. They cross to desk.* JOHNSON *hands checks to* JANE SIMMONS, *and they follow her off left. Lobby area dims.* MASTERSON, *alone in office, is spotlighted. He opens attaché case, takes out a bottle of clear liquid. He examines it carefully, smiling.*)

MASTERSON (*To himself*): Nitroglycerin! I'm sure this explosive will discourage anyone from stopping me when I leave the hotel. No, they won't give me any argument! (*Lights come up in lobby.* TOM, HELEN, SIMMONS, JOHNSON *and* FINLEY *re-enter. All but* SIMMONS *re-enter manager's office.* SIMMONS *remains at desk. Lobby lights dim. As others enter office,* MASTERSON *conceals nitroglycerin.*)

JOHNSON: The checks are in the safe deposit vault.

MASTERSON (*Indignantly*): Am I being held prisoner, Mr. Finley? (FLANNERY *rushes in, up left, dashes into manager's office, slams door.*)

FLANNERY: The Parkers were right. There's a dead man in the bridal suite. (*All register surprise.*) I've called the 10th Precinct. (*He waves fist.*) No one is to leave this room until the police arrive.

FINLEY: Nothing like this has ever happened at the Metropolitan!

TOM (*Bewildered*): Missing diamonds — and now murder!

HELEN: Mr. Masterson, your hotel room is 1439. (*He nods.*)

FLANNERY: Hey! I found the man in 1441 — the next room!

HELEN: I think the man you found is the real Mr. Masterson!

FINLEY (*Gesturing*): This is Mr. Masterson.

HELEN: I think this man is an impostor. The real Masterson is upstairs — dead!

MASTERSON (*To* FLANNERY): This young woman is mad! First, she accuses me of stealing my own diamonds, and now she'd like you to believe that I'm an impostor — and a murderer! (FLANNERY *looks intently at* MASTERSON.)

FLANNERY: I don't think you could be taken for the dead guy. He's much taller, and he has a scar on his right cheek.

TOM (*Quickly*): Was he dressed in a black trench coat?

FLANNERY (*Nodding*): Yes, a black coat. (*Suddenly*) How did you know that?

TOM: I can't tell you now, Flannery, but I'm beginning to get the picture. If you wait here, I'll get someone who might be able to identify the murdered man. (FLANNERY *grabs* TOM's *arm.*)

FLANNERY: Wait a minute, Butler. You're not leaving this room.

TOM: There's a young woman at a booth in the lobby who saw someone take Masterson's attaché case. He switched it for his own at the registration desk.

HELEN: I didn't know that.

TOM: She told me while you were getting the checks. (*To others*) She said that the stranger was a tall man with a scar, dressed in a black trench coat. He followed Masterson after he registered.

MASTERSON: Then it's obvious that man stole the Damocles Diamonds and left this case with the false stones. (*He gestures at desk. To* HELEN) Young lady, I think you owe me an apology.

FLANNERY: I'll speak to the woman at the booth. (*To* MASTERSON) I'd like to look into your room. May I have your key?

MASTERSON (*Angrily*): Positively not! I won't permit anyone to search my room.

FLANNERY (*Strongly*): I'm afraid I'll have to insist. I promise that none of your belongings will be harmed.

MASTERSON: I absolutely forbid it.

FLANNERY: I can have the police bring a search warrant.

FINLEY: I'll be glad to escort Flannery to your room. (MASTERSON *quickly moves to the door. He holds up the small bottle.*)

MASTERSON (*Coldly*): There's no need for that. I'm leaving! (*To* FLANNERY) You're a detective. Can you imagine what's in this bottle?

FLANNERY: What are you trying to pull? I'm going to hold you for further investigation.

MASTERSON: Hardly, detective. There's enough nitroglycerin in this bottle to blow the Metropolitan a mile high — and everyone in it!

HELEN: No!

MASTERSON: If I hurl it to the ground, there will be little left of this room — or the lobby. (*Everyone steps back.* TOM *puts his arm around* HELEN.) I'm leaving this room now, and I'm going to walk to the lobby. No one is to stop me or give any alarm. (*He laughs.*) I have nothing to lose. If anyone leaves this room in the next ten minutes, it will be his last step on earth. (TOM *moves forward, but* HELEN *grabs his arm.*)

HELEN (*Hoarsely*): Tom, wait. I think he means it.

MASTERSON (*To* HELEN): You're very wise, Helen. (*To others*) Remember — ten minutes. (*He swings the bottle defiantly, opens door, steps into the lobby section. Lights come up on lobby. Quickly,* MASTERSON *exits up left. Meanwhile,* GUESTS *re-enter and gather at booth.*)

JOHNSON (*Excitedly*): We must do something.

FINLEY: No. We have to do what he says. I can't jeopardize my guests.

TOM (*Impatiently*): But Masterson can travel across town in ten minutes, if he leaves the hotel. (FLANNERY *waves his hand.*)

FLANNERY: Relax, Butler! I'm an old precinct man. That's how I finally recognized you.

TOM: Yes, but what can you do?

FLANNERY: All the exits from this hotel are heavily guarded — the front lobby, the service doors and fire exits. I hired special guards to protect the diamonds, just in case something went wrong. If they see Masterson acting suspicious, they'll be on his tail.

HELEN (*Worried*): Suppose Masterson decides to hide in the hotel. It would be virtually impossible to find him.

FINLEY (*Nodding*): The Metropolitan has 1,000 rooms.

JOHNSON: And 10,000 places for Masterson to hide.

FLANNERY (*Shaking head*): But, he didn't take the diamonds. (*Points to stones on desk*)

HELEN: No, those stones are not valuable.

JOHNSON: And he didn't get the checks for $500,000. I have them.

FLANNERY (*Bellowing*): Then what did Masterson steal? After all, Masterson's attaché case was taken by the dead guy. (HELEN *shakes her head.*)

HELEN: I feel as if Masterson were acting a part. Something about this seems unreal.

FLANNERY: One thing is real. He's running around the hotel with a bottle of high explosives. (*He waves his hand, steps cautiously to the door.*) Maybe we can look outside now. I don't think he'd stay in the lobby. (FLANNERY *opens office door, steps into lobby, right.* HELEN, TOM, FINLEY *and* JOHNSON *follow.* CINDY *and* MARION *begin to demonstrate a spray can of whipped cream to* GUESTS, *in pantomime.* FLANNERY *motions to* HELEN, TOM *and* JOHNSON. *They join him down center.*) I was right. There's no sign of Masterson.

TOM: You should alert the guards at the entrance, right?

FLANNERY: No, they already know what to do. Where's the witness who told you about the guy with the scar?

TOM: In the booth. (TOM *points to* MARION *in booth.* FLANNERY *crosses to booth, while* TOM, HELEN *and* JOHNSON *remain together, center, cautiously glancing around lobby. Other* GUESTS *enter and exit.* BELLHOPS *enter and exit with luggage.* CINDY *continues to demonstrate whipped cream in pantomime.*)

FLANNERY (*To* MARION): I'm Flannery, the house detective.

MARION (*Quickly*): Yes, sir. (*They move down right.*)

FLANNERY: I understand you saw a man switch an attaché case at the desk tonight.

MARION: Yes, sir. A tall man with a scar.

FLANNERY: With a black trench coat?

MARION: That's the one.

FLANNERY: Do you think you'd recognize his picture if I showed it to you?

MARION: I could try. (FLANNERY *takes out plastic case containing several photographs. He flips through the pictures while* MARION *repeatedly shakes her head. Suddenly she points to photograph.*) That's the man!

FLANNERY (*Nodding*): Freddie Silver. (*Slowly*) I was afraid of that. (*He turns.*) Thank you, young lady. (FLANNERY *returns downstage.* MARION *returns to booth.*)

TOM: Do you know who made the diamond switch?

FLANNERY (*Nodding*): Yes, I know. (*He sighs.*) I wondered how an intruder could have entered the hotel, switched cases with Masterson in plain view, and escaped without being seen by the guard at the front entrance. (*Pauses*) The intruder was one of the guards working here. I hired him myself.

HELEN: Then you knew him.

FLANNERY (*Bitterly*): Yes, I trusted Silver. I knew he was once a con man in jewelry heists, but he said he had gone straight and I wanted to give him a second chance. (*He points to* MARION.) I showed that young woman pictures of all my guards. She identified Freddie as the one who made the switch.

TOM: He was foolish to switch the attaché cases in the lobby, wasn't he?

HELEN: Yes, that troubles me too, Tom. (*Slowly*) It seems as though he wanted to be seen!

FLANNERY: We don't have to worry about him anymore. He's in the Parkers' closet with a bullet in his head.

TOM: And his killer must have the Damocles Diamonds. (MASTERSON, *dressed in his original dark suit, stumbles in up right. The ring is missing from his finger. He has removed his wig, and his hair is parted on the side, as before. There is blood on his face. He has a dazed expression, and he shakes*

*his head groggily. Everyone stares and ad libs surprise at his
appearance.*)

SIMMONS: That man! He's been hurt!

FLANNERY (*Turning*): Masterson! (*He rushes upstage, takes
MASTERSON's arm, and helps him into office. Lights in lobby
remain up. Office lights go up. HELEN, TOM, JOHNSON and
FINLEY go into office. MASTERSON drops at desk, holds his
head in his hands.*)

HELEN: What happened?

MASTERSON (*Dazed*): Someone attacked me in my room. He
must have been hiding there when I entered. (*MASTERSON
notices the diamonds on the desk.*) The Damocles! They're
safe.

TOM (*Soberly*): They're not the real diamonds. Someone
switched cases with you at the desk, then got himself killed
for his effort.

MASTERSON: The one people say was found in the Parkers'
suite? (*TOM nods.*) But why? Why was I attacked *after* the
Damocles had been stolen? (*He touches his cheek, winces.*)
He must have hit me with the gun butt. All I can remember
is some sweet-smelling stuff.

FLANNERY: You must have been drugged. (*MASTERSON tries to
stand, grips desk for support. He turns to FLANNERY.*)

MASTERSON: I'm all right. But the diamonds! You must find
them at all costs.

FLANNERY: The guards are alerted. I'll check them out.

JOHNSON: I'll come along in case the diamonds are recovered. I
can easily identify them.

FINLEY (*To MASTERSON*): A man tried to assume your identity
just now, and he nearly got away with the checks.

JOHNSON: He should have known that he could never sell those
false stones as the Damocles Diamonds.

MASTERSON: Jewel thieves will do desperate things. (*Groans
and rubs head*)

FINLEY: I'm going to call the house doctor. You may be seriously hurt. (FLANNERY, JOHNSON *and* FINLEY *go into lobby.* CINDY *demonstrates the whipped cream to* GUESTS, *in pantomime.* FLANNERY *exits right.* JOHNSON *and* FINLEY *exit up left.*)

MASTERSON (*To* HELEN): Why don't you go with Mr. Johnson? You and your fiancé may help find the diamonds. (HELEN *looks at* MASTERSON *intently and points to his head.*)

HELEN: Your hair is parted on the side.

MASTERSON (*Flustered*): This is hardly the time to discuss my grooming habits!

TOM (*Impatiently*): Helen, isn't it time we looked for the Damocles?

HELEN: It isn't necessary, Tom. I think the case — and the diamonds — are in room 1439.

MASTERSON: That's my room! The attaché case was stolen at the registration desk. It wouldn't be in my room.

HELEN: Perhaps you're carrying the Damocles Diamonds now.

MASTERSON (*Angrily*): Are you accusing me of stealing my own diamonds?

HELEN: They weren't your diamonds. They belonged to the London System. You were just an intermediary in the sale to Mr. Johnson. You were to deliver the diamonds, receive $500,000, and return to London. The System would have paid you the customary ten percent.

TOM: What are you driving at, Helen?

HELEN: It would be far more profitable if Masterson kept the diamonds himself and, after a reasonable period, sold them on the open market for one million dollars. That's what Mr. Johnson intended to make on individual sales. (*To* MASTERSON) It was a matter of fifty thousand against one million dollars! You contrived a neat scheme to get the Damocles Diamonds and convinced everyone that they had been stolen.

MASTERSON: That's absurd.

HELEN: You hired Freddie Silver as an accomplice. You knew

he had a record in jewel robberies. You instructed him to switch attaché cases at the desk. You wanted someone to see him. It would give strength to the belief that the diamonds had been stolen.

TOM (*Nodding*): I think I understand. (MASTERSON *jams his hands into his pockets, walks to desk, turns, glares defiantly.*)

MASTERSON: Those are lies. Perhaps in handling the attaché case I was negligent, but that hardly makes me a jewel thief.

HELEN: There's more evidence. You're a convincing actor, Mr. Masterson, but you were too theatrical when you pretended to impersonate yourself.

MASTERSON: What are you talking about?

HELEN: You put on a wig without a part and put the diamond ring on your right hand. An impostor would have copied your hair style and worn the ring on the correct finger. But you wanted us to believe there was a second person involved when it was you all along.

MASTERSON (*To* TOM): Your fiancée has a vivid imagination.

HELEN: That's further proof! You must have been here a few minutes ago, or else you wouldn't have known that Tom is my fiancé, not my brother.

TOM (*Brightly*): That's right, Helen!

MASTERSON (*Surly*): And I suppose I killed the man in the Parkers' suite.

HELEN: Yes, you killed your accomplice. Why should you share the profit with him?

TOM: I get the picture now. After you threatened us with the nitro, you returned to your room, changed your appearance, put a superficial scratch on your face, and stumbled into the lobby as if you had been unconscious.

MASTERSON (*Coldly*): You're correct. There was no second Masterson. As for Freddie, he threatened to turn me in if I didn't give him most of the diamonds. I couldn't let him stand in my way then, and I can't let anyone stand in my way now. (*He takes a gun from his pocket.* TOM *and* HELEN *step back, in alarm.*) This is the gun that killed him. (*Gestures at door*) We're going through the lobby and out of the hotel. (*To* TOM) You will hail a cab and the three of us will ride to the city limits. (*Laughs*) I'll leave the false stones that I bought from the System many years ago. That way it won't be a total loss for Johnson, even if he doesn't get the Damocles. (*Levels gun at them*) Remember, I killed once tonight. I won't hesitate again. (MASTERSON *opens door with free hand, conceals gun in pocket.*) Don't try anything. I'm ready to pull the trigger at a moment's notice. (HELEN *and* TOM *walk slowly into the lobby.* MASTERSON *follows them closely. At the demonstrator's booth,* CINDY *is showing can of whipped cream to* GUESTS. *She waves to* HELEN *and* TOM.)

CINDY: Would you like to see our demonstration? This whipped cream will flow freely and evenly onto your favorite dessert, thanks to the miracle of modern packaging.

MASTERSON: Now now.

HELEN (*Brightly*): Yes! We'd like to see the demonstration. (MASTERSON *jams the hidden gun into* HELEN's *back.*)

MASTERSON: I said, not now. (HELEN *remains near the booth.*)

CINDY (*Proudly*): Zip! Zip! Modern living! (*She presses cap on the can, but nothing happens. She presses harder, strains, turns to* MARION.) This can doesn't work either.

MARION (*Brightly*): Modern packaging is wonderful! You'll lose weight trying to open the packages. (*Desperately,* CINDY *presses the can, which is pointed in* MASTERSON's *direction. Whipped cream suddenly spurts into his face. Sputtering, he tries to wipe off cream.* TOM *quickly grabs* MASTERSON *and wrestles him to the floor.* GUESTS, CINDY, MARION *and* JANE SIMMONS *register shock.* TOM *takes* MASTERSON's *gun from his pocket and keeps him covered.* FLANNERY *rushes in, right.*)

FLANNERY: What's going on here?

TOM: Here's your criminal, Flannery. (*Indicates* MASTERSON) You can read all about it in my paper.

FLANNERY: What are you talking about? Where's the second Masterson?

HELEN: You're looking at both of them. The jewel thief — and Freddie Silver's murderer! (FLANNERY *helps* MASTERSON *to his feet, collars him.*)

FLANNERY: Come along. The police are outside. (MASTERSON *and* FLANNERY *move to right and exit.*)

TOM (*Calling*): Watch out, Flannery. He's carrying a fortune in diamonds.

CINDY (*To* TOM): Diamonds! That sounds important. I hope I didn't do anything wrong. (GUESTS *slowly exit.* JANE SIMMONS *exits up left.*)

HELEN: On the contrary. You helped us catch a murderer.

TOM: And you saved our lives.

MARION (*Nudging* CINDY): I told you modern packaging was wonderful!

CINDY (*Helplessly*): But nothing works! (MARION *and* CINDY *gather packages, exit.* TOM *and* HELEN *move down center.*)

TOM (*Sighing*): It's been quite a night.

HELEN: You wanted a story and a byline. (*Happily*) And now you have it! Tom, you were wonderful.

TOM: You solved the case, Ms. Sherlock Holmes. You deserve a reward. How about a diamond engagement ring?

HELEN: No, thanks! (*As* TOM *registers surprise*) I'm going to settle for a plain gold band. I've had enough of diamonds for a lifetime! (TOM *and* HELEN *embrace as curtains close.*)

THE END

Production Notes

THE DAZZLING DIAMOND CAPER

Characters: 7 male; 6 female; as many male and female extras as desired for bellhops, waiters, and guests.

Playing Time: 45 minutes.

Costumes: Modern dress. Business suits for male principals. Masterson wears a dark suit, later changes into a gray suit and, finally, into the original dark suit. On his first appearance, his hair is parted on the side. He later changes into a wig or hair style without a part, as directed. A diamond ring is moved from his left hand to his right hand, as indicated in the script. Silver wears a black trench coat. He has a scar on his right cheek.

Properties: Box of cereal reading ZIPPOS; container of whipped cream; box of crackers; knife; hammer; wallet with photographs; suitcases; umbrella; two identical attaché cases for Masterson and Silver; small bottle containing colorless fluid; gun; manila envelope containing black velvet cloth and diamonds; pen; pad and pencil; envelope containing five certified checks; telephones; piece of celluloid; jeweler's loupe.

Setting: Divided stage. Lobby of the Metropolitan, a large New York hotel, is in right half of stage. Entrance to lobby is at right. Another entrance, up center, leads to elevators and stairs. Down left is wall with working door to manager's office. Office is in left half of stage, and is furnished with desk, chairs, and telephone. The exposed front of the office faces audience. Down right is a booth with large poster reading, WELCOME TO THE PACKAGERS' CONVENTION. Up center is the registration desk, with pen, cards, telephone, etc., on it. Exit up left leads to other rooms in hotel. Chairs, rugs and flowers complete the furnishings in the fashionable lobby. The extras should simulate the constant activity in a busy hotel.

Lighting: Because of simultaneous onstage action, individual scenes may be spotlighted. Stage lights may be dimmed during pantomime scenes.

Sound: No special effects.

Don't Pet My Rock!

When avid collectors gather for the annual Pet Rock Convention, they don't expect to be involved in a jewel theft!

Characters

TOM SUTTON, *a young businessman*
AUDREY SUTTON, *his wife*
TV ANNOUNCER
TWO TV CAMERAMEN
TWO MEN ⎫
　　　　　⎬ *visitors to the Convention*
THREE WOMEN ⎭
SPECTATORS, *12 or more*
NEWSPAPER REPORTER, *a woman*
HARRY GRIMES, *an insurance man*
BELLHOP
PROFESSOR OGILVIE
DINNY
MAMIE
POLICEMAN
UNCLE ABNER

TIME: *The present, afternoon.*
SETTING: *The Grand Ballroom of Rockefeller Center. Aisles of tables displaying pet rocks are at right and left.*
AT RISE: MEN *and* WOMEN *walk up and down aisles, inspecting pet rocks.* TWO TV CAMERMEN *move a camera on*

96

casters along aisles, focusing on displays. ANNOUNCER, *carrying cordless mike, enters right, followed by* SPECTA- TORS. *During the play,* SPECTATORS *enter, inspect displays of pet rocks, comment in pantomime and exit.* CAMERAMEN *move camera forward and focus on* ANNOUNCER, *who smiles into camera.*

ANNOUNCER: Good afternoon, ladies and gentlemen. Wel- come! This afternoon we are bringing you live all the fun, all the excitement of the annual Pet Rock Convention, here in the Grand Ballroom at, appropriately enough, Rockefeller Center. (*He indicates displays.*) We are surrounded here by the beloved pet rocks of members of the Federated Geologi- cal Society, known as the Jolly G's! Pet rocks from every corner of the globe have been entered — from the Appala- chians to the Alps, from Tanganyika to Timbuktu. No stone has been left unturned. A highlight of the show will be the naming of the Pet Rock of the Year, with the winner re- ceiving an all-expense-paid trip to the Rock of Gibraltar. In addition, we will feature a rare television appearance by the pet rock owned by Audrey Sutton, a rock found in the rubble of the Great Sphinx of Egypt! Yes, the Sphinx — that fabulous monster with the body of a lion, the head and torso of a man. And we will be meeting one of its descen- dants today. (*As he crosses left, 1st* MAN *and* 1ST WOMAN *move forward.*)

1ST MAN (*To* 1ST WOMAN): I understand the Sutton pet rock is definitely not just another pebble on the beach.

1ST WOMAN (*Agreeing*): Yes, I can't wait to see Petronella. (*They examine other exhibits.*)

ANNOUNCER (*At mike*): Yes, ladies and gentlemen, we are sur- rounded by pet rock lovers. And what is a pet rock? It is the ideal pet for people who are allergic to cats and dogs or plants. It is just right for those who are not allowed to have a pet. The perfect companion for the man or woman with a heart of stone. The more than one million proud pet rock owners never have to worry about violating the law, never have to clean up messes, never fear that their pet will keep the neighbors awake at night. (2ND WOMAN *taps his arm.*)

2ND WOMAN: Oh, Mr. Announcer, a pet rock *can* keep you awake at night.

ANNOUNCER: Really?

2ND WOMAN: Of course. Take our little Peter, for instance. He's still very young, only the size of a pebble, but he had a terrible cold and a gravelly throat last week, and coughed for three nights. (*Gestures to* 2ND MAN) Didn't you hear Peter coughing, Bill? (2ND MAN *stares glassily at camera.*)

2ND MAN: Oh, yes, I heard him cough. (*Wildly*) I also hear bells — and whistles — and hoot owls. And I see dancing ostriches — great big purple dancing ostriches. (*He lifts the ends of his coat and dances on his toes.*) Whoops! I'm a dancing ostrich! (*He pirouettes off left.* 2ND WOMAN *follows.*)

2ND WOMAN (*Calling*): Oh, Bill! You're off your rocker again! (*She exits.*)

ANNOUNCER: As you can see, folks, pet rock lovers certainly are unique! (*Gesturing to* CAMERAMAN *to move to table on right aisle.*) Why don't we all take a moment now to look at one of these intriguing displays? (*As camera moves closer to display,* 3RD WOMAN *goes to* CAMERAMAN *and grips his arm.*)

3RD WOMAN: Take that dreadful camera away from Petunia. She's terribly timid.

1ST CAMERAMAN (*Disgruntled*): I'm only doing my job.

3RD WOMAN: I don't care. Petunia isn't used to people. Why, when anyone comes to the house, she runs into the closet and hides.

2ND CAMERAMAN (*In disbelief*): She runs into the closet and hides?

3RD WOMAN: Well, maybe I give her just a little push; then she rolls into the closet and hides. You've heard of rock 'n' roll!

1ST CAMERAMAN (*Shaking head*): And I gave up working on the Merv Griffin Show for this! (*Goes back to camera as* 3RD WOMAN *moves away*)

ANNOUNCER (*At mike*): All this exciting action is being brought to you by the Nighty-Night Mattress Company, the world's largest manufacturer of mattresses for pet rocks. Is your precious pet sleeping on a lumpy mattress? Does your pet rock complain of fissures in its back after a sleepless night? Then see your Nighty-Night dealer. He or she has the mattress for your pet. A Nighty-Night mattress will assure your pet of a perfect night's sleep — she'll sleep like a rock! (ANNOUNCER *gestures left.*) While we are waiting for Mrs. Sutton, the proud owner of the celebrated Sphinx pet rock, we will take our cameras to the next exhibit area of pet rock displays. (*He gestures to* CAMERAMEN *who follow him left.* SPECTATORS *follow.*) Coming up next — an original chip off Plymouth Rock, a rock from the Great Wall of China, and an actual shard from the Rock of Gibraltar. (CAMERAMEN, *with camera,* ANNOUNCER *and several* SPECTATORS *exit left, while several remain onstage examining rocks.* TOM *and* AUDREY SUTTON *enter right.* AUDREY *carries a covered shoe box, a newspaper and a large purse. They walk to center table.* AUDREY *deposits box and newspaper.* TOM *nods impatiently. His annoyance is apparent.*)

TOM (*Angrily*): Well, here we are, Audrey. I hope you're satisfied. (*Looking back offstage.*) At least we got rid of that nosy newspaper woman. We lost her in the crowd out in the lobby. (*Exasperated*) Ever since you brought that pet rock from the Sphinx the press hasn't left us alone. My job could be in danger if this goes on much longer.

AUDREY: Tom, you promised not to start complaining again.

TOM: Other guys' wives want dogs or cats for pets. A tropi-

cal fish, maybe. A parakeet. But not my wife. Oh, no! Tom
Sutton's wife has to go out and buy a pet rock! (AUDREY
shakes her head cautiously.) I've heard of marriages being
on the rocks, but this is ridiculous.

AUDREY (*Indicating box*): Be quiet, Tom. Petronella will hear
you! Don't take her for granite!

TOM (*Angrily*): Stop it, Audrey! Rocks can't hear!

AUDREY: An ordinary rock can't hear, and it can't talk, and it
can't eat. But Petronella's different — she's pedigreed!

TOM (*Shaking his head*): Why did you have to buy a pet rock?

AUDREY: Because I was lonesome in our apartment when you
were away on sales trips. I needed companionship. I wanted
a pet.

TOM: But why a rock?

AUDREY: Our lease says that we can't have any pets, but I
didn't think anyone would object to Petronella.

TOM: So you went to a pet shop and picked out a rock! What
a waste of five bucks!

AUDREY: Professor Ogilvie didn't think it was a waste. He
telephoned right after I bought Petronella and he was very
excited. He said a shipment of valuable geological specimens from Egypt had accidentally been sent to the pet shop.
The rock I bought was actually a piece of the Egyptian
Sphinx!

TOM: Don't remind me! There must have been a dozen newspaper articles about it. (TOM *gestures dramatically*.) Priceless
rock sold as pet! (*Normal voice*) We haven't had a moment's peace since.

AUDREY: Petronella *is* a pretty little thing, though. Did you
ever see how she sparkles in the sunlight? Why, she looks
like a cluster of diamonds.

TOM: Diamonds, indeed! They're pieces of quartz. Oh, we
shouldn't have come to this convention — and we should get
rid of that pet rock. Put her out to pasture in the rock garden, maybe.

AUDREY (*Shocked*): Get rid of Petronella? Never! Why, she's as steady as — as a rock.

TOM: But what about me? All the other salesmen make terrible puns. I'm the laughing stock of the company. "There goes Tom Sutton — the guy with rocks in his head!" I tell you, Audrey. Something's got to be done about your obsession with this rock. (*He wipes forehead.*) Thank goodness Uncle Abner is in Europe.

AUDREY: What does your Uncle Abner have to do with it?

TOM: You seem to have forgotten that I'm Uncle Abner's favorite nephew. He's considering making me a full partner in his oil business. (TOM *clears his throat and speaks in deep voice.*) "My nephew, Tom Sutton. Now, there's a solid-minded young man. Stability and all that. Yes, sir! Give me a man with his two feet planted solidly on the ground — right on top of an oil well!" (*Resumes normal voice*) If Uncle Abner finds out that I've become stepfather to a rock, he'll disown me.

AUDREY: I never thought of that.

TOM: Audrey, the more I think about it, the more nervous I get about all of this publicity. Let's get out of this place before it's too late. (NEWSPAPER REPORTER *enters. She waves a pad and pencil. When* TOM *sees her, he sighs glumly.*) It's too late!

REPORTER: What a mob in that lobby! I almost lost you both.

TOM: We were worried about that.

REPORTER: And such excitement! Police are swarming all over the place.

AUDREY: Police?

REPORTER: Haven't you heard? The Slope Diamond is missing.

AUDREY: Isn't that the famous uncut stone found in the African diamond mine?

REPORTER: That's the one. It was kept in its natural state and sold to a New York dealer. The diamond was on display in this hotel.

TOM: But why all the police? Are they bodyguards — or something?

REPORTER: No, the Slope Diamond was stolen under their very noses! It was on display in the Rainbow Room, and one of the attendants just found the case smashed.

AUDREY: How terrible!

REPORTER: It's great news! I phoned the story in to my paper. No one is permitted to leave the hotel.

TOM (*Sadly*): Then we can't leave, even if we tried.

REPORTER: Not a chance. The police think the robber is still in the hotel. What a story! (*Suddenly*) Why would you want to leave?

TOM: This pet rock business is too much for me.

REPORTER: But you're a celebrity! The owner of a pet rock — a descendant of the famous Egyptian Sphinx! After this convention, your name will be a household word.

TOM (*Nodding*): Big deal! I don't want any publicity.

REPORTER: You can't avoid it. My editor told me that Professor Ogilvie is coming from the university and he has a statement about your pet rock that will make headlines!

TOM: More publicity! (REPORTER *glances around.*)

REPORTER: Where's that TV crew? I want them around when you introduce Petronella to the convention. (*She grins.*) I'm anxious to see her myself. She must be a perfect little jewel.

AUDREY: Do you like pet rocks?

REPORTER: Sure. I have one myself. Of course, Patricia is only a piece of limestone, but she's descended from Mount Rushmore and that makes her a member of the D.A.R.

TOM: The D.A.R.?

REPORTER: Daughters of American Rocks. (*To* AUDREY) Will you let me see her now?

AUDREY: No, I'm sorry. It's too soon to disturb her. (*She glances at* TOM.) The man in the pet shop told me I should let Petronella rest after a trip.

TOM: That guy had rocks in his head, too!

AUDREY: Don't rock the boat, Tom. I'm only following instructions. I guess I can remove the cover, but Petronella must stay in her little box. Pet rocks need fifteen minutes to acclimatize — get used to new surroundings. If Petronella gets too excited — well, I brought some old copies of *Rolling Stone*, her favorite newspaper, in case she has an accident.

REPORTER: A wise idea. (AUDREY *slowly uncovers box, smiles.*)

AUDREY (*Softly*): Good afternoon, Petronella. (TOM *frowns.* REPORTER *bends over box.*)

REPORTER: Oh, she's a beauty! (*She smiles.*) Kitchy-kitchy-koo!

TOM: Let me show you how strongly I feel about dear little Petronella! (*He steps forward, stares at box, wiggles his fingers in his ears, sticks out his tongue.* AUDREY *and* REPORTER *register shock.*)

AUDREY: Tom, stop that! Why, Petronella is frowning!

REPORTER (*Strongly*): Rock bottom male chauvinist! (AUDREY *delicately removes pet rock from box, places it on newspaper.*)

AUDREY: There! I think she's comfortable. (AUDREY *opens purse, takes out alarm clock, places it near rock.*)

REPORTER: What's the clock for?

AUDREY: The pet shop owner found that the ticking of an alarm clock has a soothing effect. Petronella just loves it!

REPORTER: Do you have difficulty with her feeding? My Patricia won't eat a thing. (*As* AUDREY *answers,* REPORTER *jots in notebook.*)

AUDREY: I sprinkle her with rock candy and rock salt each morning. She needs her minerals, you know. She seems to like it, but she still has trouble with solid foods. She can't digest marble chips.

TOM (*Angrily*): Audrey, I'm warning you!

AUDREY: Sometimes if she's eaten especially well, I reward her by playing her favorite composer on the stereo.

REPORTER: Oh! Who's that?

AUDREY: Rachmaninoff.

REPORTER: Of course. (*Looking around impatiently*) Where's the TV crew? History is being made in here, and those cameramen are off after diamonds or some useless stones like that. (*She covers her mouth quickly, nods at pet rock.*) Oh, I'm sorry, Petronella, I didn't mean to say that about your relatives. (*She exits left.*)

TOM (*Slowly, with mounting anger*): I can't believe all of this. Reporters, TV cameras, a major convention — all because of a lot of nutty people who practically *worship* a bunch of lousy rocks! (AUDREY *looks at rock, clucks angrily.*)

AUDREY: You hurt Petronella's feelings again. (AUDREY *picks up rock.*) Come along, baby, it's time for your exercise. (*She places rock on floor.*)

TOM: Exercise? You didn't tell me about that.

AUDREY: I wanted to surprise you. I've taught Petronella so many tricks! I even enrolled her at obedience school. She enjoys meeting other pet rocks.

TOM: And how much has that enjoyment cost me?

AUDREY: Oh, the school is reasonable enough. Petronella can attend the entire course for only seventy-five dollars.

TOM (*Exploding*): Seventy-five dollars? That's my commission for five sales!

AUDREY: Look at all the things she's learned. She can heel, sit, and roll over.

TOM: (*Scoffing*): Do you expect me to believe that? (AUDREY *stands with her back toward rock, five feet away.*)

AUDREY: I'll show you. (AUDREY *looks over her shoulder.*) Heel! Heel! (*Very slowly,* AUDREY *takes a small step backward. She nods triumphantly.*) You see? Petronella moved! She's much closer to me now!

TOM: Petronella didn't move forward. You moved backward.

AUDREY: You don't have any imagination. Here! I'll show you another one. Petronella will come forward anytime I command it.

TOM: Ha! (AUDREY *faces rock, bends and places her hands on her knees.*)

AUDREY: Come, Petronella. Come to Mommy! (AUDREY *takes a small step forward. She whispers.*) Can't you see it, Tom? Petronella is actually moving forward!

TOM: You're the one who's moving. (AUDREY *straightens.*)

AUDREY: No, I actually saw Petronella move. (AUDREY *bends, pets stone.*) That's a good girl. Daddy doesn't understand you!

TOM: Daddy? (REPORTER, CAMERAMAN, *with camera,* ANNOUNCER *and* MEN, WOMEN *and* SPECTATORS *enter left.*)

ANNOUNCER (*At mike*): Mr. and Mrs. Sutton, our newspaper friend told us all about you. This is a pleasure! Ladies and gentlemen, the owners of Petronella, the famous Sphinx pet rock, are with us now in the Grand Ballroom. (ANNOUNCER *smiles fondly at rock. Camera moves in for a closeup.*) And this must be Petronella!

1ST WOMAN: Isn't she lovely?

1ST MAN: Why, I think she resembles Cleopatra.

3RD WOMAN (*Nodding*): On her father's side.

AUDREY (*Nervously*): I — I don't know what to say. I've never been on TV before.

TOM: Just tell everyone that Petronella eats rock candy for breakfast every morning, or that she takes her orange juice on the rocks.

AUDREY: Please, Tom! (*To* ANNOUNCER) I was just demonstrating some tricks that Petronella learned at obedience school.

ANNOUNCER (*At mike*): Ladies and gentlemen, you are about to see Petronella perform her amazing feats. Please demonstrate, Mrs. Sutton. (AUDREY *steps backward, points at rock.*)

AUDREY: Stay! Stay! (*Everyone stares at rock, gasps in admiration*)

1ST MAN: Look how she stays!

1ST WOMAN: Remarkable!

REPORTER: I've never seen such coordination. She's so well trained.

3RD WOMAN: Why, I've been trying to teach that trick to my pet for months. She simply won't stay. She insists upon rocking around.

TOM: What's your pet — a Mexican jumping rock?

3RD WOMAN: No, but I have a very uneven floor. (HARRY GRIMES *rushes in, right. He waves an insurance policy.*)

HARRY: Stop! Stop! (*He points at rock.*) Is that Petronella? (*Everyone nods.*) How could you possibly have her lying on that cold floor? She'll be petrified. (HARRY *picks up rock, places it on table, pets it.* AUDREY *reacts angrily as camera follows action.*)

AUDREY: Don't pet my rock! Who are you, anyway?

HARRY: Grimes is my name. Insurance is my game.

AUDREY: Insurance? We're not interested.

TOM (*Nodding*): I'm worth more dead than alive right now.

HARRY: Who wants to insure you? I represent the Rock-of-Ages Insurance Company. We carry every type of no-fault insurance for pet rocks — chipping, cracking, erosion, landslides, crazing, Blue Rock health insurance, the works! You know our motto — "A piece of the rock for every rock."

AUDREY: Well, I don't know. Petronella seems pretty healthy to me. (ANNOUNCER *covers mike, looks angrily at* HARRY)

ANNOUNCER: Get out of here, Grimes. You're cutting into my territory. (ANNOUNCER *smiles at camera, uncovers mike.*) A little interruption, ladies and gentlemen — all part of the excitement at the Pet Rock Convention. (ANNOUNCER *glares at* HARRY.) I'll sue your company!

HARRY: It's a free country, and this hotel is a public place. I'll sell my insurance if I want. (*To* SPECTATORS) Ladies and gentlemen, I have a little policy that will cover your pet rock's old age. We have complete Medicare and Medicaid coverage — not to mention liability, disability, and maternity benefits.

1ST WOMAN: I suppose I should think of my pet's future.

HARRY: You're right — who knows when there's going to be a rockfall or something? What if the Rockies crumble? (*He gestures left.*) Now, if you'll follow me, I'll be glad to sign your pets.

ANNOUNCER (*Angrily*): You're forgetting this is the Nighty-Night Mattress hour!

HARRY (*Triumphantly*): Nighty-Night? Oh, I've waited for this moment for ages. Yes, I knew that someday I would meet a Nighty-Night Mattress representative. Revenge is mine!

ANNOUNCER (*Uncomfortably*): What do you have against Nighty-Night?

HARRY: I slept on your water bed mattress once — and it sprang a leak! (*Wildly*) But I am prepared! (*He takes water pistol out of pocket. Everyone gasps.*) You and Nighty-Night will pay! (*He squirts water at* ANNOUNCER.) Ha! Ha! (HARRY *rushes off left.* ANNOUNCER *smiles feebly, wipes water from face. He smiles at camera.*)

ANNOUNCER: Yes, ladies and gentlemen, we have all kinds here this afternoon. (*To* AUDREY) Do you have any other pet rock tricks for our audience?

AUDREY: Petronella seems to learn easily. I taught her to play dead, and I even tried to teach her to fetch. (*Sadly*) Rarely, if ever, did she return with the object.

1ST WOMAN: It's all a matter of time, my dear.

TOM (*Sarcastic*): Why don't you teach her to shake hands? (BELLHOP *enters right.*)

BELLHOP: Paging Mr. Sutton. Telephone call for Mr. Sutton.

TOM: I'm Mr. Sutton.

BELLHOP: There's a telephone call for you, Mr. Sutton. You can take it on the lobby phone. (BELLHOP *gestures right, exits.*)

TOM: Now what? I've probably lost all my accounts because of this foolishness. And that last one was a beauty!

AUDREY: I hope not, Tom. (*Suddenly*) What was the last account?

TOM (*Feebly*): The Sleepy-Eyed Bed Pet Rock people.

ANNOUNCER: Sleepy-Eyed? Our arch rival! (*He quickly covers mike.*)

AUDREY: I didn't think you believed in pet rocks, Tom.

TOM: A sale is a sale — so I thought I'd get on the bandwagon. (TOM *exits right.*)

ANNOUNCER (*Quietly, to* AUDREY): My company will sue your husband!

AUDREY: Tom didn't mean any harm. After all, he is a super salesman, and if you do anything to hurt him, Petronella and I will leave this silly show right now!

ANNOUNCER: (*Tearfully*): Oh, you can't do that. We'd be ruined! (PROFESSOR OGILVIE *enters right. He approaches rock, glances at watch.*)

PROFESSOR: Thank goodness I got here in time.

REPORTER (*Brightly*): Why, you're Professor Ogilvie from the State University! I can't tell you what an honor it is to meet one of the world's most renowned geologists!

PROFESSOR: Thank you, young lady. (*He points at rock, smiles.*) And this must be Petronella. (*He examines rock closely.*) A rare prize, indeed.

AUDREY: How do you do, Professor? You telephoned me about Petronella's ancestry.

PROFESSOR (*Solemnly*): What a momentous occasion! The mere presence of this stony souvenir from long ago makes me tremble with excitement! (PROFESSOR *addresses camera; dramatically*) We are on the threshold of history! (*Everyone gasps, whispers in pantomime.*)

ANNOUNCER: Professor Ogilvie, world-famous rock connois-
seur, can you mean that Petronella's presence on this show
could affect the course of history?

PROFESSOR (*Dramatically*): You have heard of the riddle of the
Sphinx, haven't you?

ANNOUNCER (*Nodding*): Of course! It has mystified people for
ages!

PROFESSOR (*Excitedly*): The riddle is a wonder of the ages.
Once in every century, it is reported that the Great Sphinx
speaks. It recites the famous riddle and then remains silent
for another hundred years.

SPECTATORS (*Ad lib*): Amazing! Remarkable! Unbelievable!
(*Etc.*)

ANNOUNCER: But what does that have to do with our show?

PROFESSOR: This is the very day! The Great Sphinx will speak
today!

AUDREY (*Proudly*): My little Petronella is going to say her first
word.

ANNOUNCER: A talking pet rock! (*He shakes his head in disbelief, shouts hoarsely into mike.*) Ladies and gentlemen, you
will hear the riddle of the Sphinx from Petronella's very own
lips. (*Suddenly*) She does have lips, doesn't she?

AUDREY: Well, there's a little indentation where her mouth
should be. I — I don't know whether she can talk. (*Fearfully*) Oh, dear. I do hope this doesn't get Tom into trouble!

REPORTER: You'll be the most famous woman in the world.

AUDREY: I don't want to be famous. I just want to be a good
parent to my rock. Remember what they say about the hand
that rocks the cradle, I mean, cradles the rock . . .

ANNOUNCER: When will the pet rock speak, Professor Ogilvie?

PROFESSOR: If my calculations are correct, the Sphinx should
speak in exactly fifteen minutes.

ANNOUNCER: We don't have much time. (*To* CAMERAMEN) We
have to make certain that this is covered by satellite. We'll
need more cameras, more cables, more worldwide coverage.

Call the network. Call the President! Petronella is going to
speak! (ANNOUNCER *grabs* PROFESSOR*'s arm.*) We'll have to
get you ready for the camera. There's a makeup kit inside.
(CAMERAMEN, REPORTER, PROFESSOR, ANNOUNCER *and* SPEC-
TATORS *exit left.* AUDREY *stands alone, stares at rock.*
TOM *rushes in right, grabs* AUDREY*'s arm, quickly tugs her
toward right exit.*)

TOM: Audrey, we have to get out of here — fast!

AUDREY: What's the matter, Tom?

TOM (*Gesturing*): That was Uncle Abner on the phone. He
decided to come back unexpectedly from a business trip and
he just landed at the airport. On the plane he read those
ridiculous newspaper articles about Petronella, and he's
fuming!

AUDREY: What did he say?

TOM: He said something about doubting my stability, my sure-
footedness, and my sanity. If I repeated his exact words,
though, I'd be rated X. If I can't convince him that I'm entirely innocent in this pet rock nonsense, I'll lose the partnership — and probably my life!

AUDREY: Is he coming here?

TOM (*Nodding*): I told him to meet us here, but I'm losing my
nerve fast. Let's go before he gets here. I can't face him.

AUDREY: But I can't leave now. Petronella is going to speak.

TOM (*Abruptly*): Who cares whether Petronella is going to
speak? Audrey, let's — (*He stops; in disbelief*) Did you say
that rock is going to speak?

AUDREY: I can't believe it either. My head is spinning.

TOM: I'm not surprised. You've been in the clouds for days.

AUDREY: Professor Ogilvie said that Petronella would recite
the riddle of the Sphinx. It happens once every hundred
years.

TOM: I'll wait until the next time. Look! We're going to mingle
with the crowd and try to find the back exit. The police

won't let anyone out the front way. Why did those confounded robbers have to steal the Slope Diamond today?

AUDREY: But I can't leave without Petronella!

TOM: I never want to see that pet rock again. If Petronella ever crosses my path again, she'll be a rolling stone — rolling right to the bottom of the nearest lake. (TOM *and* AUDREY *exit left.* DINNY *and* MAMIE *enter right. They glance around cautiously.* DINNY *carries a rock hidden under his coat. Slowly, they approach the center table, glance around anxiously*)

MAMIE: All right, Dinny, what do we do now?

DINNY: Have a heart, Mamie. How did I know those guards were going to find that the Slope Diamond was missing as soon as I stole it? (DINNY *displays rock.*) Imagine! Fifty huge uncut diamonds in this dirty rock!

MAMIE: We'll be on a rock pile if the police catch us with the goods. I told you it was a bad caper.

DINNY: So you know all the answers. Klepto-Mamie! The gal who sees all, knows all.

MAMIE: I should have known better than to tie up with you.

DINNY: Well, we can't leave the hotel until the heat's off.

MAMIE (*Pointing at stone*): And we can't carry that thing around. It's a dead giveaway.

DINNY (*Nodding*): If we can only stash it until the coast is clear. (*He glances at the various pet rocks.*) Say, what kind of place is this, anyway?

MAMIE (*Glancing around*): Looks crazy, if you ask me. I guess it's a display of some kind. (MAMIE *picks up a sign on right table, reads.*) "Federated Geological Society." (*She replaces sign.*)

DINNY (*Righteously*): A man's religion makes no difference to me.

MAMIE: Maybe it's a political convention.

DINNY: Do you think it's one of those subversive groups?

MAMIE: Maybe. You can't trust anybody these days. (*Quickly*) But all these rocks. I have a great idea! (*She taps her fore-head.*) My brain's working!

DINNY: Impossible!

MAMIE: Quiet! Listen — what's the best place to hide a rock?

DINNY: That's what I'd like to know.

MAMIE: We'll hide the Slope Diamond with these rocks, of course!

DINNY: You mean we should leave it here — in plain sight?

MAMIE: It's worth a chance. Haven't you ever heard of Edgar Allan Poe?

DINNY: Wasn't he that check forger from Schenectady?

MAMIE: Naw, that was Fingers Poe. Edgar Allan wrote short stories and poems. Real weird-o stuff. Well, he turned out a story about a letter. A guy wanted to hide it — so what did he do? He mailed it with a lot of letters. Nobody ever thought of looking for it with other letters.

DINNY: So what do we do — mail the Slope Diamond to ourselves?

MAMIE: No, no! We'll hide the diamond with these other rocks. (MAMIE *points at* AUDREY*'s rock.*) Take that one, for instance. It's about the same size as the Slope Diamond, and it's speckled with all those fancy little stones. No one will notice the difference.

DINNY: Sounds risky, if you ask me.

MAMIE: It's a risk we have to take. If we're sent up for another rap, they'll give us a one-way ticket. (MAMIE *picks up rock, replaces it with the Slope Diamond. She glances around, places* AUDREY*'s rock and the uncovered box on first table, right. She dusts off hands.*) There! The diamond is safe. We'll pick it up later.

DINNY: Mamie, I have to hand it to you. Your brain does work once in a while.

MAMIE: Thanks, Dinny — a girl always likes a compliment.

(*She gestures left.*) We'll hide in there until the police leave. I hope we won't have too much trouble getting the Slope Diamond back.

DINNY: No one will stop us. (DINNY *removes gun from his coat pocket.*) This friendly persuasion will see to that! (DINNY *and* MAMIE *exit left.* ANNOUNCER*'s voice is heard off left.*)

ANNOUNCER (*Offstage*): And now, ladies and gentlemen of the TV audience, we'll return to the Grand Ballroom where the world-famous Sphinx rock will speak to the world! (ANNOUNCER, NEWSPAPER WOMAN, TOM, AUDREY, PROFESSOR, CAMERAMEN, *with camera,* HARRY *and* SPECTATORS *enter left.* ANNOUNCER *talks in pantomime while* TOM *and* AUDREY *walk downstage.*)

TOM: It's no use. The rear exits are blocked. We can't get out of here.

AUDREY: I'm glad. I simply couldn't desert Petronella. (AUDREY *pets Slope Diamond.*) Poor little thing! She looks terribly tired.

TOM: Audrey, I'm warning you — (AUDREY *stares at diamond.*)

AUDREY: Something's wrong with Petronella. She — she looks so dirty and grimy.

TOM: Maybe she went out to play in a sandpile.

AUDREY: Be serious! I'm sure that Petronella is frightfully ill. (PROFESSOR *snaps to attention, rushes forward.*)

PROFESSOR: Ill? Did someone say that Petronella is ill?

AUDREY: Something's wrong, Professor. She seems so disconsolate, so lusterless. I'm sure the trip has been too much for her. I think she's lost a little weight.

PROFESSOR: This is terrible, terrible! (PROFESSOR *pushes* SPECTATORS *aside.*) Quick, I must take her pulse. (PROFESSOR *places his hand tenderly on diamond, studies his watch. He sighs, wipes his forehead.*) No, her pulse is normal.

AUDREY: Thank goodness for that.

PROFESSOR: Now to check her respiration. (*He removes stethoscope from his pocket, puts it on and listens to rock. Everyone waits anxiously.*)

HARRY: I told you that you should have taken out pet rock insurance.

AUDREY: I don't want to think about it.

HARRY: My company pays up to sixty days in a semi-private gravel bed — and even out-patient care.

3RD WOMAN: My Petunia looked the same way a few weeks ago. She came down with chips and erosion.

AUDREY: How dreadful!

3RD WOMAN: It was a mild case. Besides, her health isn't what it was — she's so old, she used to dance with the Rockettes.

AUDREY: I hope Petronella hasn't caught anything serious. She's never been ill before.

1ST WOMAN: Our little pet wasn't well for three days before we found out what was ailing her.

AUDREY: What was wrong?

1ST WOMAN (*Happily*): She's now the proud parent of three little pebbles! (PROFESSOR *removes stethoscope.*)

PROFESSOR: Just as I suspected. Petronella has had an attack of gall stones!

AUDREY: We'd better cover her right away before she becomes petrified. (AUDREY *removes a small blanket from her purse, spreads it over the diamond. The top of the diamond still shows.*)

PROFESSOR: She'll be all right, I'm sure. (PROFESSOR *bends over, presses his ear against the diamond. He straightens.*) Petronella has a case of laryngitis. It's a common ailment with pet rocks. That's why they don't speak too often. (*Suddenly*) Laryngitis! If Petronella has lost her voice, she won't be able to speak today! (ANNOUNCER *covers mike.*)

ANNOUNCER: What's all this about laryngitis? If that stupid rock can't speak, the network will lose a bundle. We'll sue the Suttons for fraud!

AUDREY: You can't do that! We didn't do anything wrong.

ANNOUNCER: The network spent a fortune to bring this telecast to the world, Mrs. Sutton. If that rock is sick, it's all your fault.

1ST CAMERMAN (*Sighing*): I even gave up Sesame Street for this! (*Commotion is heard offstage.* UNCLE ABNER *and* POLICEMAN *enter.* POLICEMAN *holds onto the protesting* UNCLE ABNER.)

ABNER (*Struggling*): Unhand me — you — you young idiot!

POLICEMAN: Don't tell me my business — I know how to deal with you. You're definitely the criminal type. (*Gesturing to others*) I found this old codger trying to break into the hotel. He said his nephew is up here. (TOM *emerges from crowd, waves his greeting, smiles weakly.*)

TOM: Uncle Abner! Er — you're looking very well.

ABNER: Bah! I never felt worse in my life. (ABNER *shakes loose from* POLICEMAN.) What's going on here, anyway?

TOM: You'd never believe it, Uncle Abner.

AUDREY: It's all my fault, Uncle Abner. You see, I bought a pet rock and —

ABNER: Yes, yes, I read that nonsense in the paper.

AUDREY: Things got out of hand. Petronella is a pedigreed pet rock. (*Proudly*) She's your grandniece. (ABNER *points accusingly at* TOM.)

ABNER: Are you responsible for this? (TOM *shakes his head.*)

AUDREY (*Quickly*): Petronella is descended from the Egyptian Sphinx. She's going to say the riddle of the Sphinx in a few minutes.

ABNER (*To* POLICEMAN): You'd better take me to headquarters. Everybody's crazy here!

TOM: No, no, Uncle Abner — you don't understand. Everything will be all right, after Petronella recovers from laryngitis.

ABNER (*Nodding*): Stark raving mad! (DINNY *and* MAMIE *enter left and watch the proceedings, unobserved.*)

PROFESSOR (*To* ABNER): It's obvious that you know nothing about pet rocks. They are lovable, gentle pets. All they require is a little understanding and attention.

1ST WOMAN: Under no circumstances should you turn your pet rock loose.

3RD WOMAN (*Nodding*): The world is already overcrowded with unwanted rocks, and millions must be destroyed each year.

1ST WOMAN (*Sobbing*): These poor little rocks meet brutal ends in roadbeds and cement mixers. (*She takes out handkerchief, rushes off right, sobbing.*)

ABNER (*To* POLICEMAN): I'm warning you, you'd better get me out of here. I'll confess to anything if you let me leave this nutty place.

TOM: Uncle Abner, they can't arrest you! You haven't done anything wrong. Stand up for your rights!

UNCLE ABNER: Oh, no! Don't *you* try to help me! You're as bad as the rest. No nephew of mine ever played with pet rocks!

TOM: But what about our partnership?

ABNER: Partnership, ha! The only partnership I'd offer you is an equal share in a gravel pit. (TOM *sinks against a table. Table tilts slightly. Diamond falls.* SPECTATORS *gasp.* MAMIE *and* DINNY *register interest. Quickly,* AUDREY *picks up diamond, fondles it.*)

AUDREY: Oh, you poor little dear. I hope you're not hurt.

2ND WOMAN: Try singing a chorus of "Rockabye, Baby." That always soothes my pet rock whenever she falls down and goes "boom." Of course, when she landed on my husband's foot, he sang a different tune. (AUDREY *frowns at diamond.*)

AUDREY: Why, one of her little stones has fallen out. (AUDREY *picks up chip of stone.*) My, see how it gleams! (DINNY *and* MAMIE *exchange glances.*)

POLICEMAN: Let me see that thing! (*He examines chip, then points to diamond.*) I think this is the missing Slope Diamond! (*Everyone registers surprise.*)

ANNOUNCER (*At mike*): Nighty-Night Mattress is bringing you all the action, folks. Stand by for new developments. (CAMERAMEN *move camera.*)

POLICEMAN (*To* ANNOUNCER): Enough TV talk, buddy. I'm throwing you into the clink, too. You can spend the rest of your life sleeping on a Nighty-Night mattress. (AUDREY *examines diamond.*)

AUDREY: You're right, officer. This isn't Petronella. (*She places diamond on the table, glances around anxiously.*) Where is my pet rock?

POLICEMAN: Maybe she went out for a little walk. (*Soberly*) I'm warning you. I won't stand for any nonsense.

AUDREY: You don't understand. Petronella is missing! She's been rocknapped!

POLICEMAN: We'll settle this entire matter at headquarters. (*He picks up diamond.*) I'm taking the Slope Diamond along as evidence. (*With authority*) Everyone is under arrest! (ABNER *shakes his fist at* TOM.)

ABNER: I'll disown you — after I've broken every bone in your body!

REPORTER: What a story! (*Waves dramatically*) "Geological Society Sent to Rockpile!"

POLICEMAN: You're coming along, too.

REPORTER: I protest. I'm a member of the press.

POLICEMAN: You'll get pressing, all right. In the prison laundry room! (MAMIE *looks nervously at* DINNY. DINNY *nods, takes gun from his pocket, rushes forward. He waves gun.*)

DINNY (*Shouting*): All right! Everyone up against the wall. (MAMIE *grabs diamond from* POLICEMAN.)

2ND CAMERAMAN: Oh, great. This guy thinks he's another Kojak. (DINNY *jams gun into* CAMERAMAN*'s ribs.*)

DINNY: We're getting out of this place, and nobody's going to stop us. (*To* POLICEMAN) You're coming along, too. (*Everyone registers shock.*)

TOM (*To* DINNY): You'll never get away with it.

DINNY (*Menacingly*): Would you like to stop us?

TOM (*Nervously*): Me? Oh, no! Ha! Ha! Go right ahead. (TOM *steps back near right table. He glances at table, sees* AUDREY's *rock in box on table.*)

PROFESSOR (*Indignantly*): What have you done to Petronella?

DINNY: I'm only interested in one rock — the Slope Diamond, and we're clearing out with it now. (*As* DINNY *talks, he turns his back to* TOM. TOM *quickly removes rock from box. He brings it down against* DINNY's *head.* DINNY *drops his gun. He wears a dazed, stupid expression.* MAMIE *screams.* POLICEMAN *retrieves* DINNY's *gun, quickly unholsters his own gun, levels it at* DINNY.)

POLICEMAN (*To* DINNY): Get moving! And I recognize you, too. You're Dinny the Dip — Public Enemy Number Fourteen.

DINNY (*Offended*): Public Enemy Number Thirteen.

MAMIE (*Thoughtfully*): I think it's Thirteen and a half, Dinny. The guy ahead of you is a midget!

POLICEMAN (*To* TOM): I'll need your testimony at headquarters, young man. I suspect there'll be a nice reward for Dinny's capture.

TOM: A reward? (POLICEMAN, DINNY *and* MAMIE *exit right.*)

ABNER: I don't know what's going on, but it's too much for me. First I find my nephew and his wife talking to a rock. Then my nephew apprehends a dangerous criminal with that stupid rock. (TOM *grins, hands rock to* AUDREY, *and looks over other rocks on table.*)

AUDREY: Please, Uncle Abner! Tom found Petronella for me, and she needs peace and quiet, after such a shattering experience. (TOM *holds up rock.*)

TOM: Uncle Abner, these are not just stupid rocks — this one, for example, is a piece of oil shale, and could lead somebody to a fortune.

ABNER: What's that? Where does it come from?

TOM: The exact location at which it was found is here. (*Holds up card*)

ABNER: Tom Sutton is a chip off the old block. (*Thumps* TOM *on the back*) If you're that good at spotting oil shale in the middle of this rockpile, you're the right partner for me. We'll make a fortune. (ABNER *smiles at* AUDREY's *rock.*) She's a cute little devil, isn't she? (ABNER *straightens, frowns*) Ahem . . . come to my room at this hotel when you've finished with the police, Tom, and we can discuss your future. (*Exits*)

PROFESSOR: I hope we're not too late. Petronella was supposed to speak a little while ago. (PROFESSOR *approaches rock dramatically.*) Speak to us, O descendant of the Sphinx. Tell us the riddle of the ages! (*Everyone focuses attention on rock.*) Speak, I command you. The world awaits your message. Speak! (PROFESSOR *smiles persuasively.*) Won't you say one little word to us? (PROFESSOR *straightens, shrugs.*) It's no use. Petronella will not speak!

AUDREY (*Nodding*): After all this excitement, she's probably too frightened. (*Pats rock*)

PROFESSOR: I'm afraid we'll have to wait another century!

ANNOUNCER (*At mike*): And while you're waiting, ladies and gentlemen, you can sleep in luxury on a Nighty-Night mattress! (*Brightly*) Petronella didn't speak, but she helped capture a dangerous criminal. (AUDREY *tugs at* TOM's *arm.*)

AUDREY: He's right. Petronella saved the Slope Diamond.

TOM: What about me?

AUDREY: If it hadn't been for her, you couldn't have conked Dinny the Dip.

ANNOUNCER (*At mike*): Petronella is the unanimous choice for

Pet Rock of the Year! (*Everyone cheers.* 1ST WOMAN *re-enters and joins* ANNOUNCER.)

1ST WOMAN: My friend has a pet rock on display in there. (*She gestures left.*) Her pet can recite "Twinkle, Twinkle, Little Star"!

PROFESSOR: Yes, yes, there are such rocks. They are descendants of the star sapphire.

ANNOUNCER (*At mike*): An unforgettable moment! A pet rock who recites "Twinkle, Twinkle, Little Star!"

REPORTER: What a story! Let's go see that rock! (*Everyone exits left except* TOM *and* AUDREY. TOM *sighs.*)

TOM: It's been quite a day.

AUDREY (*Smiling*): Everything turned out perfectly. Petronella is a national heroine — and you're going to be Uncle Abner's partner.

TOM: We'd better get to headquarters and see about that reward. (AUDREY *blows a kiss at pet rock.*)

AUDREY: We'll be right back, darling.

TOM (*Shaking head*): I still don't believe that pet rocks can heel and roll over and sit. And I don't believe that they can speak.

AUDREY: You have no imagination! You've got to believe! (*Filtered voice is heard from offstage microphone.*)

PETRONELLA (*Over microphone*): I'm tired now. This convention is boring. If you can spare me for the afternoon, I wish you'd take me to a rock concert. The Rolling Stones are playing my song. (TOM *and* AUDREY *stare at each other.*)

TOM: What did you say? I never knew you liked rock music.

AUDREY: I didn't say a word. I though that was you.

TOM: Not me. I didn't say anything.

AUDREY: Then it must have been. . . .

TOM: You don't mean . . . (*Both whirl on* PETRONELLA *and gasp, pointing at rock.*) Was it really? I wouldn't have believed it if I hadn't heard it with my own ears. Audrey, you were right all along. Hooray!

AUDREY: And you thought I had rocks in my head! (*They embrace as curtain closes.*)

THE END

Production Notes

Don't Pet My Rock!

Characters: 10 male; 6 female; 2 male or female for TV Cameramen; as many male and female as desired for Other Spectators.

Playing Time: 35 minutes.

Costumes: Modern everyday dress. Policeman and Bellhop wear appropriate uniforms. Audrey carries purse.

Properties: Cordless mike, TV "camera" on casters, shoe box containing large light-colored rock, newspaper, notebook, pencil, alarm clock, large rock for Slope Diamond, stethoscope, small blanket, water pistol, guns for Dinny and Policeman.

Setting: The Grand Ballroom of Rockefeller Center. Entrances are right and left. Two long tables right and left are covered with displays of pet rocks. Another empty table is at center. Banner at back may read: PET ROCK CONVENTION. WE LEAVE NO STONE UNTURNED TO WELCOME YOU.

Lighting: No special effects.

Mystery Liner

Little do passengers on board the cruise ship Venture
*expect that in addition to sun, good food, and pleasant com-
panions their ocean voyage will include — murder.* . . .

Characters

WAYNE COLLINS
LINDA COLLINS, *his wife*
ADAM MASTERS
JOAN
CONNIE
MRS. VAN CLEEF
ROBERTA GREGORY, *a debutante*
DONALD BLAINE, *steward*
CAPTAIN WATSON
DR. HOLLAND
MISS ATKINS, *social director*
ALAN DIRKSON
WAITER
PASSENGERS

SCENE 1

SETTING: *The Nautilus Lounge on board the S. S.* Venture, *a
cruise ship. There are sofas down left and right, and dining
tables and chairs up left and right. Exit at upstage center
leads to deck. Backdrop of ship's railing, with a life preserver attached to it, is seen through center exit. Exit at left
leads to galley and main dining room.*

AT RISE: *The Nautilus Lounge is full of activity as* PASSENGERS *enter, talking happily, and sit at tables upstage, or exit left.* WAYNE *and* LINDA COLLINS *sit on sofa down right, conversing animatedly.* MRS. VAN CLEEF, *holding a green traveling case, and* MISS ATKINS, *ship's social director, sit on sofa left, talking.* WAITER, *carrying tray of dishes, enters left, serves* PASSENGERS *at table up left, then crosses to another table and takes order.* ALAN DIRKSON *enters at center, looks around room, sees* MRS. VAN CLEEF *and watches her steadily as he sits alone at a table, up left.* JOAN *and* CONNIE *enter center and cross downstage.* JOAN *beams, but* CONNIE *looks worried.*

JOAN (*Happily*): Here we are, on board the *Venture*. How do you like the ship, Connie?

CONNIE (*Glumly*): I don't know why you persuaded me to change our plans. We were supposed to return to New York on the *Iberia* the day after tomorrow.

JOAN: Every eligible male on that ship was positively ancient — at least thirty-five. It made our trip to Puerto Rico a disaster. But did you see Donald Blaine, the steward on this ship? (*Sighs loudly*) He's beautiful!

CONNIE (*Impatiently*): Never mind that, Joan. Let's find our cabin.

JOAN: There's — uh — something I forgot to tell you. There are so many people traveling this time of year, you see.

CONNIE (*Interrupting*): What's the number of our cabin?

JOAN (*Sheepishly*): I wasn't able to get a cabin.

CONNIE: Do you mean — we're stowaways? Joan, how could you?

JOAN (*Desperately*): I simply had to meet the steward! It'll take only two days to reach New York, and we can sleep in the lifeboats and the theatre.

CONNIE: We'll probably sleep in the brig! (*Suddenly*) Where are our suitcases? I thought you sent them to our cabin.

JOAN: I had them flown to New York by air express. (*Pointing to tables*) I'm starved. Let's eat!

CONNIE: Our travelers' checks — all our money — are in those suitcases! We don't have a dime.

JOAN: We'll eat. Don't worry. I have a plan. Come on. (*Pulls* CONNIE *to table upstage. They sit.* WAITER *crosses to them, pantomimes taking their order. During the following scene, he serves them. Meanwhile* WAYNE COLLINS *stands, stretches.*)

WAYNE: Ah, this is the life! A sea voyage! No noisy cities, no telephones, no public appearances — and no Leslie Popinjay.

LINDA: Don't mention that name! I came on this cruise to forget that I'm Leslie Popinjay, author of four mystery novels. I just want to be Mrs. Wayne Collins, wife of a very promising — but very stubborn — architect.

WAYNE: Now, Linda.

LINDA: My novels have been very popular, I might add.

WAYNE (*Reciting titles*): *The Headless Corpse — Blood on the Snow — The Cringing Cadaver — The Case of the Fabulous Fiend!* I'm married to a major crime wave! (ROBERTA GREGORY *enters center and stands near table looking around impatiently.* LINDA *brightens, tugs at* WAYNE*'s arm.*)

LINDA: Wayne, that's Roberta Gregory!

WAYNE: Who?

LINDA: You know — the famous debutante. She's always in the newspapers.

WAYNE (*Shrugging*): So what? That doesn't mean anything. It looks as though she's waiting for someone. (ROBERTA *paces back and forth.*)

LINDA: It's more than that. She's acting so nervous — so worried. Oh, I'm sure she's in trouble.

WAYNE (*Strongly*): You're looking for material for a new mystery novel, are you?

LINDA: Don't be silly. (*Mysteriously*) Do you think she's in danger?

WAYNE (*Exploding*): There you go again! I'm warning you, Leslie Popinjay, stop butting into other people's lives! (MRS. VAN CLEEF *looks up and sees* LINDA.)

MRS. VAN CLEEF: Leslie Popinjay! (*She jumps up and rushes to* LINDA, *gesturing to* MISS ATKINS *to follow her.* DIRKSON *watches.*) Leslie Popinjay! (*Pumps* LINDA*'s hand*) Oh, this is an honor, indeed. (*Pulls* MISS ATKINS *forward*) Miss Atkins, the ship's social director, pointed you out. I'm so excited! I am Mrs. Eugene Van Cleef, and I simply adore Puerto Rico at this time of year. It's so much better than Europe, don't you think? (WAYNE *and* LINDA *stare, bewildered.*) Now, what was I talking about? Of course — Leslie Popinjay! I simply adore mysteries. *The Headless Corpse* and all those things. (*Looking her over*) But you seem dreadfully young to be murdering all those people.

LINDA (*Weakly*): I'm pleased to meet you, Mrs. Van Cleef.

WAYNE (*Disgruntled*): Same here.

MRS. VAN CLEEF: You must join me tonight. The Captain's table, of course. Miss Atkins will arrange it.

LINDA: Miss Atkins, you look so familiar. I'm sure we've met before.

MISS ATKINS: No, no — I don't think so.

LINDA: But I'm sure I recognize you. Have I seen your picture?

MISS ATKINS (*Nervously*): If you'll excuse me . . . . The other passengers — I have an appointment. (*Exits*)

MRS. VAN CLEEF: I'm exhausted, simply exhausted! (*Pats her traveling case.* DIRKSON *leans forward, watching.*) My little friends and I must retire to our stateroom now. But don't forget, Leslie Popinjay — dinner tonight. (*To* WAYNE) You're included too, Mr. Popinjay! (*Exits, followed quickly by* DIRKSON.)

WAYNE: How dare she call me Mr. Popinjay!

LINDA: Please, Wayne. Something's wrong.

WAYNE: What now?

LINDA: That man just followed Mrs. Van Cleef! He was watching her all the time. (*Worried*) And Miss Atkins. I know I've seen her before. Could there be some connection?

WAYNE (*Annoyed*): For Pete's sake!

LINDA: Mrs. Van Cleef must be very rich. What did she mean by her little friends? What does she carry in that case?

WAYNE: I've had enough mysteries for one morning. (*Takes her arm and steers her to sofa right. They talk in pantomime. ADAM MASTERS enters center, sees ROBERTA and crosses to her chair. She tries to rise, but he grabs her arm, pushes her into chair. He sits beside her.*)

MASTERS (*Coldly*): Good morning, Miss Gregory.

ROBERTA (*Nervously*): There must be some mistake. I'm not Miss Gregory.

MASTERS: Come now, Roberta. Anyone would recognize you from your pictures. I've been looking for you. (*Grimly*) I am deeply interested in three people aboard the *Venture*.

ROBERTA: What do you want?

MASTERS (*Suddenly wincing in pain*): Ouch! I have a splitting headache. I've just taken something for it. (*Takes note from pocket*) I'd like you to read this note. You'll find my cabin number at the bottom. I'm sure I'll hear from you. (LINDA *turns, watches them.*)

ROBERTA (*Frightened*): What do you want with me? (*He brushes his hand across his face.*)

MASTERS: All in good time. (*Smiles faintly*) One meets such interesting people on an ocean voyage. (*Exits center. ROBERTA quickly reads note, crumples it and drops it into ashtray, then exits center. LINDA crosses to table, seizes note. WAYNE follows.*)

WAYNE: What are you going to do?

LINDA: I want to read this note, of course. (*She smooths paper, reads aloud.*) "If you don't want Donald Blaine to know the truth about your father's investments, I'll expect to hear from you within the hour." (*Puts note into purse*) I was right! That man's trying to blackmail Robert Gregory.

WAYNE (*Musing*): Donald Blaine — that name's familiar.

LINDA (*Nodding*): He's the ship's steward. Oh, don't you see? Donald's probably in love with Roberta Gregory, and that man, whoever he is, is threatening to expose her.

WAYNE (*Waving his hand*): Hold on! This sounds like the first three chapters of a Leslie Popinjay novel. Maybe he's just a bill collector.

LINDA (*Determined*): I'm going to find the Captain and show him this note.

WAYNE: Linda, you're just asking for trouble. I think we should mind our own business. (*Firmly*) Now, let's sit down and talk this over. (*They cross to sofa, sit, pantomime conversation.* WAITER *enters, crosses to* JOAN *and* CONNIE.)

WAITER: Ladies, did you enjoy the sautéed snails?

JOAN: Snails? I thought they were mushrooms! (*Covers mouth with napkin.* WAITER *offers* JOAN *check and pen.*)

WAITER: If you will kindly sign the check —

CONNIE (*Nervously*): The — the check!

JOAN (*Quickly*): Of course I'll sign the check. (*Takes pen, signs. Gives check and pen to* WAITER.) There!

WAITER (*Reading*): Cabin U-19. But you've made a mistake.

JOAN (*Affectedly*): The very idea!

WAITER: Cabin U-19 is the Captain's washroom!

CONNIE: The washroom?

JOAN: I did make a mistake.

WAITER (*Suspiciously*): To be sure! (DONALD BLAINE, *steward, enters left.* WAITER *signals him.*) Mr. Blaine, these young ladies claim that they are sleeping in the Captain's washroom.

JOAN: It was just a mistake. I —

CONNIE: Oh, why don't you tell him the truth?

BLAINE: If I can be of any assistance —

CONNIE: You might escort us to the brig. You see, we don't sleep in the Captain's washroom. We don't sleep anywhere. We were supposed to sail on the *Iberia*, but we stowed away on the *Venture* instead.

JOAN: Connie! You promised you wouldn't tell.

WAITER (*Indignantly*): Shall I call Captain Watson to deal with — with these stowaways?

BLAINE: That won't be necessary. I'm sure I can handle this matter. (WAITER *glares, picks up tray, bill, and pen, and turns to exit. Suddenly* ADAM MASTERS *staggers in at upstage center, grasping his throat in pain. Several* PASSENGERS *notice him and watch in surprise.* LINDA *sees* MASTERS, *impulsively cries out.*)

LINDA: That's the man who threatened Roberta Gregory!

WAYNE (*Putting arm around* LINDA *as if to hold her back*): Something's wrong with him. (MASTERS *looks about frantically, sees pen in* WAITER*'s hand, crosses to him and pulls pen out of his hand.* WAITER *watches, stunned.* MASTERS *walks haltingly to wall up left, lifts pen and draws a large* "R" *on wall. He draws short diagonal line to the right of it, then suddenly drops pen, gasps as if choking, falls to floor.* CONNIE *screams.* PASSENGERS *talk excitedly to each other.* BLAINE *and* WAYNE *rush to* MASTERS. LINDA *stands, watching.* BLAINE *feels for* MASTERS' *pulse and presses head to* MASTERS' *chest, then lifts his head.*)

BLAINE (*To* WAITER): Call Dr. Holland immediately. (PASSENGERS *begin to move closer to* MASTERS. BLAINE *stands, speaks loudly.*) Will you all please return to your cabins?

LINDA (*Crossing to stand with* WAYNE): What's wrong — is he hurt?

BLAINE: I'm afraid he's dead. (*Turns to look at "R" on wall, as curtains close*)

* * * * *

TIME: *A few hours later.*

SETTING: *The same as Scene 1.*

AT RISE: LINDA, WAYNE, MISS ATKINS, ROBERTA GREGORY, BLAINE, DOCTOR HOLLAND *and* CAPTAIN WATSON *are assembled in Lounge.* LINDA *and* WAYNE *sit on sofa at right.* MISS ATKINS, ROBERTA *and* BLAINE *sit on sofa left.* DOCTOR HOLLAND *stands down left.* WATSON *stands center, addressing group.*

WATSON: As Captain of the *Venture* it is my duty to conduct a preliminary investigation into the death of Adam Masters, who died in this room just two hours ago. We have established Masters' identity through a check of the passenger list. Dr. Holland, will you acquaint us with the cause of death?

HOLLAND (*Clearing his throat*): I would like to run a few more tests, but I'm almost certain Adam Masters died of strychnine poisoning. Strychnine is one of the fastest-acting poisons, so it must have been administered to Masters only a short time before his death.

WAYNE (*Standing*): I want to know why we have been detained. Linda and I didn't even know the man's name.

LINDA: Please, Wayne! Captain Watson has to speak to all the witnesses.

WATSON: Thank you, Mrs. Collins. (*Smiling*) I've read several of your mysteries. You're very knowledgeable about poisons.

LINDA (*Shocked*): Surely you don't think I had anything to do with that man's death, simply because I know something about poison!

WATSON: No, no, Mrs. Collins. Don't jump to conclusions.

Perhaps you'll be able to help me with my investigation. (*To* ROBERTA) Now, Miss Gregory, I understand from one of our waiters that you talked to Masters not long before his death.

ROBERTA (*Flustered*): I — I never met him before. It was a mistake.

WATSON: The waiter also informed me that Masters gave you a letter which you read and dropped on the table. After you left, the letter was retrieved and read by Mrs. Collins.

LINDA (*Quickly*): I thought it might be important. I was going to return the letter to Miss Gregory.

ROBERTA (*In disbelief; to* LINDA): Did you read that letter? (LINDA *nods.*) Then you know . . . . There was a question about a stock transfer my father put through several years ago. He didn't do anything wrong, but if it were brought to light, it would cause a scandal. My father has a weak heart. He couldn't take the shock. (BLAINE *embraces* ROBERTA.)

BLAINE (*Tenderly*): Roberta, why didn't you tell me about that blackmailer?

ROBERTA: I didn't *know* he wanted to blackmail me, until I read the note.

WATSON: Mr. Blaine, you are acquainted with Miss Gregory, I see.

BLAINE: We were married in San Juan. (*All turn to them, surprised.*)

LINDA: You're married?

ROBERTA (*Shakily*): Donald and I decided to keep our marriage a secret until we arrived in New York. We didn't want any publicity.

BLAINE (*Nodding*): People would be bound to think I married Roberta for her money.

ROBERTA: Donald, I would have paid that dreadful man anything to keep him from hurting us.

BLAINE: Do you think it would have mattered? Do you think that anything could have come between us?

WATSON: Miss Gregory — or I believe it is now Mrs. Blaine — exactly what did Masters say to you?

ROBERTA: I can't remember. He insisted that I come to his cabin within an hour. That was all.

WATSON: He spoke of nothing else?

ROBERTA: He mentioned that there were three people aboard the *Venture* in whom he was interested.

BLAINE: Three people?

ROBERTA (*Nodding*): He didn't mention their names, but I'm sure he had something terrible in mind.

WATSON (*Musing*): It seems that Masters may have been a blackmailer on a large scale. (*To* ROBERTA) He attempted to blackmail you, and there are two other people on board that he may have approached for money. Two other people who might have wanted him out of the way . . . . (MISS ATKINS *drops her purse, quickly picks it up. She starts to speak.*) Yes, Miss Atkins? Did you wish to say something?

MISS ATKINS: No, no, Captain Watson. It was nothing at all. (*Fumbles nervously with purse.* LINDA *watches her.*)

WATSON (*To* ROBERTA): Did Masters give you any clue to the identity of the other two persons?

ROBERTA: No. He mentioned something about a headache, though, before he left.

BLAINE: A headache? Did Masters say that he wasn't feeling well?

ROBERTA (*Nodding*): Something like that.

BLAINE: Then maybe he had already been poisoned when he spoke to you.

LINDA: I don't think that's possible. Strychnine is too fast-acting.

HOLLAND: I must agree with you, Mrs. Collins.

LINDA (*Suddenly*): Unless the poison were enclosed in some kind of capsule, something that would have to melt.

WATSON: That's a possibility. We'll have to trace Masters'

actions from the time he left the salon until he staggered in here and died a short time later. (*A scream is heard offstage.* MRS. VAN CLEEF *rushes in upstage center, clutching her traveling case.*)

MRS. VAN CLEEF (*Breathlessly*): Oh, that dreadful man! (WATSON *crosses to her, helps her to chair.*)

WATSON: Calm down, Mrs. Van Cleef.

LINDA: What happened?

MRS. VAN CLEEF: I — I saw a man looking into my cabin. From the porthole on the main deck.

LINDA: What man?

MRS. VAN CLEEF: I don't know his name, but I thought I saw him in the lounge a little while ago.

WAYNE (*Snapping fingers*): I think I saw him, too. He left shortly after Mrs. Van Cleef and Miss Atkins.

MISS ATKINS: Is there anything I can do for you, Mrs. Van Cleef?

MRS. VAN CLEEF: No, no, my dear. I'm all right now. (*To others*) You see, Miss Atkins took me to my cabin earlier, and then I watched from my porthole as she entered her own cabin. Then I slept for a while, and when I woke up — I felt someone watching me! And then I saw him — looking through the porthole. I screamed, and he ran away. (*Clutches traveling case*) I know he was trying to steal my traveling case! (*Glances around*) Why is everyone so solemn?

LINDA: A man has been murdered. I'll tell you all about it. (*She sits by* MRS. VAN CLEEF, *pantomimes conversation.*)

WATSON (*To* BLAINE): I want you to find out the identity of the man who was watching Mrs. Van Cleef.

BLAINE: Yes, sir. (*To* ROBERTA) I'll take you to your cabin, dear. (*They exit.* CONNIE *and* JOAN *rush in.*)

JOAN: I hope we haven't missed the excitement!

WATSON: I've been looking for you two — I want to see you in my quarters, at once.

JOAN: We didn't mean to do anything wrong.

HOLLAND: Captain, will you excuse me? There are several prescriptions I must fill.

WATSON: Of course, Dr. Holland. Thank you for your help. (HOLLAND *exits up center.*) Come along, young ladies. (WATSON, JOAN *and* CONNIE *exit left.* MRS. VAN CLEEF *jumps up, excited.*)

MRS. VAN CLEEF: A murder mystery! Why, Miss Popinjay, this is just like one of your novels. *The Headless Corpse* — or something like that. You're simply marvelous at thinking up poisons and murder weapons.

WAYNE (*Uncomfortably*): This is hardly the time to mention that.

MRS. VAN CLEEF: Well, it's still an exciting voyage. And Miss Atkins has been wonderful. Why, she's as good as any nurse I've ever had.

LINDA: A nurse? Of course! (*To* MISS ATKINS) Why didn't I recognize you before?

MISS ATKINS: I don't know what you're talking about.

LINDA: You're a nurse. I read about you in one of the detective magazines. Only your name wasn't Atkins — it was Adams.

MISS ATKINS: That's not true!

WAYNE: What are you talking about, Linda?

LINDA: I never forget a face. I recognized her from the story about an unsolved crime.

WAYNE: I wish you would tell me what this is all about.

LINDA: Miss Atkins — or Adams — was the nurse for a wealthy old woman.

MISS ATKINS: Miss Kramer. She died.

LINDA (*Slowly*): And the coroner's report showed that Miss Kramer died from strychnine poisoning!

MISS ATKINS: There was an inquest, and I was cleared. I didn't know what to do after that. All the publicity! I had to get away. I found this job on the *Venture*. You won't tell the Captain, will you? He must never know.

MRS. VAN CLEEF: You poor dear! Of course your secret is safe with us.

LINDA: It wasn't safe with Masters. He threatened to expose you — isn't that right?

MISS ATKINS (*Nodding*): Yes. He gave me a note, too, telling me to come to his cabin, if I didn't want the Captain to know about my past.

LINDA: And you went there shortly after you left Mrs. Van Cleef.

MISS ATKINS: How did you know that?

LINDA: Simple. Mrs. Van Cleef said she watched you enter your cabin. Your cabin isn't on this deck at all — but Masters' cabin is next to Mrs. Van Cleef's.

MISS ATKINS: You're right. I went there. Masters threatened to tell the Captain everything about the Kramer case. I pleaded with him, but he insisted that I pay him two hundred dollars a month.

LINDA: There was someone else aboard the ship whom he intended to blackmail. First, Roberta Gregory — second, Miss Atkins — and the third . . . .

WAYNE: The third suspect. (*To* MISS ATKINS) Did Masters mention anyone else aboard ship?

MISS ATKINS: No, no one.

LINDA: Did he mention anything about a headache?

MISS ATKINS: No.

LINDA: Did you see any capsules or headache pills in his cabin?

MISS ATKINS: No, I didn't look for anything like that. There might have been a glass of water on his table — I'm not sure.

MRS. VAN CLEEF (*Impatiently*): Headaches? Blackmail? Fiddlesticks! Leslie Popinjay, I'm surprised at you! You overlooked the most important thing.

LINDA: I don't understand.

MRS. VAN CLEEF: Masters' clue to the identity of his murderer. (*She points to* "R" *on upstage wall.*) You told me that he wrote the letter "R" on the wall just before he died. (*Crosses to wall and points to small diagonal line right of* "R") It looks as though he tried to write something else here, too.

LINDA: The letter "R." The name of his murderer! (*Suddenly*) Roberta Gregory!

WAYNE: Hey! Don't jump to conclusions! Of course "R" is Roberta's initial, but Masters might have meant something else. (JOAN *and* CONNIE *enter.*)

JOAN: That's a relief!

CONNIE: The Captain assigned us to a small cabin, and he's going to let us pay for it in New York.

JOAN: Not only that — he asked us to help Miss Atkins with the ship's ball tomorrow night.

CONNIE: A masquerade ball!

MISS ATKINS: I certainly do need help. (*To others*) We always have a talent show and masquerade ball the night before we land.

JOAN: Just think of all the men!

MRS. VAN CLEEF: I'm going to my cabin now.

MISS ATKINS: Of course. It's been a very trying day for you. You must be exhausted.

MRS. VAN CLEEF: Don't be absurd! I'm going to work on a costume for the masquerade tomorrow night. I feel simply marvelous! (*She exits center with* MISS ATKINS.)

LINDA (*To* JOAN *and* CONNIE): You two can give me some help, too.

JOAN: It'll be a pleasure!

WAYNE (*Warningly*): Now, Linda.

LINDA (*Continuing*): We're going to my cabin, and I'm going to give you a list of people who are involved in this murder. You're going to visit each of them and say that Linda Collins knows the identity of the third suspect.

WAYNE (*Angrily*): Are you out of your mind? I'm not going to let you be a sitting duck for a murderer just to get an idea for a thriller. Whoever killed Masters will try anything to silence you!

LINDA: Please, Wayne! We'll be in New York the day after tomorrow, so we have only a short time to catch the murderer. (*To* JOAN *and* CONNIE) Come with me. We have a lot of work to do! (LINDA, JOAN *and* CONNIE *exit up center.* WAYNE *follows them off. In a moment,* DIRKSON *enters left. He glances around room nervously, then crosses to upstage wall and stares at letter* "R" *as curtains close.*)

* * * * *

<h2 align="center">SCENE 3</h2>

TIME: *The following night.*

SETTING: *The Lounge, as in Scene 1, now decorated with streamers and balloons. Letter "R" remains on upstage wall.*

AT RISE: PASSENGERS, *in masquerade costumes, are dancing downstage to recorded music from offstage. Other* PASSENGERS *in costume stroll in upstage center, talking softly.* CAPTAIN WATSON *and* BLAINE, *in uniform, enter left and cross downstage, followed by* ROBERTA *and* MISS ATKINS, *both wearing everyday dress.*

ROBERTA: I'm terribly frightened.

BLAINE: There's nothing to worry about, dear.

MISS ATKINS: But — a masquerade ball! It seems so strange — after the murder.

WATSON: I'd like to know what Joan and Connie have been up to all day.

BLAINE: Yes — they were very mysterious.

ROBERTA: I think they're working with Linda.

WATSON: I hope Linda Collins knows what she's doing. (JOAN *and* CONNIE *rush in center, in vaudeville costumes. They join others.*)

JOAN (*To* WATSON): Captain, this is the most exciting cruise I've ever taken!

CONNIE: This is the *first* cruise you've ever taken. And the last — with me! (MRS. VAN CLEEF *enters, wearing a long gown and Gay Nineties hat trimmed with feathers.*)

MRS. VAN CLEEF: Hello, everyone. (*Joins others.*)

MISS ATKINS: You look marvelous, Mrs. Van Cleef. But I must admit, I'm not used to seeing you without your traveling case.

MRS. VAN CLEEF: I know, but Wayne Collins insisted I leave it in my stateroom.

BLAINE: What is in that case?

MRS. VAN CLEEF (*Casually*): My jewels, of course.

BLAINE: Jewels? No wonder you were followed yesterday! (*To* WATSON) Captain, we'd better lock up those jewels in the safe at once.

WATSON: You're right. Take care of it, will you, please? (BLAINE *nods and exits.*)

MRS. VAN CLEEF: But you're making a terrible fuss about nothing. Please let me explain! (*She breaks off as* WAYNE *and* LINDA *enter, up center, calling greetings.* LINDA *wears a ballerina costume, and* WAYNE *a clown suit. Both wear half-masks. They cross to group downstage, remove masks.*) Linda, how lovely you look!

WATSON: Collins, I'd like a word with you. Mrs. Van Cleef tells us she left her case in her stateroom — at your insistence.

WAYNE (*To* MRS. VAN CLEEF): Didn't you tell the Captain about your jewels?

MRS. VAN CLEEF: I tried to tell him, but — (*Shouts are heard offstage.* BLAINE *enters, with* DIRKSON. *He holds* DIRKSON'*s arms pinned behind his back, and pushes him center.*

BLAINE: Here's our man, Captain. I found him in Mrs. Van Cleef's cabin.

DIRKSON: I knew I'd get into trouble when I accepted this

assignment. (*He pulls free from* BLAINE, *produces wallet, takes out card, hands it to* WATSON.)

WATSON (*Reading*): Alan Dirkson — Licensed Private Investigator!

JOAN: A detective!

DIRKSON: I was hired by Mrs. Van Cleef's brother to guard her.

MRS. VAN CLEEF: My brother Horace?

DIRKSON: She's carrying a fortune in jewels in her traveling case.

MRS. VAN CLEEF: Nonsense! Let me tell you all something. My jewels are paste — fakes! My brother is an idiot, but he does come up with a good idea occasionally. I listened to him and decided to have my jewels duplicated in paste before I left on this cruise. The real jewels are in a bank vault in New York.

DIRKSON: All this — for nothing!

WAYNE: I persuaded Mrs. Van Cleef to leave the jewels unguarded in her cabin. Linda and I have been watching it all night.

LINDA (*Nodding*): We thought that the jewel thief might be the murderer.

DIRKSON: You can't pin a murder rap on me!

LINDA: Calm down, Mr. Dirkson. We had no idea you were a detective. (*To others*) Now, what do we do? We'll be in New York tomorrow and the murderer is still at large.

MRS. VAN CLEEF: I don't know about the rest of you, but all this excitement has given me an appetite. Captain, where's the food?

WATSON: A midnight supper is being served in the main dining room.

MRS. VAN CLEEF: Oh, Captain, this is just what the doctor ordered! (*They exit left, followed by* CONNIE, JOAN *and* PASSENGERS.)

WAYNE (*Snapping fingers*): That's it!

LINDA: What are you talking about?

WAYNE: It's an incredible idea — but I just might be right. (*Pointing to upstage wall*) I think I've cracked Masters' secret message.

BLAINE: Who is the murderer?

WAYNE: I'm not sure yet, but I think (*Pauses*) — why don't you all go in to supper. I'll join you soon.

LINDA: No! I'm going with you.

WAYNE: Leslie Popinjay isn't the only one who can solve mysteries in this family. I'll see you later. (*He puts on his mask, exits center.*)

LINDA (*Calling after him*): Wayne! (*She starts to go up center, but* BLAINE *takes her arm.*)

BLAINE: I think you should come to supper with us.

LINDA: No, no. I want to wait for Wayne.

BLAINE: Are you sure?

LINDA: Please! I'll be all right. (*Reluctantly,* BLAINE, DIRKSON, MISS ATKINS *and* ROBERTA *exit left.* LINDA *paces nervously.*) That husband of mine! (*Crosses to upstage wall, traces letter "R" with finger, then traces short diagonal line at right of "R" with finger. Excited.*) Of course! The answer to the mystery was there all the time. I'd better find Wayne before he gets into trouble! (DOCTOR HOLLAND *enters, wearing clown suit identical to* WAYNE*'s and half-mask.* LINDA *takes his arm.*) Wayne, I'm so glad you're safe! When I guessed who the murderer was, I began to worry about you. (HOLLAND *squeezes her arm.*) I've figured it all out. Masters had a headache and he was going to take something for it. Who was the most logical person to give him a painkiller? The ship's doctor! I'll bet Masters recognized Dr. Holland. Maybe Holland was guilty of some crime, and Masters tried to blackmail him, so Dr. Holland gave him a pill for his headache that was really a capsule of strychnine! (*Tugs at* HOLLAND*'s arm*) Please, Wayne, let's go find Captain Watson and tell him.

HOLLAND (*Coldly*): You're a very clever woman, Mrs. Collins. (*Rips off his mask.*)

LINDA (*Terrified*): Dr. Holland!

HOLLAND: But you're just a little too clever, I'm afraid.

LINDA: Where's Wayne?

HOLLAND: I found him searching my cabin — so I had to silence him.

LINDA (*Frightened*): What have you done to him?

HOLLAND: He's not hurt. I didn't have time to dispose of him, because I had to find you — I didn't know how much he'd told you. I borrowed his costume, but all that was an unnecessary precaution, because I found you alone. Now, please, Mrs. Collins, come with me.

LINDA (*Fearful*): What are you going to do with me?

HOLLAND: There are many unfortunate accidents at sea. A slippery deck — a broken railing — and you and your husband will disappear. (LINDA *starts to scream, but* HOLLAND *clamps his hand over her mouth. He drags her up center. Suddenly* WAYNE *enters center, in shirt and pants, rubbing his head, dazed.*)

WAYNE: Holland! Let go of her! (*They struggle.*)

LINDA (*Screaming*): Help! Captain! Help! (WATSON *and* BLAINE *rush in left and hold* HOLLAND.)

WAYNE (*Pointing to* HOLLAND): Here's the murderer, Captain. (HOLLAND, *still struggling, is forcibly led off by* BLAINE. LINDA *collapses on sofa as* MRS. VAN CLEEF, MISS ATKINS, DIRKSON, JOAN *and* CONNIE *hurry in left.*)

ROBERTA: What happened?

LINDA (*Weakly*): We just caught a murderer — that's all.

WAYNE: You mean, *I* did. After all, I caught Dr. Holland. (*All gasp, surprised.*)

MRS. VAN CLEEF: Dr. Holland? Was he the murderer?

WAYNE: Yes, Dr. Holland murdered Adam Masters. Actually, you gave me the clue to the murderer's identity, Mrs. Van Cleef.

MRS. VAN CLEEF: Did I really? How exciting!

WAYNE: Earlier tonight you said, "Just what the doctor ordered!" And everything fell into place. A doctor is the logical person to have administered poison to Masters without arousing suspicion.

ROBERTA: You mean — headache pills?

LINDA: That's right. When Masters visited the doctor, he recognized Holland and tried to blackmail him. Holland suddenly decided to kill him. Masters' dying clue. (*Points to* "R" *upstage*) That told the rest of the story.

MRS. VAN CLEEF: That symbol is still Greek to me!

WAYNE: It's not Greek, it's Latin.

LINDA: Masters wanted to leave a clue after he realized that he'd been poisoned. He didn't have time to write Holland's name, but he gave us a clue. Unfortunately, he didn't live to finish it. (*Crosses to wall, points*) Do you see this little diagonal line? (*Takes pen from purse*) I believe this is what he intended to write. (*She draws diagonal line down through leg of* "R.")

CAPTAIN: I see! It's not "R" — it's "Rx" —symbol for a doctor's prescription.

JOAN: How dramatic!

WAYNE: When I confronted Holland with the evidence, he bashed me over the head with something and I passed out. He must have taken my costume. I knew he'd try to find you, Linda, so I headed here as soon as I came to.

LINDA: You didn't get here too soon! (*Snaps fingers*) This would make a wonderful plot for a mystery novel!

WAYNE (*Rubbing head*): Don't tell me you're thinking about another book.

LINDA: Yes, dear. It takes place on board a ship.

WAYNE: But we came on this cruise to relax!

LINDA: Who cares about that? This is a great idea, and it will be my best book. I'm going to start writing at once.

WAYNE (*Shrugging*): You've forgotten about me again, haven't you?

LINDA: No, darling, of course not. I'm going to make you the hero! (WAYNE *groans. Others laugh. Quick curtain.*)

THE END

Production Notes

Mystery Liner

Characters: 7 male; 6 female; male and female extras for Passengers.

Playing Time: 35 minutes.

Costumes: Casual vacation dress. Watson and Blaine wear uniforms. In Scene 3, Joan and Connie wear vaudeville costumes: striped blazers, white slacks, straw hats. Mrs. Van Cleef wears a Gay Nineties hat with feathers and a flowing gown, Wayne wears a clown suit and half mask, and Linda wears a ballerina costume and half mask. Holland enters wearing clown suit identical to Wayne's, and Wayne re-enters in shirt and pants. Passengers in Scene 3 wear various masquerade costumes.

Properties: Traveling case; trays with dishes of food; check; pens (thick marking pen should be used, so that writing can be seen by audience); Linda's purse; Miss Atkins' purse; wallet and card for Dirkson.

Setting: Nautilus Lounge on board the S. S. *Venture,* a cruise ship. Sofas are down left and down right. Dining tables and chairs up left and up right. Exit at upstage center leads to deck. Through doorway, portion of ship's railing, with life preserver attached, is seen (this can be on backdrop). Exit at left leads to galley and main dining room. In Scene 3, Lounge is decorated gaily with balloons and streamers.

Lighting: In Scene 3, lighting may give a nighttime effect.

The Vagabond Vampires

Thurston Tempest and his wife Voracia, two happy vampires, will have their house demolished unless they can solve a baffling "whodunit" . . .

Characters

THURSTON TEMPEST, *a vampire*
VORACIA, *his wife*
MR. GRIGSBY, *middle-aged man*
MRS. GRIGSBY, *his wife*
TOM MARTIN, *22*
SUE LANG
JEFF, *Tom's cousin, 24*
MRS. MARSHALL, *the housekeeper*
OFFICER GROGAN

TIME: *Evening, the present.*
SETTING: *The living room of the Martin house. Two coffins are down center. A large window is up center, with a closed door to its right and a cabinet to its left. A high-backed chair facing away from audience is in front of window. A table with a large box on it is at center. Exits are at right, left, and center. Furniture is covered with dust sheets, and lights are dim.*
AT RISE: *Moonlight shines through window. Baying of hound is heard from offstage. Slowly the cover of one coffin opens with a creak, and* THURSTON TEMPEST'S *hand appears. Then*

slowly THURSTON *sits up. He is dressed as a vampire in black suit and cape. He gets out of coffin, closes lid, and points dramatically to other coffin, with a flourish of his cape.*

THURSTON: Arise, wife! We must walk through the night. (THURSTON *looks at coffin, taps foot impatiently. Dramatically*) Arise, I command you! Our search must begin. (*Lid remains closed.* THURSTON *strides forward and hammers on coffin, shouting.*) O.K., Voracia, get out of the sack! (*Lid opens.* VORACIA *sits up, rubs her eyes sleepily, then stands.*)

VORACIA: Oh, Thurston, I don't know why you insist on waking me every night at this terrible hour.

THURSTON: We are not supposed to sleep at night. (*Proudly*) We are vampires! (VORACIA *arranges her long white gown.*)

VORACIA: Nonsense! That's all because of your Uncle Bela and his insomnia. He couldn't sleep at night like ordinary people, so he used his influence with the American Hysterical Society, the Peace Corpse, and the U-frighted Nations to get them to pass a resolution saying that vampires should sleep only during the day. (VORACIA *gestures dramatically, imitating* THURSTON.) We must search the night! (*In normal voice*) Really, Thurston. I don't know how I've put up with you all these centuries. (*During the ensuing dialogue,* THURSTON *and* VORACIA *fold the sheets in the coffins, fluff pillows, and set coffins in upright positions near right entrance.*)

THURSTON (*Angrily*): Knock it off, Voracia! And don't criticize Uncle Bela. (*He points to box on table.*) After all, he just sent us that package from Transylvania. We haven't even opened it.

VORACIA: Well, I don't want his surprise gifts. Uncle Bela and his gifts can stay in Transylvania for all I care. I'll stay here. (*She gestures.*) I love this marvelous old house. It has such a morbid atmosphere. After all, an unsolved murder was committed in this very room.

THURSTON: I wonder who did kill Joseph Martin.

VORACIA: It's none of our concern. He was a mean, vindictive old man, and, besides, no one else will live here as long as the mystery stays unsolved. (VORACIA *takes two dust sheets from chair and drapes them over upright coffins.*) There! Our beds are made, although I don't care for these old-fashioned coffins. I'd prefer a waterbed casket. They're so nice and clammy!

THURSTON: I'll get the evening paper from next door.

VORACIA: Good! I love to read the local news, especially the obituaries. The Grigsbys must miss their paper, though.

THURSTON: Mrs. Grigsby is always snooping around. I'm sure she suspects that we live here, although she can't prove it — no mortal has ever seen us.

VORACIA: I don't know why the Grigsbys should mind. (*Proudly*) Not everyone can have vampires for neighbors. (THURSTON *exits right.* VORACIA *surveys room, clucks in disapproval.*) I wish we could hire someone to clean this place. (*She straightens a dust sheet and sings to tune of "A-Tisket, A-Tasket."*)

A-tisket, A-tasket — I lost my little casket.

I sent a letter to my mummy and on the way I dropped it.

(THURSTON *returns hurriedly, waving a newspaper which he places on table.*)

THURSTON: We're in trouble. The Grigsbys saw me take their newspaper.

VORACIA: That's impossible. We're invisible!

THURSTON: The newspaper isn't invisible. As I picked it up, Mrs. Grigsby came out. (THURSTON *smiles.*) It gave her quite a scare to see the paper floating in space.

VORACIA: The poor dear! (*Footsteps are heard from offstage.*) Goodness! That must be the Grigsbys. Are you sure we're invisible at will? (THURSTON *nods.* MR. *and* MRS. GRIGSBY *rush in, right. They do not see* THURSTON *and* VORACIA. MRS. GRIGSBY *gasps, points to newspaper.*)

MRS. GRIGSBY: I told you, Warren. There's our newspaper.

GRIGSBY: So what? Maybe a strong wind blew it here.

MRS. GRIGSBY: And I suppose the strong wind opened the front door. You know, there have been strange goings-on in this house for six months — ever since old Joseph Martin was murdered.

GRIGSBY: Maybe the house is haunted. (*He laughs fiendishly. MRS. GRIGSBY cringes.*)

MRS. GRIGSBY: Please be serious! I'll certainly be glad when they tear this house down. (THURSTON *and* VORACIA *exchange glances.*)

GRIGSBY: It's only a proposal. Nothing's been decided.

MRS. GRIGSBY: Well I'm all for getting rid of this house. There's something uncanny about the place. (*Turns away; GRIGSBYS do not hear following dialogue*)

VORACIA (*To* THURSTON): Uncanny? I'll teach that old bat to talk about me.

THURSTON: Remember your blood pressure, Voracia.

VORACIA: I haven't had blood pressure for centuries. I'm going to get rid of the Grigsbys.

THURSTON: All right, I'll help you. (THURSTON *crosses to* MRS. GRIGSBY *and tweaks her ear.*)

MRS. GRIGSBY (*Turning; happily*): Oh, Warren, you haven't done that in years.

GRIGSBY: What are you talking about?

MRS. GRIGSBY (*Coyly*): You tweaked my ear.

GRIGSBY: You've been at the rum candy again. (*Walks away*)

MRS. GRIGSBY (*Indignantly*): I know when my ear has been tweaked, Warren Grigsby! (VORACIA *rubs back of* GRIGSBY'S *neck.*)

GRIGSBY (*Turning, pleased*): You're acting very romantic, Alma.

MRS. GRIGSBY: Romantic? You're imagining things!

GRIGSBY (*Perplexed*): Didn't you rub the back of my neck just now?

MRS. GRIGSBY: Don't be silly. (*Suddenly*) Didn't you tweak my ear? (GRIGSBY *shakes his head. They glance at each other, nod slowly.*)

GRIGSBYS (*In unison*): This place is haunted! Let's get out of here! (*They run out.* THURSTON *dusts his hands.*)

THURSTON: Good riddance!

VORACIA: Never mind them. What's all this about tearing down the house?

THURSTON: It must be in the newspaper. (*He picks up newspaper, turns several pages.*) Yes, here's the story. (*He reads.*) "Martin Estate considered for city park."

VORACIA: Then it's true!

THURSTON: Listen. (*He reads.*) "The town planning committee has decided to purchase the house owned by the late Joseph Martin. The house will be razed and a new recreation center built on the site. The Martin house was the setting of one of the country's most baffling crimes. Joseph Martin, elderly financier and art collector, was brutally murdered in his sitting room six months ago. His nephew, Thomas Martin, was held for grand jury investigation, but was released for insufficient evidence. The case has never been solved. Tom Martin and his cousin, Jeff, have decided to sell the house to the town." (THURSTON *sighs, places newspaper on table.*) We'd better start house-hunting.

VORACIA: But I love this house. The rooms are so cold and dismal and gloomy — just perfect for us. And we have a lovely view. (VORACIA *walks to window, points.* THURSTON *joins her.*)

THURSTON: Ah, you mean the family graveyard.

VORACIA (*Nodding*): It recalls such happy memories. We first met in a graveyard, Thurston. (*Fondly*) It was love at first fright.

THURSTON: Well, we can't stay here. You know what people do to vampires.

VORACIA (*Cringing*): Don't remind me. They'd drive a stake

through my heart — and it would ruin this lovely dress. (*Valiantly*) We must do something. (*Paces*)

THURSTON: I don't like that look in your eye.

VORACIA: Quiet! I'm thinking.

THURSTON: The last time you had a bright idea, we had to turn into bats and fly away. (*Distastefully*) And you know I get airsick. (VORACIA *brightens, snaps her fingers.*)

VORACIA: Of course! The perfect solution! Tom and Jeff Martin want to get rid of this place — because of its unhappy memories, probably. Now, if we could solve the mystery of Joseph Martin's death, they might decide to keep the house. We'd have a happy home for centuries.

THURSTON: How are you going to solve the Martin case?

VORACIA: We're going to find the murderer! (THURSTON *begins to protest, but* VORACIA *waves him to silence.*) Listen to me. Someone killed Joseph Martin, that much is certain. If we can find the killer, everything will be all right.

THURSTON: Uncle Bela always warned me that you were a flighty little thing. We'd have to investigate the case, question all the suspects, prove the killer's identity. And we'd have to do our work at night.

VORACIA (*Determined*): Right. We'll start this very night! (*She points at box on table.*) The package Uncle Bela sent us — maybe it contains something that'll help. (*She opens box, removes book. She reads title.*) "How To Win Fiends and Incriminate People." (VORACIA *shakes her head.*) Isn't that like Uncle Bela? The one time we need his help he sends us a useless book.

THURSTON: Maybe the book will give us a clue. (VORACIA *flips pages, reads contents.*)

VORACIA (*Reading*): "How to Be the Death of the Party." "Always Leave Them Gasping." "How To Handle a Grave Situation." (VORACIA *brightens.*) Here's something. (*Reads.*) "How to Solve Old Murders"!

THURSTON: Good old Uncle Bela. I knew he'd come through.

VORACIA (*Reading*): "Assemble all the suspects, preferably at the scene of the crime. A dark, stormy night is best." (VORACIA *stops reading, faces window, gestures dramatically.*) Aha! (*Moonlight fades. She raises her arms. Rumble of thunder is heard in distance. Howling of wind increases.*)

THURSTON: You always had a way with vampire magic. (VORACIA *continues to read.*)

VORACIA: "After the suspects are assembled, recreate the murder. The murderer will display signs of nervousness, and his capture will follow." (VORACIA *lowers book, places it on table.*) Oh, Thurston, do you think it will work?

THURSTON: It's worth a try.

VORACIA: We should assemble the suspects now. If I scream, we'll be able to get them all here in a jiffy.

THURSTON (*Trace of panic*): Not one of those screams!

VORACIA (*Proudly*): I was the champion wolf caller of Cadaver County. (*She walks to window, cups her hands, emits a soul-chilling scream.* THURSTON *covers his ears.* VORACIA *screams again. Sound of glass shattering is heard offstage.*)

THURSTON: Oh-oh! You broke the picture tube of the Grigsbys' television set again.

VORACIA: No, the sound didn't come from that direction. (*She points to right.*) It came from the road. (*Footsteps are heard offstage.* VORACIA *grabs* THURSTON's *arm, points at door right.*) Someone's outside! (TOM MARTIN *and* SUE LANG *enter cautiously.* SUE *shivers.* VORACIA *and* THURSTON *watch with interest.*)

SUE: What made us come here, Tom?

TOM (*Shrugging*): I — I don't know, Sue. We were driving past when my headlights shattered. And that scream!

SUE: Yes, the scream. It sounded — well, almost supernatural. (SUE *gestures.*) I haven't been in this room since your uncle — since Mr. Martin was murdered.

TOM (*Nodding*): Something made us return to this house — where Uncle Joseph was murdered! (*Thunder is heard from offstage.*)

SUE: Please don't think about it.

TOM: How can I help but think about it? I was the last one to see Uncle Joseph alive. I'm still the prime suspect.

SUE: The grand jury cleared you.

TOM (*Bitterly*): Everyone in town still thinks I killed Uncle Joseph. "There goes Tom Martin," they say. "You know, the actor fellow — the one who killed his uncle." (TOM *pounds on table.*) I'll be glad when this house is torn down.

SUE (*Pointing at chair near window*): I found your uncle in that chair. The dagger! The blood! (*She covers her face.*)

TOM: And I had been in this room talking to Uncle Joseph a few minutes before. (*Footsteps are heard offstage.*) What's that?

SUE (*Regaining her composure*): There's someone in the hall. (*Footsteps grow louder.*) Someone is standing outside the door. (*She points right.* TOM *signals* SUE *to be quiet and leads her to stand beside door right.*)

VORACIA (*To* THURSTON): Isn't this exciting? I feel just like a character in a Kojak case!

THURSTON: Quiet! (*Flashlight shines into room, moves over various objects.* JEFF MARTIN *enters, carrying flashlight.* TOM *steps forward, grabs* JEFF. JEFF *drops flashlight and turns, startled.*)

TOM: Who are you? Oh, it's you, Jeff. (TOM *quickly releases* JEFF, *who picks up flashlight, turns it off, and places it on table.*) What are you doing here?

JEFF: I might ask you the same question, cousin Tom. (*He turns.*) And Sue! Ah, the loyal woman, faithful to the bitter end.

SUE: This is no time for flippancy, Jeff. As for our being here, well — we heard a scream.

JEFF: So did I. I'm staying in the caretaker's cottage, and the noise shattered my bedroom window. It was the worse shriek I've ever heard.

VORACIA (*Indignantly*): How dare he insult my lovely voice? Why, I once played the lead in Peter Pan.

THURSTON: You were the only one who could fly across the stage without assistance. Now, will you be quiet?

TOM (*Soberly*): Here we are, together again. The three of us were the only ones in the house on the night of the murder.

JEFF: The windows and doors were found locked. No one broke in.

SUE: And that means that one of us murdered Joseph Martin. (*Thunder sounds offstage.* SUE *cringes.*) The only other person who lived here was Mrs. Marshall, the housekeeper, and she was out for the night.

TOM (*Suddenly*): If only I knew what really happened. People still suspect me.

SUE: But you had no reason to kill him. You had been on tour with your new play. You only returned that very day. (*She shakes her head.*) There had to be a motive for the crime.

JEFF: The motive is obvious enough. Someone had stolen Uncle Joseph's jade statue. It was worth a fortune. He thought one of us was responsible, and he was going to turn the guilty one over to the police.

VORACIA (*Happily*): Oh, Thurston, a stolen jade statue! I think the same thing happened in a Charlie Chan mystery.

THURSTON: You read too many mysteries. I'm more interested in solving a real one here tonight.

SUE: Mr. Martin kept the statue on display in his cabinet. (SUE *points at cabinet.*) The jade was valued at fifty thousand dollars.

TOM: On the day I arrived home, the statue was stolen. Uncle Joseph suspected me — he was always bitter about my acting career. On the night of the murder Uncle Joseph intended to question the three of us separately. (*To* JEFF) You were the first to see him, Jeff.

JEFF (*Nodding*): The old boy really let me have it. He shouted at me — said I couldn't wait to get his money. Of course he accused me of stealing the statue. Our tempers flared. I got out of here — fast.

TOM: Yes, when I came in, you were gone. (*He points at chair.*) Uncle Joseph sat in that chair, in the dark. I really didn't have a good look at him when he spoke. He condemned my acting career. I could see the movement of his hand as he stroked his moustache. He sat there like my judge and jury.

VORACIA (*Nudging* THURSTON): This is the perfect time to re-enact the crime. I learned a supernatural formula for re-creating the past from the Bride of Frankenstein.

THURSTON: The Bride of Frankenstein is an empty-headed female.

VORACIA: Male chauvinist vampire! Watch this. (VORACIA *gestures at* TOM, SUE *and* JEFF, *who freeze in position.*)

THURSTON: What have you done to them now?

VORACIA: I put them in a trance. Now they will be able to relive the night of the murder. (*She recites in low, dramatic voice.*)

Backward, O days — turn backward in time,
Let us relive the night of the crime.

(*She gestures magically. As if in a trance,* TOM, JEFF *and* SUE *walk mechanically to right exit.*) Oh, it's working! Their spirits are traveling back in time.

THURSTON: If you miscalculated, they'll probably wind up in Napoleon's court. (TOM, SUE *and* JEFF *exit right.* VORACIA *points left.*)

VORACIA: Wait! Something's going to happen. (*Points left*) I hear someone in the other room. (MRS. MARSHALL, *in housedress and apron, enters left. She stares apprehensively around the room.*)

THURSTON: Who's that?

VORACIA: I don't know. (*Brightly*) Didn't Jeff mention a housekeeper?

THURSTON (*Nodding*): Mrs. Marshall. Now we know she was in this room shortly before the murder.

VORACIA: Let's see what she's going to do. (MRS. MARSHALL *crosses to cabinet from lower left. She stoops, takes statue from lower shelf, which is not visible to audience. She straightens, looks at statue, then hides it under apron. She glances around, exits left.*) Why, it was the housekeeper who stole the jade statue!

THURSTON (*Nodding*): It's settled. Mrs. Marshall killed Joseph Martin to silence him.

VORACIA: Not so fast. Didn't Jeff say that Mrs. Marshall was out of the house at the time of the crime? We mustn't jump to conclusions.

THURSTON: You're making me jumpy. Why, I think you're enjoying this murder. And at your age! You must be three hundred years old.

VORACIA: The very idea! I'm not a day over two hundred and fifty. (*Closet door up center opens.* JEFF *enters, disguised as Joseph Martin in a long robe, gray wig and moustache.*) Look! That must be the recreated spirit of Joseph Martin. (JEFF *hobbles to chair and sits facing window, away from audience.* TOM *enters right. He walks to back of chair, rubs his hands nervously. He now wears different jacket.*)

TOM: Did you want to see me, Uncle Joseph?

JEFF (*In strained, cracked voice*): Yes, indeed. You took your sweet time getting here.

TOM: Mrs. Marshall told me you were talking to Jeff. I didn't want to interfere.

JEFF (*Mockingly*): Such a considerate nephew! You'd do anything to continue that nonsensical acting career, and live on my charity.

TOM (*Angrily*): You asked me to live in this house. If you're trying to insult me, I'd like you to know that I'm leaving tomorrow. I have a job in the city.

JEFF: A likely story! You're as worthless as your cousin Jeff.

TOM: What do you want, Uncle Joseph?

JEFF (*Hoarsely*): I want my jade statue! One of you took it. If it's not returned tonight, I'll call the police.

TOM: Is the statue missing? I don't know anything about it. (TOM *and* JEFF *talk in pantomime as* VORACIA *tugs at* THURSTON'*s cape.*)

THURSTON: What's the matter now?

VORACIA: Part of the story's missing. Jeff Martin was the first person to be questioned, but we didn't see it. This is Tom's interview.

THURSTON: Maybe something went wrong with the Bride of Frankenstein's magic poetry.

VORACIA (*Impatiently*): So she's not Dylan Thomas. Now we'll have to solve the murder without hearing Jeff's interview.

JEFF (*Bluntly*): Did you take the statue, Tom?

TOM: I don't know anything about it, Uncle Joseph. If you think I'm guilty, why don't you call the police? (TOM *pounds on back of chair.*) You're a hateful old man. It's a wonder someone doesn't murder you. (*Shouting*) I'll be glad to get out of this house tomorrow! (TOM *storms out right.* VORACIA *applauds.*)

VORACIA: Good for Tom! (*Suddenly all stage lights go out.* JEFF *exits unseen.*)

THURSTON: Where are the lights?

VORACIA: Something must have gone wrong with the magic chant again. Listen! I hear footsteps. Someone is in this room with us.

THURSTON: Well, if it's the murderer, I'd like to give him a fat lip. Transylvania was never like this! (*Stage lights come up. Thunder is heard.* SUE *enters right. She wears a different dress. She approaches chair.*) That's Sue. It's her turn to be interviewed.

SUE (*Calling softly*): Mr. Martin. I understand you wanted to see me. Mr. Martin, is there anything I can do for you? (*She faces chair, screams, covers her face with her hands.*) He's dead! (SUE *screams, rushes from room right.* VORACIA *shakes her head.*)

VORACIA: I feel strange.

THURSTON: I do, too. Maybe it's the sautéed spider legs we had for dinner.

VORACIA: No — we must have returned to the present. (*She crosses quickly to chair.*) There's no one in the chair. Yes, we're back to normal — if a vampire is ever normal. (*Crestfallen*) And we still don't know who killed Joseph Martin.

THURSTON: If we're going to be good detectives, we must examine the facts. We know that Joseph Martin was alive after Jeff's questioning.

VORACIA (*Insistently*): We didn't see Jeff's interview.

THURSTON: It doesn't matter. Joseph Martin was alive when Tom came into the room. Tom spoke to him. We know that.

VORACIA: And immediately after that, Sue found the body. Why, that means —

THURSTON (*Slowly*): Tom Martin killed his uncle.

VORACIA: That nice boy! I simply can't believe it.

THURSTON: Nice boy, my foot! If we can find evidence to convict Tom, we'll be able to live in this house for the rest of our lives — er, rather — deaths.

VORACIA: But there was a time lapse when something important might have happened. If we could only find the right clue, we could employ our supernatural powers and name the murderer! (*Suddenly*) Maybe there's something else in Unlce Bela's book. (*She picks up book, leafs through pages.*) Yes, here's a chapter called "How to Inspire a Vampire." (*She reads.*) "If a vampire wishes to solve an old murder, he must break a speckled egg laid at midnight on Friday the thirteenth and scatter the contents around the scene of the crime. Such an egg, properly broken, will force all those assembled to tell the truth, and the murderer will confess his crime.''

THURSTON: That's great! But where in the name of Wolfman's beard are we going to find a speckled egg laid at midnight on Friday the thirteenth? (VORACIA *searches package, produces an egg.*)

VORACIA: I must admit that Uncle Bela leaves no gravestone unturned. This is an egg, and it's labeled ''Strictly fresh. Laid on Friday, March 13, 1850, at midnight.''

THURSTON (*Impatiently*): Well, get on with it, Voracia. Break the egg!

VORACIA (*Hesitating*): I really don't think I should.

THURSTON: Are you doubting Uncle Bela's instructions? He was an experienced vampire when we were just little bats. I want you to break that egg!

VORACIA: Very well, Thurston. (VORACIA *places egg on* THURSTON*'s head, gives it a resounding smack. Particles of egg and shell drip down his face.*)

THURSTON (*In long-suffering tone*): Now, why did you do that?

VORACIA: I was following Uncle Bela's instructions. Here they are. (*Opens book, reads*) ''The most effective method of breaking the egg is to shatter it on the head of another vampire.''

THURSTON (*Shrugging helplessly*): Now she tells me. (*He removes handkerchief from pocket, dabs at his face.* VORACIA *quickly takes handkerchief.*)

VORACIA: Now we have the magic ingredient. (*She walks around the room, shaking handerchief and scattering egg and shell in various places. She recites mysteriously.*)

Monster's claw and dragon's tooth —
Let the suspects tell the truth!

(VORACIA *returns handkerchief to* THURSTON *who puts it into his pocket. Happily*) There! Now we'll see what develops.

THURSTON (*Shaking head*): That spell to tell the truth won't have any effect on me. I don't feel different. (*Suddenly, speaks in a high voice, smiling sheepishly.*) Voracia, I'd like to tell you what really happened when I went to the Vampire's Convention in Atlantic City.

VORACIA (*Suspiciously*): I often wondered about those three days.

THURSTON: I met Dracula's daughter and we had dinner together at the local blood bank.

VORACIA: That vixen! I always knew she had designs on you. (*Suddenly*) How wonderful!

THURSTON (*Puzzled*): Aren't you angry?

VORACIA: The supernatural truth potion. It works, Thurston! It forced you to tell the truth. It will surely help us to find the murderer. (VORACIA *grabs* THURSTON*'s arm.*) I hear someone in the hallway. (MRS. MARSHALL, *wearing hat and coat, enters right.*) It's Mrs. Marshall.

THURSTON: Why did she come here tonight?

VORACIA: She's a prime suspect, remember. (MRS. MARSHALL *walks to cabinet, removes statue from beneath coat.* VORACIA *gasps.*) Look, it's the jade statue! (MRS. MARSHALL *puts statue on cabinet shelf, looking around nervously.*) We knew that Mrs. Marshall stole the statue — and now she's returning it.

THURSTON: Why would she do a thing like that?

VORACIA: The truth potion! It forced her to return the statue that she had stolen. (TOM, *wearing original jacket, enters right.* MRS. MARSHALL *turns quickly, gives a frightened cry.*)

TOM: Mrs. Marshall! I haven't seen you for six months! What are you doing here?

MRS. MARSHALL (*Dazed*): I did a terrible thing, Mr. Tom. (*She *points at cabinet.*) I had to make up for my crime. (TOM *looks behind her, sees statue.*)

TOM: Why, that's the missing statue. Did you put it there? (MRS. MARSHALL *nods.*) Then you must have stolen it!

MRS. MARSHALL: Yes, I took it. I was going to sell it to an art dealer, but I realized I could never get away with it. I wanted to put the statue back, but your uncle was in the room for the rest of the night.

TOM (*Sternly*): You should have told the police.

MRS. MARSHALL: I couldn't do that! Your uncle had been murdered. If the police knew I stole the statue, they'd think that I — that I — (*Breaks down*) Tom, I didn't murder Joseph Martin. I swear it!

TOM (*Relenting*): I believe you, Mrs. Marshall.

MRS. MARSHALL (*Submissively*): I'll call the police. I'll tell them about the statue. I'll tell them everything. Maybe they'll believe me. (*She reaches into coat pocket, takes out false moustache. She hands it to* TOM *who studies it, frowning.*)

TOM: It's a false moustache! Why, it looks like the one I wore in *Cyrano de Bergerac*. (TOM *examines moustache closely.*) Yes, I think it's the same one. Where did you find it?

MRS. MARSHALL (*Pointing to closet, center*): I found it in that closet on the morning after the murder. (TOM *shakes his head, puts moustache on table.*)

TOM: I don't understand it. I kept some makeup in that closet. Wigs — beards — grease paint. But I'm sure I left the moustache in my room upstairs. I didn't put it in the closet with the other things.

MRS. MARSHALL: I found it in the box with the makeup. I knew it belonged to you, but I didn't think too much about it at the time.

TOM: The police searched the closet.

MRS. MARSHALL: They must have overlooked it. It was hidden in the box — and it was wrapped in something else. A bloodstained handkerchief!

TOM: What? I can't believe it!

MRS. MARSHALL: It was your handkerchief, Tom. I recognized the monogram. (MRS. MARSHALL *turns her head.*) Shh! Someone is out in the hallway!

TOM: Jeff and Sue are here tonight. They're making coffee in the kitchen. The electricity in the house was never turned off. (TOM *waves his hand.*) Never mind that now. Where is that handkerchief?

MRS. MARSHALL: I burned it. I should have gotten rid of the moustache, too. I knew the things belonged to you. I didn't want them to think that you murdered your uncle.

TOM: If I killed Joseph Martin, it would have been foolish to leave such evidence at the scene of the crime. The moustache, the handkerchief — they could be traced to me. I can't think of any reason for leaving them in the closet unless — (TOM *shakes his head.*) No, that's too incredible.

MRS. MARSHALL: Incredible? What do you mean?

TOM: We'd better find the others right away. This old house — this very room — we'll force the murderer to tell the truth. (TOM *and* MRS. MARSHALL *exit.* VORACIA *smiles.*)

VORACIA: Thurston, there are some clues at last.

THURSTON: The clues indicate that Tom killed his uncle.

VORACIA: Hogwash! I still don't trust that Marshall woman. And what about Tom? He seemed so excited just now that I'm sure he must suspect something.

THURSTON (*Nodding*): He was excited about the handkerchief and the moustache.

VORACIA (*Excited*): The moustache! That's it, of course! It makes a perfect disguise.

THURSTON: What are you talking about?

VORACIA: You're going to disguise yourself as Joseph Martin, so the murderer will break down and confess.

THURSTON: I won't fool the murderer. I — I don't know anything about acting.

VORACIA: You're a marvelous actor. Remember the season we spent with the Haunted Hollow summer stock? Everyone simply adored you in *The Thing and I* — and you were wonderful in *Barefoot in the Dark.*

THURSTON: Well, I don't know. What am I going to use as a disguise?

VORACIA: Tom said that he kept his stage makeup in that closet. (*She points at closet.*) I'm sure you'll find something useful there. And you saw the spirit of Joseph Martin in our recreation of the crime.

THURSTON: But I don't know who the murderer is yet.

VORACIA: Well, then, remain invisible until we think we know the murderer's identity. You can appear in your disguise to that person. The others won't see you, of course.

THURSTON (*Sighing*): You'll be the death — er, life — of me yet, but I'll try it. (*Sudden blackout. Sound of running is heard from offstage.*)

VORACIA: Thurston, where are you? What's happening?

THURSTON: It's the lights again. (*From offstage, a gunshot is heard.* SUE *screams offstage.*)

VORACIA: Thurston, are you all right? (*Lights come up.*) This house is enough to frighten even a vampire. Where are the others?

THURSTON: I don't know, but I might as well get into the Joseph Martin disguise. (*He walks to closet, opens door, turns.*) Stay out of trouble, Voracia! (*He enters closet, closes door.* TOM, SUE *and* JEFF *enter right. All wear original outfits.* SUE *is dazed.* TOM *helps her to sofa. She sits.*)

SUE: It's terrible, simply terrible.

TOM: I can't believe it. I was talking to Mrs. Marshall only a few minutes ago. And now she's dead!

SUE: It happened so quickly. I was in the kitchen with Tom when someone came in. It must have been Mrs. Marshall.

TOM: I saw her, too.

SUE: That's when the lights went out. Someone rushed past me, and then I heard the shot. (*Suddenly*) Where were you, Jeff?

JEFF: I went to see about my suitcase. I left it in the hall.

SUE: Then Tom and I were the only ones in the kitchen with Mrs. Marshall.

TOM (*Quickly*): You don't think I killed her, do you?

SUE: No, no. Why would anyone kill Mrs. Marshall?

JEFF (*Pointedly*): Maybe Tom can tell us. (*He faces* TOM.) Maybe the grand jury was wrong. Maybe you do know a great deal about Uncle Joseph's death.

VORACIA (*Nervously, to herself*): Oh, dear, I feel a crisis coming on. (*As* TOM, JEFF *and* SUE *argue she rushes to closet, throws door open.* THURSTON *enters. He has removed black cape and now wears long robe and a thick, gray wig.*) Thurston! The disguise is perfect!

THURSTON: I feel as ridiculous as I did the time we went to the witches' masquerade as Adam and Eve. (VORACIA *grabs his arm, leads him down center.*)

VORACIA: Someone has just killed Mrs. Marshall.

THURSTON (*Nodding*): I overheard them talking. What was the motive?

VORACIA (*To* THURSTON): The false moustache, of course. (*She points at moustache on table.*) I knew it was a vital clue. (*Suddenly*) If I could put the moustache on the killer, I'm sure the others would know the truth.

THURSTON: My dear Voracia! You don't know who the murderer is.

VORACIA: I'll think of something. I'd like to put the lights out again. Now, let me see. (VORACIA *stands transfixed, recites slowly.*)

Creatures of long and fearsome nights,
Conduct thy deeds — put out the lights.

(*There is a rumble of thunder offstage, accompanied by flash of lightning. Sudden blackout.*)

JEFF: Now what?

TOM: Who put out the lights?

SUE: Someone is here with us. I feel someone — I feel — (SUE *screams. Lights return.* SUE *is wearing false moustache. She touches her lip, quickly removes moustache, throws it on table with distaste.*) Ugh! That moustache!

THURSTON (*To* VORACIA): You really goofed this time.

VORACIA: Oh, dear, I must have gotten confused in the dark.

TOM: The moustache again! It's part of my makeup. Mrs. Marshall found it shortly after the murder in the closet. Someone left it there for the police to find. (*To* SUE) But who tried to put it on you?

JEFF (*Slowly*): There are a lot of things that need explaining. I think you'd better start talking, Tom.

TOM (*Angrily*): Are you accusing me?

SUE: Don't talk like that, Jeff. If we start arguing, we'll never learn the truth.

JEFF: Maybe the murderer doesn't want us to find out. (*He pauses, lost in thought.*) Why did Mrs. Marshall come here tonight? Is it possible she knew something about the crime — some evidence that would point to the killer?

TOM: Do you mean that moustache?

JEFF: Perhaps she found the moustache in this room. If so, it would certainly establish that you were here with Uncle Joseph.

TOM: I've already admitted that. I told you I was the last one to see him alive. But why would I have the false moustache with me? I didn't try to disguise myself. (TOM *stops, looks at* JEFF.) Perhaps somebody else needed a disguise. (TOM *puts hand into pocket, then, surprised, withdraws gun.*)

SUE: Where did you get that gun?

TOM: I — I don't know. I don't own a gun.

JEFF: A likely story! (JEFF *grabs gun from* TOM, *sniffs barrel.*) This gun has been fired recently. I'll bet it's the gun that killed Mrs. Marshall. (*Holds gun.*)

SUE: Oh, no!

TOM: I never saw that gun in my life. Someone put it in my jacket. Someone who'd like to accuse me of murdering Mrs. Marshall. (*To* JEFF) I think you fill the bill.

JEFF: You're crazy.

TOM: No — I've just realized the significance of the false moustache. (*To* SUE) I was wrong all the time. I wasn't the last person to see Uncle Joseph alive.

JEFF: You admitted it to the police.

TOM (*Shaking head*): No. Someone else was the last to see him alive. Uncle Joseph was already dead when I came into the room.

SUE (*To* TOM): You said that you talked to him.

TOM: I spoke to someone wearing a gray wig and moustache who sat in that chair. (TOM *points to chair.*) I thought it was Joseph Martin, but I was mistaken. He had already been murdered.

JEFF: What are you trying to say?

TOM: Jeff, you were the first person Uncle Joseph questioned that night. He must have accused you of stealing the statue. You argued. In your anger you picked up a dagger from the cabinet — and stabbed him!

JEFF (*Nervously*): You don't know what you're talking about.

TOM: You knew that I was the next one to be interviewed. (Tom *points at closet.*) You hid Uncle Joseph's body in the closet, removed his robe, put on a gray wig — and went to my bedroom for the false moustache that I left there. When I came into the room, you were sitting before the window, hidden in shadows. You imitated Uncle Joseph's voice and accused me of being a good-for-nothing. You made certain I would lose my temper. After I stormed out, you put Uncle Joseph's body back in the chair, put the robe on him, and hid the moustache in the closet where you hoped the police would find it.

SUE: I can't believe that Jeff killed Joseph Martin.

VORACIA (*Shouting*): Believe it! Believe it! Thurston, isn't this exciting?

THURSTON: Button your lip, dear.

TOM: It's the only possible solution. (*To* JEFF) Mrs. Marshall found the moustache instead of the police. She brought it here tonight. You overheard her talking to me and knew you had to silence her. It was a simple matter to shoot her and slip that gun into my pocket while the house was in darkness. (TOM *points at the gun in* JEFF's *hand.*) But there's one thing you overlooked. There's a simple chemical test to determine whether or not a person has fired a gun. When I call the police, we'll both take the test. (*Slowly*) I have nothing to hide. Have you, Jeff?

JEFF (*Scoffing*): The police won't buy your ridiculous story. A murderer posing as a murdered man — chemical tests — a moustache hidden in a bloodstained handkerchief. They'll never believe you! (JEFF *laughs mockingly as* TOM *watches him intently.*)

TOM (*Coldly*): How did you know about the handkerchief?

SUE: What handkerchief?

TOM: Mrs. Marshall found the moustache in a bloodstained handkerchief with my initials. She told me about it shortly before she was murdered. I'm the only one who knew about the handkerchief, except for the person who hid it in the closet. That person is the murderer!

VORACIA: Bravo!

JEFF: I must have heard you mention the handkerchief.

SUE: Tom didn't say anything about it. (*To* JEFF) But he's right. (*Slowly*) You are the murderer. (JEFF*'s hand shakes as he levels gun at* TOM.)

JEFF: There'll be no police investigation. It will be a simple matter to kill Sue. I'll tell the police that you killed her because she knew you had committed the crime. (SUE *stares at him, afraid.*) I'll tell them that I had to kill you, Tom, in self-defense. (JEFF *laughs.*) The Martin case will be closed!

VORACIA: We must stop that dreadful man.

THURSTON (*Nodding*): He's our murderer, all right. I'm going to appear to him now. I can't let him kill those two nice youngsters. (THURSTON *picks up moustache that* SUE *has put on table, puts it on, and taps* JEFF *on shoulder.* JEFF *sees him and trembles. Gun shakes in his hand.*)

JEFF: Uncle Joseph! (SUE *and* TOM *stare at him, puzzled.*)

THURSTON (*Hollow tones*): Faithless nephew, why did you kill me?

JEFF (*Dazed*): I didn't mean to kill you. I didn't know what I was doing.

THURSTON: Will you confess to the police?

JEFF: Yes, yes, I'll confess to the police, Uncle Joseph. (*Drops gun.*)

SUE (*To* TOM): What's happened to Jeff? To whom is he talking?

TOM (*Bewildered*): I don't know, but it's saved our lives.

SUE: This house is haunted!

TOM: If it is, the ghosts can live here forever, as my special guests!

VORACIA: What a nice young man! You were wonderful, Thurston. I don't think Jeff will give us any more trouble tonight. But there's nothing like being certain. (*She removes another egg from package. She stands behind* JEFF, *intones.*)

O speckled egg of mighty power,
Remove this man within the hour!

(VORACIA *breaks egg on top of* JEFF's *head.* JEFF *stands transfixed.*)

SUE: Where did that egg come from?

TOM: I don't know, and I don't want to think about it! (VORACIA *jumps up and down excitedly as* OFFICER GROGAN, MR. *and* MRS. GRIGSBY *enter right.* GROGAN *carries a gun.*)

GROGAN: What's going on here?

MRS. GRIGSBY (*Valiantly*): Officer Grogan, do your duty! (*To* MR. GRIGSBY) I was right, Warren. I knew I heard people in this house.

MR. GRIGSBY: I still think we're interfering.

MRS. GRIGSBY: Well, I'm glad we called the police, especially after I heard that gunshot.

TOM (*To* GROGAN): Officer, here's your man. (*He points to* JEFF, *who stands in a trance.*) He killed Joseph Martin and the housekeeper. He confessed after he saw a ghost. Then someone nailed him with an egg. (*Feebly*) Does that make sense to you?

GROGAN: Of course, it makes perfect sense. These things happen to me all the time. (*He shakes his head sadly, collars* JEFF.) Come on, we're going down to headquarters. (VORACIA *ushers* THURSTON *into closet, closes door.* GROGAN *and* JEFF *exit right.*)

SUE: I'm sorry, Tom. For a minute, I thought you killed Mrs. Marshall.

TOM: Let's forget everything that happened here before now. (TOM *takes* SUE's *hand.*) I don't have to leave this house, now that my name is cleared. It will be our home — if you agree.

SUE (*Nodding*): Of course! And it will be a happy home.

TOM: With a permanent place for our supernatural friends.

MRS. GRIGSBY (*Frightened*): Supernatural? (TOM *nods.*)

TOM: Far, far out! (*He waves hand in air.* TOM *and* SUE *exit.*)

MRS. GRIGSBY: It will be nice to have real people living in this house again. (*Bravely*) Here's to our new neighbors — whatever they are! (GRIGSBYs *exit.* VORACIA *opens closet door and* THURSTON *re-enters. He wears cape, and has removed wig and moustache.*)

THURSTON (*Sighing*): It's been quite a night, Voracia.

VORACIA (*Happily*): We won't have to move, after all. The Martin house is saved! Of course, Tom and Sue might resent having vampires in their living room.

THURSTON: This house has a fine old cellar. It's full of mice, cobwebs, and spiders.

VORACIA: A home of our own! (*Sternly*) But I'm still terribly upset about your date with Dracula's daughter.

THURSTON: She can't hold a candle to you.

VORACIA (*Smiling*): Well, you can take me out to dinner tonight. Let's go to the blood bank. I'm simply dying for Type A — medium rare!

THURSTON: We will fly together! (THURSTON *wraps his cape around* VORACIA *and they move toward exit making flying motions. Curtain.*)

THE END

Production Notes

The Vagabond Vampires

Characters: 4 male; 4 female; 1 male or female for Grogan.

Playing Time: 35 minutes.

Costumes: Thurston wears black suit and cape; he changes into robe and thick gray wig. Voracia wears long white dress. Mrs. Marshall wears housedress and apron, later wears coat and hat. Modern everyday dress for Grigsbys, Sue, Tom and Jeff. Sue and Tom wear different clothes for flashback; Jeff puts on wig, robe and moustache. Grogan wears policeman's uniform.

Properties: Oblong boxes with covers large enough to hold actors; pillows, sheets, cloth covers, box containing book and two eggs, newspaper, false moustache, statue, guns, handkerchief, flashlight.

Setting: The gloomy living room of the Martin house, with large window up center and a high-backed chair facing away from audience in front of it. There is a table at center, and the two "coffins" down right. Exits are at right and left, and there is a closet at right of window. At left of window is cabinet. Other tables, chairs, etc., all covered with sheets or cloths, complete furnishings.

Lighting: Stage lights go out and come on as indicated in text. Lighting is dim throughout, and moonlight shines through window at beginning of play.

Sound: Baying of hound, thunder, gunshots, footsteps, sound of glass shattering, as indicated in text.

170

Strange Inheritance

Phineas Slag's relatives are divided in their opinions of him, but all are curious about the terms of his will. . . .

Characters

MRS. TRELAWNY, *a middle-aged dowager*
MAUREEN TAYLOR, *10*
MISS ATTERBY, *her governess*
MARY MONTROSE, *a young actress*
FRANK DAWSON, *a young man*
JOHN ATHERTON, *a tough, cynical man*
ALFRED SOUTHGATE, *solicitor*
CONSTABLE

TIME: *Late evening.*

SETTING: *Law office of Southgate, Latham, Abercrombie and Green, in London. Long conference table with seven chairs arranged around it is at center. Small table stands up left, with inkwell on it, and telephone on table is down left. Three paintings are on wall up center, and statue of Falstaff is on table below paintings. Door to outer office is in right wall, and a window covered with heavy draperies is in wall up center.*

AT RISE: MARY MONTROSE, *disguised as* MISS WAVERLY, *in a short dress and wearing heavy makeup and blond wig, enters right, followed by* MRS. TRELAWNY *and* JOHN ATHERTON.

MARY (*Gesturing toward chairs; in Cockney accent*): If you'll just sit down and make yourselves comfortable, Mr. Southgate will be here shortly.

ATHERTON: Thank you, Miss — er Miss —

MARY: Miss Waverly. (*Smiling*) But my friends call me Rose, duck!

MRS. TRELAWNY (*Gushing*): I'm so enthralled! Imagine! The reading of dear cousin Phineas Slag's will at midnight!

ATHERTON (*Suspiciously*): It's weird, if you ask me.

MRS. TRELAWNY (*Frowning*): Mr. Atherton, please! Conduct yourself as a gentleman.

ATHERTON: Come off it, Imogene.

MRS. TRELAWNY (*Haughtily*): Mrs. Trelawny, widow of the late, lamented Hector Trelawny, *if* you please.

ATHERTON (*Sneering*): You don't fool me with your airs. I know you run a boardinghouse in the West End. (*She gasps.*) You must be pretty well off, now that old Trelawny finally died.

MRS. TRELAWNY: My dear departed husband left thirty-five thousand pounds to his stepson, fifty thousand pounds to a London hospital, and his grandfather's snuff box to me! (*Dabs at eyes*) And I gave the best years of my life to that wretched man!

ATHERTON: I suppose you think you'll strike it rich in Phineas Slag's will.

MRS. TRELAWNY: I was dear Phineas' closest relative.

MARY: I'll prepare some tea while you bicker about your inheritance. (*She exits.*)

MRS. TRELAWNY (*Disapprovingly*): Frivolous girl! Somehow she doesn't fit into the dignified surroundings of a law office.

ATHERTON (*Looking around with distaste*): This morgue isn't exactly modern. (*Examines books left*) And look at these musty books. I don't think they've been touched in years.

MRS. TRELAWNY: I don't know why Phineas Slag didn't employ a solicitor with a better address. This is one of the most run-down streets in London. (MISS ATTERBY *leads in* MAUREEN. *They are followed in by* FRANK DAWSON, *impersonating* JIM FROST. ATHERTON *looks at them suspiciously, staring at* FRANK. MRS. TRELAWNY *looks annoyed.*) More relatives!

MISS ATTERBY: I'm not a relative at all. I'm here to act in the interests of my ward, Maureen Taylor, third cousin of the late Phineas Slag.

MRS. TRELAWNY: Oh, yes, I remember the Taylors. (*She sniffs.*) Dear child — how you've grown!

MAUREEN: I like the way you talk. (*Laughing*) All your chins wiggle.

MRS. TRELAWNY: Manners, my child! (*To* FRANK) And you, sir?

FRANK: The name's Frost. Jim Frost. Phineas Slag was my granduncle. (ATHERTON *starts in amazement.*)

ATHERTON: You're Jim Frost? (*He quickly regains his composure, but watches* FRANK *suspiciously.*)

MRS. TRELAWNY (*Nodding*): Of course. You're the American.

FRANK: Yes, my dad settled in Maryland.

MRS. TRELAWNY: Of course. (*She sniffs again.*)

MAUREEN: Lady, do you have a cold?

MRS. TRELAWNY: Why, no, I always talk like this. (*Haughtily*) Are you trying to insult me?

MAUREEN: Miss Atterby taught me it's impolite to sniffle in public. Here, use my hanky! (*She offers handkerchief from pocket.* MRS. TRELAWNY *turns away angrily.* MAUREEN *shrugs, returns handkerchief to pocket.*)

MRS. TRELAWNY: Please consider my position in this family. After all, I am Mr. Slag's first cousin twice removed. The rest of you are second cousins once removed.

ATHERTON (*Sarcastically*): Don't shake the family tree too hard!

MISS ATTERBY: Well, I just hope the reading will be held promptly. It's dreadfully late for Maureen.

ATHERTON: It's almost midnight. (MRS. TRELAWNY *takes letter from purse.*)

MRS. TRELAWNY: Yes, and the letter said the will would be read *at* midnight. (*Opens letter and starts reading*) "And with the passing of your cousin, Phineas Slag, an Australian resident for thirty years, it is imperative that you attend the reading of his last will and testament at the law office of Southgate, Latham, Abercrombie, and Green at midnight on Tuesday, the 19th." You see? (*She returns letter to purse.*)

ATHERTON: That's the same as mine. (FRANK *nods agreement.*)

MISS ATTERBY: Maureen received an identical letter. (*Slowly*) Southgate, Latham, Abercrombie, and Green. I don't believe I've ever heard of them before.

MRS. TRELAWNY: Where is Southgate, the one who signed the letters? It seems a bit mysterious.

MAUREEN: Maybe the ghost of old Phineas Slag is going to murder us all! (*She makes scary face, screams.*)

MRS. TRELAWNY (*Angrily*): Miss Atterby, can't you control that child? My delicate nerves, you know.

ATHERTON (*Scoffing*): You have nerves of steel. You'd stop at nothing to get Phineas Slag's money.

MRS. TRELAWNY (*Haughtily*): I didn't come here to be insulted. (*Slowly*) Of course, it must be a vast estate. Phineas was a sheep-rancher in Australia, and they're all dreadfully wealthy.

FRANK: Why did Cousin Phineas leave England?

ATHERTON: Maybe the old boy had a brush with the law.

MAUREEN: Maybe he was disappointed in love.

MISS ATTERBY: Maureen! You shouldn't know about such things.

MAUREEN: Why not? I read all your books about love. (MISS ATTERBY *gasps.*)

FRANK: Are any of you familiar with Southgate, Latham, Abercrombie, and Green?

MRS. TRELAWNY: Why, no. I'm not.

ATHERTON: Nor I, and I've been badgered by every well-known firm of solicitors in London. You see, my business has been a little shaky lately. I even made a trip to America (*Looks at* FRANK) lately to see if I could raise some funds.

MRS. TRELAWNY: Well, if you think you're going to inherit any money, you're sadly mistaken. Dear Phineas was so close to me.

ATHERTON: You hadn't seen or heard from him in thirty years.

FRANK: Well, I'd never even met Phineas Slag.

MISS ATTERBY: We didn't know the gentleman, either.

MAUREEN: I saw his picture once. Mommy had it in an old album. That's before I came to live with Miss Atterby.

MISS ATTERBY: She's lived with me since her parents' death.

MAUREEN: Phineas Slag had the nicest eyes. So warm — yet so sad.

ATHERTON (*Impatiently*): Why can't we get on with the confounded will? Are we waiting for more relatives?

MRS. TRELAWNY: I think there's another one . . . . Mary Montrose, a Shakespearean actress, I believe. I read that she recently toured Japan with a theatre company.

MAUREEN (*Happily*): An actress!

FRANK (*Slowly*): Mary Montrose. Yes, we must wait for Mary. (MARY, *still disguised as* MISS WAVERLY, *enters carrying tea tray.*)

MARY: Anyone for tea, ducks? (*She places tray on table up left.*)

MRS. TRELAWNY: Where is Mr. Southgate? This waiting is intolerable.

MARY: There's money involved. You'll wait, all right! (*Exits*)

MRS. TRELAWNY: I don't know why I came to this dreadful place. (MAUREEN *gets up, walks around room, goes over to tea tray.*) I am obviously entitled to the entire estate. (MAUREEN *looks around, grins, surreptitiously pours ink into teapot, then walks innocently back to* MISS ATTERBY.)

MISS ATTERBY (*Coldly*): I doubt that very much — and I intend to protect Maureen's interests.

ATHERTON: Maybe you'd like the estate for yourself, Miss Atterby!

FRANK: Please — let's hear the will before we jump to conclusions.

ATHERTON: I don't remember asking you for your advice, Frost. (*All turn as* SOUTHGATE *enters and coughs loudly. He is bald with white sideburns and white beard, and carries a briefcase.*)

SOUTHGATE (*Looking around*): The survivors of Phineas Slag. Yes, yes, of course. (*He goes to chair at table, left, sits.*) I believe everyone is acquainted. (*He opens briefcase.*)

FRANK: Are you Alfred Southgate?

SOUTHGATE (*Gruffly*): Southgate — of Southgate, Latham, Abercrombie and Green. Yes, yes, I wrote to all of you. (*Nodding to* FRANK) You must be the American one — Mr. Frost, I believe. (*He glances around.*) Yes, yes, everyone looks exactly as I expected. (*Pauses*) But Miss Montrose. Where is Mary Montrose?

ATHERTON: She hasn't arrived.

SOUTHGATE: I gave explicit instructions for everyone to be here at midnight. I will not tolerate any interruption of the reading of Phineas Slag's last will and testament. (*He stands, storms to door, calls.*) Miss Waverly! Miss Waverly! (*He looks out right, turns.*) And now my secretary is gone.

FRANK: She was here a few minutes ago. Where do you suppose — ?

SOUTHGATE: Questions! Questions! We'll conduct the reading

without the services of Miss Waverly. (*He returns to table, looks at group.*) Your departed cousin was most generous. Most generous.

MRS. TRELAWNY: Dear Phineas! I loved him so!

ATHERTON: You just said you hadn't seen him for thirty years!

MRS. TRELAWNY (*Tearfully*): But I thought of him constantly. Out there in Australia — alone and friendless — without anything to live for.

ATHERTON (*Bitterly*): Except his money!

MRS. TRELAWNY: Mr. Atherton, you are incorrigible!

MISS ATTERBY: Mr. Southgate, may we hear the will, please! (SOUTHGATE *ignores her and smiles at* MAUREEN.)

SOUTHGATE: You're a young one, all right.

MAUREEN: And you're a nice man. I think I met you before . . . without all those whiskers. (SOUTHGATE *coughs gruffly.*)

SOUTHGATE: A very outspoken child. (MARY *re-enters, now wearing simple dress and moderate makeup, with blond wig removed. She closes door behind her, stands in front of door with her hands behind her back.*)

MARY: Mr. Southgate? (SOUTHGATE *turns.*) I am Mary Montrose.

SOUTHGATE (*Rising*): We've been waiting for you, my dear. (*Gestures*) Come in. Have you met your relatives? (*As* MARY *walks to table he introduces others, who nod to her.*) Mrs. Trelawny — Miss Atterby — Maureen Taylor — Mr. Atherton — and this is your American cousin, Jim Frost. (MARY *freezes, gasps.*)

FRANK (*Quickly*): Miss Montrose, this is a pleasure. (*Goes to her, taking her arm*)

MARY: Jim Frost? (*In shock*) Oh, no! (*Brushes her hand across her face.* FRANK *leads her downstage.*)

SOUTHGATE: Miss Montrose — Mr. Frost — will you all take your places at the table. (*Others take seats at table.* MARY *stares at* FRANK.)

MARY (*Bewildered*): What are you doing here? Who are you?

FRANK: Sh-h-h. Please, trust me for a little while. (SOUTHGATE *coughs impatiently.*)

SOUTHGATE: Miss Montrose, are you all right?

MARY: Yes — yes, of course. (*Goes to table, followed by* FRANK. *Both sit.* SOUTHGATE *takes long legal document from briefcase, raps on table for attention.*)

SOUTHGATE: As the hour is very late, and the provisions of this will are rather — ahem — unusual, I will omit the preliminaries and begin by reading the specific bequests. (*Looks over his glasses at group*) I'm certain that's the main interest of everyone here!

MRS. TRELAWNY: What an unkind thing to say! Phineas Slag was a warm, sympathetic, lovable, old man — my dearest relative.

SOUTHGATE: I found him to be an aggressive, hateful skinflint!

ATHERTON (*Rising*): I won't permit you to talk about Cousin Phineas like that — even though it's true!

SOUTHGATE: May I continue? (ATHERTON *sits down.* SOUTHGATE *strokes his whiskers, looks around, adjusts his glasses, then turns his attention back to will. Reading*) "I amassed a fortune in Western Australia, but my life was a solitary one — without friends or family, and in order to amuse myself during the lonely years, I indulged in many puzzles and games of my own device. The wording of the will is a kind of puzzle in itself. The quotations which each of you will hear as my solicitor, Alfred Southgate, reads the will, are clues to places in this room where you will find hidden the specific bequests I have made."

ATHERTON (*Angrily*): Slag must have been crazy. I'm not here to play games.

SOUTHGATE (*Dryly*): A man may set up his estate in any way he wishes. Mr. Slag was of sound mind at the time of his death. Are all of you ready to hear the clues to your fortunes? (*All nod.*) Very well. (*Reading*) "First, to Mrs. Hector Trelawny, I leave this message . . . .

". . . She is intolerable curst,
And shrewd and forward. . . ."

MRS. TRELAWNY (*Angrily*): Phineas Slag said that about me? Why, the despicable old reprobate!

ATHERTON (*Laughing*): Maybe he wasn't so crazy after all.

MISS ATTERBY: But I don't understand. What did Phineas Slag mean — "shrewd and forward"?

SOUTHGATE: I have taken a solemn oath not to divulge any information. (*Smiles*) In accordance with the will, I have hidden letters to all of you in this room — but it's for you to find them. (*Indicating* MARY) Perhaps Miss Montrose can help you?

MARY: How can I help? Those lines are familiar, and yet — "She is intolerable curst." Of course! Those lines are from *The Taming of the Shrew!*

MRS. TRELAWNY: A shrew, am I? Why, that miserable scoundrel! (MARY *stands, points at first picture hanging on wall, up right.*)

MARY: That picture — I'm sure it represents Kate and Petruchio.

FRANK (*Standing*): The principal characters in *The Taming of the Shrew.*

MAUREEN (*Excitedly*): I'll bet there's a message hidden in that picture! (MRS. TRELAWNY *rushes over to picture, takes it off wall, turns it over, revealing an envelope attached to the back, puts picture on table. She rips off envelope, opens it and takes out letter, which she reads quickly to herself, frowning.*)

MRS. TRELAWNY: That skinflint! Just listen to this. (*Reading aloud*) "To my not-so-beloved cousin, Imogene Trelawny, I bequeath the sum of ten pounds." (*Throws letter down*) Ten pounds! Can you believe it? (*She storms over to table.*) I'm leaving this dreadful place this very minute — and I'll see my lawyer in the morning! (*She rushes to door, tries unsuccessfully to open it.*) The door is locked! (*She returns to table and begins to shout at* SOUTHGATE.) You locked us in this room!

SOUTHGATE: Precisely. I warned you that this will had rather unusual provisions. No one is to leave the room until the entire will has been read. My secretary locked the door after all of you came in.

MRS. TRELAWNY (*Enraged*): I'll scream! Someone will hear me.

SOUTHGATE: I doubt that. We're the only persons in this building at this hour. That's why Mr. Slag insisted that his will be read at midnight.

MRS. TRELAWNY: I'll have you arrested.

SOUTHGATE: On what grounds? You came here of your own volition, and, after all, Mr. Slag did not forget you in his will. Everything is perfectly legal and binding — have no doubt of that. (MRS. TRELAWNY *sighs, sits down.*) Now, if we can continue . . . . (*He continues reading from will.*) "To John Atherton, who has an uncanny knack for spending and wasting money, I leave this message:
    "Thou art too wild, too rude and bold of voice . . .' "
(*He looks up.*) Can you find your bequest in that message, Mr. Atherton?

ATHERTON: If it's Shakespeare, forget it. I'm not the type!

MARY: I recognize the lines. They're from *The Merchant of Venice.*

FRANK (*Pointing to second picture on wall*): That's a picture of the courtroom scene from *The Merchant of Venice*, isn't it? (*Walking over to it and looking at picture more closely*) Yes — there's Portia. (*Going back to table*) Do you suppose there's a message there for you, Atherton? (ATHERTON *rises, walks over to picture, takes it down, turns it over and re-*

veals envelope attached to back. He rips it off, opens it and takes out letter.)

ATHERTON (*Reading*): "In order to save you the time and tribulation of wasting my fortune, I leave you absolutely nothing — except for one pound, deposited to your account in the Bank of England. I bid you to save the pound, but I doubt whether it will be in your possession before the passing of another day." (ATHERTON *rushes back to table.*) One pound! Why, the old tightwad!

SOUTHGATE: Please take your seat, Mr. Atherton, and listen to the rest of the will.

ATHERTON: I'm leaving — now — and you're not stopping me!

SOUTHGATE (*Pointing*): You'll find the door is solid oak, much too strong to be smashed by a contingent of men.

ATHERTON (*Suddenly*): The door, yes — but you forgot the window! (*He rushes over to window, pulls back draperies, revealing window covered with steel bars. He bangs on them and tries to pull them loose, to no avail, then returns to sit at table.*)

SOUTHGATE (*Blandly*): Steel bars — the windows are as impregnable as the door.

ATHERTON (*Wildly*): You're as crazy as Phineas Slag! I need that money for my business!

SOUTHGATE: It's quite obvious that you've always needed another person's money. (*Quietly*) If I may continue? (*He reads.*) "To Maureen Taylor, my young cousin, who was placed in the care of Miss Atterby after her parents' tragic deaths, I can only say:

"What made me love thee? Let that persuade
Thee, there's something extraordinary in thee."

MAUREEN: I don't need Miss Montrose to tell me where that quote is from. Miss Atterby has read *The Merry Wives of Windsor* to me many times. We've even acted scenes of the play.

MISS ATTERBY (*Nodding*): Maureen always liked to play Falstaff.

MAUREEN: I used a pillow to make me look fat. (*Pointing to statue on table near window*) See that statue? That's Falstaff. (*She rushes over to table, lifts up statue and turns it over, revealing envelope, which she removes, then puts statue down, tears open envelope and pulls out letter. She glances at it briefly, then starts reading.*) "To my cousin, Maureen Taylor, I leave the sum of twenty-five thousand pounds to provide for her further education and welfare."

MISS ATTERBY: Oh, that dear, generous man!

MAUREEN: Mr. Slag didn't have to leave me anything. I always liked him — and I always will.

MRS. TRELAWNY (*Shocked*): Twenty-five thousand pounds to that horrid little child! (MAUREEN *sticks out her tongue.*)

ATHERTON: I'd like to wring her neck! (*He rises suddenly.*) The telephone! Why didn't I think of that before? (*He rushes to phone, left, lifts receiver, jiggles button several times, listens, then bangs receiver down.*) Dead — the phone is dead! (*Angrily to* SOUTHGATE) And I'll bet you saw to that. Why, it's just a prop.

MRS. TRELAWNY: Everything about this dreadful place is unreal. (*Suddenly*) Mr. Southgate, who are you, anyway? What are you planning to do?

SOUTHGATE: You're perfectly safe, I assure you. I am deeply grieved that you never knew your cousin, Phineas Slag. It might have changed so many things.

MRS. TRELAWNY: He was the meanest, most hateful man!

SOUTHGATE: And you, Mr. Atherton? What do you think of Mr. Slag — now that he has bequeathed you one pound? (ATHERTON *bangs on table.* SOUTHGATE *raises his hand.*) But it is getting late, and we must cover two more stipulations of the will. Mr. Frost, I believe you will be interested in the next bequest.

MARY (*Suddenly*): Mr. Southgate, there's something I must tell you. Something you must know —

FRANK: Mary, please! (*He grips her arm.*) You must trust me
— for a little while longer.

MARY (*Sadly*): I'm so confused. (*She buries her head in her
hands.*)

MRS. TRELAWNY (*Sighing and shaking her head in resignation*):
Well, I might as well have a cup of tea, at least. (*She gets
up, walks over to tea tray, pours tea into cup. She stares
at cup, screams, puts it down. Everyone rushes to tea table.
She points at cup.*) Look! That tea! It's a dreadful blue! It
— it's been poisoned! Someone is trying to kill us!

SOUTHGATE: There's nothing wrong with the tea. (*He examines
pot, then cup, frowns.*) But the color . . . . No, I don't
understand, either.

MRS. TRELAWNY (*Hysterically*): There's a murderer in this
room!

FRANK: Stop being melodramatic. (*He examines teapot.*) Ink!
Someone poured ink into the teapot! (MISS ATTERBY *gasps,
grabs* MAUREEN's *hand, examines it.*)

MISS ATTERBY: Maureen, what did you do to the tea?

MAUREEN (*Uncomfortably*): I didn't think anybody would
drink it. (*Reluctantly*) Yes, I put ink into the tea.

ATHERTON: You little brat!

MRS. TRELAWNY (*Wearily*): Well, at least one mystery's solved.
(*All return to table and sit down.*)

SOUTHGATE (*Adjusting his glasses and picking up will again*):
I think we should continue. I believe we are ready to hear
your bequest, Mr. Frost. (*Reading*)
    "Fair youth, come in! . . .
    We'll mannerly demand thee of thy story,
    So far as thou wilt speak it."
(SOUTHGATE *lowers document.*) What do you make of that?

FRANK: I don't know. (*Repeats slowly*) "So far as thou wilt
speak it." (*He turns.*) Mary, can you help us?

MARY (*Slowly*): It's from *Cymbeline* . . . .

FRANK: *Cymbeline?*

MARY: One of Shakespeare's last plays. Cymbeline was a faithful old servant who raised two princes in a cave. (*Pointing at third picture on wall*) I think that's a scene from *Cymbeline.* (FRANK *rushes over to picture, pulls it off wall and turns it over, revealing attached envelope. He tears it open, takes out letter.*)

FRANK (*Slowly*): My turn now. (*Begins to read.*) "To Jim Frost, sole survivor of my favorite cousin, I will and bequeath one hundred thousand pounds." (FRANK *whistles.*) That's a quarter of a million dollars. (*Others look obviously upset and angry.*)

MRS. TRELAWNY: That's unfair!

ATHERTON: I'll sue the estate!

SOUTHGATE: Silence, all of you!

MARY (*Coldly*): "We'll mannerly demand thee of thy story."
(*To* FRANK) Could you clear this mystery up for us now?

FRANK: Mary, I asked you to — (*She turns, faces* SOUTHGATE.)

MARY: There's something you must know.

FRANK (*Quickly*): I know what she wants to tell you. You might as well know the truth. I'm not Jim Frost!

ATHERTON: A fraud!

MRS. TRELAWNY: Incredible!

MISS ATTERBY: Then you don't deserve the inheritance. (FRANK *waves everyone to silence.*)

FRANK: Listen to me, please! Jim Frost was my best friend. Jim and I shared an apartment in New York for two years. When your letter arrived, Mr. Southgate, I knew something was wrong and — well, I came here in Jim's place.

SOUTHGATE: Were you aware of this deception, Miss Montrose?

MARY: I knew this man wasn't Jim Frost. (*To* FRANK) You must be Frank!

FRANK: That's right. My name is Frank Dawson, Jim's best friend.

MARY (*Nodding*): I should have known. Jim wrote me about you many times. He described you. Maybe that's why I trusted you, although I was terribly afraid.

ATHERTON: This is too much for me. Mistaken identities, frauds — I protest! If this man isn't Jim Frost, then how can we be sure that he's the one who shared an apartment with Frost in Brooklyn?

SOUTHGATE: This is all highly irregular. (*To* FRANK) You speak of Jim Frost in the past tense, as if —

FRANK (*Grimly*): Jim Frost is dead. He was murdered a month ago.

MRS. TRELAWNY: Murdered!

MARY (*Brokenly*): Jim and I — were engaged. Then a telegram came, telling me that he had been killed. The — the case is still unsolved.

FRANK: I sent the telegram to Mary. (*To* SOUTHGATE) When your letter addressed to Jim arrived, Mr. Southgate, I realized you didn't know that Jim had been killed. Then it occurred to me that there might be someone else who was likely to inherit from Phineas Slag — someone who would stop at nothing to get rid of Jim, in the hope that with Jim out of the way, he or she could inherit Jim's share of the estate.

MISS ATTERBY: Why, that means that one of us is a murderer!

FRANK: Exactly. (*Looks around at group slowly*) The murderer must have been surprised and frightened when I walked in here tonight and said I was Jim Frost. He must have wondered whether he'd killed the wrong man, or whether I was an impostor — and if so, who I really was. I must have made him pretty nervous. (ATHERTON *rises suddenly*.)

ATHERTON (*Turning quickly and pointing at* SOUTHGATE): There's your murderer — Southgate of Southgate, Latham, Abercrombie and Green. Who ever heard of them before? All of this set-up is phony — this office, the locked door

and barred windows, reading the will at midnight. Southgate, you deliberately lured us here to kill us.

MAUREEN (*Excited*): This is just like the movies.

MISS ATTERBY: Maureen, please!

MRS. TRELAWNY: Oh, my poor nerves. I — I think I'm going
to faint! (MRS. TRELAWNY *swoons, sinks back into her
chair.*)

SOUTHGATE: I think we're all being a trifle — ah — emotional.
I can see how my actions might arouse suspicion. I did call
you here under somewhat mysterious circumstances, but not
for the purpose of murder. Mr. Dawson was quite right. I
did not know that Jim Frost was dead. (*Turning to* MARY)
You were engaged to Jim Frost, Miss Montrose?

MARY (*Sadly*): Yes. Jim and I met and fell in love last summer
when he was in England, and he planned to come back this
year so we could be married . . . . (*Begins to cry*)

FRANK: We understand, Mary.

MARY (*Regaining her composure*): I'm all right, Frank. It was
just that seeing you here tonight, posing as Jim, was such a
shock.

SOUTHGATE: Then it appears that at least two persons in this
room knew about Jim Frost's death. Miss Montrose, Mr.
Dawson —

FRANK (*Grimly*): And the murderer!

MISS ATTERBY: I simply must get Maureen home. All this talk
of violence is bad for her.

MAUREEN (*Sullenly*): Oh, please, Miss Atterby. This is a lot
more fun than a stuffy birthday party!

SOUTHGATE: We will all leave in good time, Miss Atterby.
However, we must not forget to read the final clause of
Phineas Slag's will.

FRANK: The final clause? Of course! We haven't heard Mary
Montrose's inheritance.

MARY: I'm not interested in that now. Nothing matters with Jim gone. (SOUTHGATE *clears his throat, picks up the will.*)

SOUTHGATE: But I must finish the reading. (*Adjusts glasses, then reads*) "Forty." (*He puts will down.*) That completes the reading of the will of Phineas Slag.

ATHERTON: Forty? What does that mean?

MRS. TRELAWNY: Why did Phineas have to be so mysterious?

FRANK (*Musing*): Forty years in the wilderness . . . forty days and forty nights in the Ark . . .

MAUREEN (*Brightly*): Ali Baba and the forty thieves!

MARY (*Slowly*): Forty. All of Mr. Slag's other references were found in the works of Shakespeare, but I can't recall any play that mentions "forty." Forty what?

FRANK (*Frowning*): A play? (*Suddenly*) But Shakespeare wrote poems, too.

MARY: The sonnets, of course! Wait. There must be a copy of Shakespeare here. (SOUTHGATE *smiles and nods, as* MARY *and* FRANK *rush to shelves, scanning them quickly.*)

FRANK (*Excitedly, reaching for a volume*): Here it is . . . *The Complete Works of Shakespeare.* (*He takes book from shelf and goes back to table, followed by* MARY. *They sit down and* FRANK *leafs through volume, scanning pages, and finally stopping and looking up briefly.*) Listen. This is Shakespeare's sonnet number forty. (*He reads.*)

"Take all my loves, my love, yea take them all:
What hast thou more than thou hadst before?"

MARY (*Slowly*): "Take all . . ."

ATHERTON (*Bitterly*): She'll receive the bulk of Slag's estate.

SOUTHGATE (*Quickly*): An impressive inheritance. A half-million pounds!

MARY (*Dumbfounded*): Oh, I couldn't accept all that money.

MRS. TRELAWNY (*Sweetly*): A wise thought, my dear. Now if you'll consent to share the estate with all the heirs —

SOUTHGATE (*Quickly*): That is quite impossible. The terms of the will must not be violated.

MARY: It — it can't be true.

FRANK (*Suddenly*): It's quite evident that our murderer can't believe it, either. It seems as though he killed the wrong person!

MRS. TRELAWNY (*Brightly*): Why, he must have thought that Jim Frost would receive the entire estate.

ATHERTON: Rubbish!

FRANK: I don't think so, Atherton. Perhaps Slag told one of his relatives that he planned to leave his money to someone in a foreign country. That person naturally thought he meant Jim Frost — in America!

MISS ATTERBY: That seems logical.

FRANK: Wait a minute. Mrs. Trelawny mentioned that she's read that Mary Montrose recently traveled with a theatre company in Japan. That must be it. The murderer didn't know about Mary and thought that the only relative in a foreign country was Jim.

MRS. TRELAWNY: So the murderer decided to kill Jim, so he wouldn't receive the major part of the estate.

FRANK: We have to start by eliminating those obviously innocent, those who couldn't possibly have killed Jim.

MISS ATTERBY: It's quite evident that Maureen didn't kill Frost.

MAUREEN: Oh, bother, Miss Atterby! I wanted to be a suspect!

FRANK: No. I think we can safely say that Maureen is innocent. The murderer would have to be someone who was in America when Jim was killed.

MRS. TRELAWNY: Well, I was running my boardinghouse in the West End.

FRANK: And I know Mary was in England when I sent her the telegram about Jim's death. That leaves one suspect. (*Looks at* ATHERTON)

ATHERTON (*Nervously*): What are you talking about?

FRANK (*Pointing*): It had to be you, Atherton! You admitted that you were in America on a business trip. It must have been at the time that Jim was murdered.

ATHERTON: No, no, that's not true! (*He stands.*)

FRANK: I think it is. You gave yourself away a little while ago.

SOUTHGATE: Will you please explain, Mr. Dawson?

FRANK (*Nodding*): Atherton specifically mentioned that Jim Frost's apartment was in Brooklyn. Now, whenever one thinks of New York he immediately thinks of Broadway, Times Square, the Great White Way — in short, he thinks of Manhattan, not Brooklyn.

SOUTHGATE: A very good point, young man.

FRANK: Naturally, I knew the apartment was in Brooklyn, and Mary had Jim's New York address. But only one other person could have known the exact location.

MRS. TRELAWNY: The murderer!

FRANK (*Quickly*): You, Atherton. Somehow you thought that Jim was Mr. Slag's principal heir — and you intended to do something about it. You said a few minutes ago you needed money for your business. You went to New York, found out where Jim lived, went there and murdered him! That's how it had to be. (ATHERTON *draws gun from his pocket and levels it at* FRANK.)

ATHERTON: Very clever, Mr. Dawson, but I'm afraid the discovery may prove very costly. One of you locked this door, and I want it opened! (MRS. TRELAWNY *screams.* MISS ATTERBY *clutches* MAUREEN.) If the door isn't opened in one minute, I'll — I'll kill that kid!

MRS. TRELAWNY (*Angrily*): You monster, you! (*She picks up her large purse and hits* ATHERTON *with it, catching him off guard. He staggers.* MISS ATTERBY *screams as* FRANK *lunges forward, scuffling with* ATHERTON. SOUTHGATE *watches in alarm.* MARY *backs toward door, stands in front of door with hands behind her back.* FRANK *grabs* ATHER-

TON's *arm, forces gun out of his hand, pins him against wall. Door bursts open and* CONSTABLE *rushes into room.*)

CONSTABLE: All right, now. What's going on here?

SOUTHGATE (*Standing up and pointing at* ATHERTON): There's your man, Constable! He's a murderer!

MISS ATTERBY: Yes, he's dangerous — thank goodness you're here, Constable.

MRS. TRELAWNY: But what brought you here at this moment? How did you know we would need you?

CONSTABLE: Why, Mr. Southgate's secretary telephoned me and said the police might be needed. The secretary was gone when I arrived, but I listened at the door, and when I heard the scuffle and the lady screaming, I came right in. (*Crossing to* ATHERTON) You'll have to come with me. (*Handcuffs* ATHERTON, *starts toward door with him*)

SOUTHGATE: You'd better take his gun as evidence. (*Points to gun*) It's probably the same one that was used to kill a man in the States a month ago. (FRANK *takes out handkerchief, picks up gun with it and hands it to* CONSTABLE, *who puts gun into his pocket.*)

CONSTABLE: I'm much obliged to you, sir. I'll put in a call to the inspector, and you can give him your statement shortly. (*Exits with* ATHERTON)

MARY: Mrs. Trelawny, you saved the day! How do you feel?

MRS. TRELAWNY: I'm too excited to faint!

SOUTHGATE: Mr. Slag would have been delighted with your performance. You have a remarkable aim with that purse.

MRS. TRELAWNY: I've had a lot of practice. I threw things at dear Mr. Trelawny for years.

SOUTHGATE: I think that a reward of ten thousand pounds from the estate might be in order. As executor, I could arrange that.

MRS. TRELAWNY: Ten — ten thousand pounds! Oh, my dear, sweet, generous cousin. Ten thousand pounds!

SOUTHGATE: I believe you called him a despicable old reprobate earlier.

MRS. TRELAWNY: Did I? Well, all men are despicable old reprobates, at times.

MISS ATTERBY (*To* SOUTHGATE): Would it be all right if I take Maureen home now?

MAUREEN (*Pouting*): I want to see the rest of the show.

MISS ATTERBY: Show indeed! Dear child, you're terribly distraught.

MAUREEN: But it's just like the movies, Miss Atterby. (*She walks to* SOUTHGATE.) You can't fool me, Mr. Whiskers.

MISS ATTERBY: Maureen! (MAUREEN *quickly tugs at* SOUTHGATE*'s beard. It falls off. Everyone ad libs surprise.*)

MAUREEN: You see? I knew it was a disguise. (*To* SOUTHGATE) *You're* Phineas Slag.

OTHERS (*Ad lib*): What? It can't be! What about the will? Was it a fake? (*Etc.*)

SOUTHGATE (*Smiling and shrugging in resignation*): Yes, I must confess. The child is right. I am Phineas Slag, your long-lost relative.

MISS ATTERBY (*To* MAUREEN): How did you know Mr. Southgate was Phineas Slag, Maureen?

MAUREEN: His eyes — so sad and lonely — are just like the picture of Phineas Slag in Mommy's album.

SOUTHGATE (*Musing*): Never try to deceive a child. (*To everyone*) Yes, I returned to England a short time ago. I wanted to know my living relatives, to share my wealth with them while I was still alive, but I didn't want them to be nice to me because of my wealth. That's why I staged this masquerade. I — I wanted someone to like Phineas Slag — and not just his money.

MRS. TRELAWNY: Dear cousin — I'm so sorry.

SOUTHGATE: It's all right, Imogene. (*To others*) I rented this office under the name of Southgate, Latham, Abercrombie,

and Green. Then I hired a secretary — a Miss Waverly —
and wrote those letters to my heirs at their last known address. (*Shaking his head*) I didn't know I was stumbling
onto a murder case!

FRANK: You couldn't have known that.

SOUTHGATE: No, but, in a way, I'm responsible for Jim Frost's
murder. Atherton was the only relative to whom I ever re-
vealed my plans. I thought I could trust him. (*Sighs*) I mentioned that I was leaving my estate to a relative in a foreign country. I meant Mary Montrose, of course. (*He takes
her hand.*) Oh, my dear Mary, what a terrible wrong I
committed.

MARY (*Weakly*): You couldn't have known. We've all been
wrong. We should have tried to get in touch with you long
ago.

SOUTHGATE: Because I am a devotee of Shakespeare, I devised
tonight's little game. But my plans backfired.

MAUREEN (*Smiling*): Well, I like puzzles, too, Mr. Southgate.
And guess what? I solved your other puzzle, too.

MISS ATTERBY: What are you talking about?

MAUREEN (*Proudly*): The name of the law firm. Southgate,
Latham, Abercrombie, and Green. Take the initials of those
names and you have . . . (*She spells.*) S-L-A-G, Slag!

MRS. TRELAWNY (*Wearily*): It's entirely too much for me. My
poor head is spinning.

SOUTHGATE: I'm sorry if I deceived you all.

MRS. TRELAWNY: Oh, pshaw! What's one fortune, more or
less? Now, the nicest gentleman is coming for dinner tomorrow night. Terribly rich, too — and I'd like you to join us.

SOUTHGATE (*Bowing*): My pleasure!

FRANK: One thing still bothers me, though. (*To* SOUTHGATE)
How did the constable get into this room? When we tried
the door it was locked.

SOUTHGATE: I'm puzzled about that, too. I gave orders to Miss Waverly, my secretary, to lock the door after everyone arrived. Apparently she sensed trouble, and called the constable — but she disappeared long before he arrived.

FRANK: What do you know about Miss Waverly?

SOUTHGATE: Very little, actually. She seemed competent enough when she answered my advertisement, so I hired her. But now — (MARY *takes blond wig from her purse, puts it on.*)

MARY (*In Cockney accent*): Anyone for tea, ducks?

FRANK: Mary! You were Miss Waverly all along!

SOUTHGATE (*Stunned*): Egad! My relatives are more clever than I suspected.

FRANK: Then you must have unlocked the door for the constable.

MARY: Yes. (*Takes large key ring from pocket*) After I heard the news of Jim's death, I decided to look into the case myself — and when I saw an ad for a legal secretary at this address, where I knew the will was to be read, I applied for the job. (*To* SOUTHGATE) I called the constable, then entered the room and locked the door behind me. (*Holds up keys*) When Atherton drew his gun, I unlocked the door to let the constable in — and in the confusion, no one noticed. (FRANK *takes* MARY*'s hand.* MAUREEN *jumps up and down in excitement.*)

Maureen: You see, Miss Atterby? It *is* just like the movies! (*All laugh as curtains close.*)

THE END

Production Notes

Strange Inheritance

Characters: 4 male; 4 female

Playing Time: 35 minutes.

Costumes: Modern dress. Mary, as Miss Waverly, enters wearing short dress, blond wig, heavy makeup. She later re-enters in a simple, stylish dress, without the wig and makeup. She has a key ring in her pocket. Southgate has a bald wig, white sideburns and a white beard which can be pulled off easily. He wears glasses. Constable is in uniform. Atherton has a gun in his pocket. Mrs. Trelawny has purse.

Properties: Tea tray with cups, saucers, teapot, etc., handkerchieves, briefcase, legal document, letter, gun, book of Shakespeare, envelopes containing clues, as indicated in text.

Setting: Law office of Southgate, Latham, Abercrombie, and Green, in London, an imposing, gloomy room with dark paneling. There is a long conference table with seven chairs around it at center. Small table stands up left with inkwell on it; and telephone on table is down left. Paintings representing Kate and Petruchio, Portia, and Cymbeline hang on wall up center. Statuette of Falstaff stands on small table under paintings. Envelopes containing clues are affixed to paintings and statuette. There is a window in upstage wall with "steel" bars over it; closed draperies conceal bars at rise. There are bookshelves, left. Door to outer office is at right.

Lighting; No special effects.

The Devonshire Demons

After dusk, vampires prowl the mysterious mansion of Cedric Johnson, whose terrible powers live on — two hundred years after his death . . .

Characters

BOB LANDIS, *a young newspaper reporter*
MARGE, *his wife*
MRS. PEET, *housekeeper*
FRED LAMMERSON, *a botanist*
BLANCHE, *his wife*
THE PLANT MAN
ADELE JOHNSON, *a young woman*
JIM STODDARD, *her fiancé*
DR. BRAINTREE

SCENE 1: THE DOLLMAKER

TIME: *Evening. The present.*

SETTING: *Gloomy drawing room of Devonshire Downs, Cedric Johnson's ancestral home in England.*

AT RISE: MRS. PEET, *housekeeper, stands beside table down right, examining dolls on table. Some dolls wear period dress, others modern clothes. One male doll is dressed in slacks and sport shirt. She carefully arranges doll in supine position and covers table with large cloth. She walks upstage to French window and pulls draperies aside. Mournful baying sound is heard offstage. MRS. PEET nods, smiles, closes draperies. Voices are heard from offstage,* MRS. PEET *quickly exits left.* BOB *and* MARGE *enter.* BOB *carries suitcase and typewriter case and* MARGE *carries suitcase. They put cases down near door.* BOB *glances around in dismay, whistles.*

BOB: Don't say it, Marge. Please, don't say it!

MARGE: I wasn't going to say anything, Bob. So please stop worrying and acting like a —

BOB: A new husband? (*He smiles, gives her a hug.*) All right! I should have insisted that you stay in our warm flat in London. I was crazy to bring you with me to this gloomy old barn.

MARGE: But I've always loved the Devonshire moor country. It's so mysterious — and foreboding! And this house — the ancestral home of Cedric Johnson. Why, I can almost feel his presence.

BOB: I hope you're wrong, because Cedric Johnson has been dead for two hundred years.

MARGE: Two hundred years? Wow! Bob, what do you suppose happened to Tom Trevor? Why did he leave here?

BOB: Old Jet-Set Tom? He probably went off to the International Correspondents' Convention in Paris, and is really living it up!

MARGE: I can't believe that. Tom is pretty wild, but he'd never abandon an assignment.

BOB: Well, he disappeared from this one — that's why I inherited the job. (*Gestures dramatically*) Get a feature story on Cedric Johnson's mansion, the *Times* editor said. Give it the full treatment — werewolves, vampires, the occult — the whole works! (*He looks around.*) You know, I don't blame Tom for leaving. This place gives me the creeps.

MARGE (*Nervously*): It's not so bad. But you know the legends about Cedric Johnson — that he experimented in the occult. Horrible things may have happened in this house.

BOB (*Cheerfully*): Nonsense! That's just gossip. Cedric was a weird recluse who lived with a slightly batty housekeeper. He probably never did anything worse than chase kids out of his apple orchard.

MARGE: But someone must have lived here since his death. (*She points to table and chairs.*) Everything is dusted and polished. (*Points upward*) And the lights. Whoever heard of electric lights in a two-hundred-year-old house?

BOB (*Thoughtfully*): You're right about that. Maybe Cedric's heirs kept up the place. (*Brightly*) That's it, of course. I understand that one of his descendants, Frederic Lammerson, is coming here for two weeks. They must be getting the house ready for him.

MARGE: Isn't he the one who gave your editor permission to photograph the house for the article? (BOB *nods.*) I'm sorry you got the assignment.

BOB (*Resolutely*): I have to do the London *Times* article. We'll leave as soon as the story's finished. (*Glances at watch*) If I start tonight, we'll probably be out of here by tomorrow — before sunset. (*Sound of howling is heard from offstage.*)

MARGE (*Frightened*): What's that?

BOB: Probably a neighbor's dog baying at the moon.

MARGE: There's not another house for miles around. (*She walks upstage to French window, pulls back draperies.*) I can't see a thing! The mist — it's everywhere.

BOB (*Joining her*): It's a pretty desolate place. Some of the bogs in the moor are bottomless, they say. Many people have disappeared out there. (MARGE *closes draperies, turns.*)

MARGE: Don't say that!

BOB (*Sternly*): Get hold of yourself, Marge.

MARGE: It's just that I keep thinking of Tom Trevor. Do you think he's out there — somewhere?

BOB: I told you that Paris is the best bet — and the editor will give him the sack when he returns. (*Briskly*) Now let's find a room where we can unpack. I want to start that article. (*He picks up suitcases.*)

MARGE: But I don't want to explore these dark, gloomy rooms.

BOB: You're being unreasonable!

MARGE (*Relenting*): I'm foolish, I know, and I'm sorry. No, you run along. (*Gesturing*) I'll find a place for your typewriter, and when you return I'll help with the article.

BOB (*Grinning*): That's better! I'll be right back. (*He exits, carrying suitcases.* MARGE *glances out window, shivers. She picks up typewriter, looks around, then puts typewriter on floor. She lifts table cover, stares curiously at dolls, picks up a doll in period dress and touches doll's face.* MRS. PEET *enters left. She stands behind* MARGE.)

MRS. PEET (*Coldly*): What are you doing here? (MARGE *screams, drops doll, turns. Gently,* MRS. PEET *picks up doll, smooths its dress.*) Poor Margarita! I hope she didn't hurt you. (*She turns, glares at* MARGE.) Why did you touch my dolls?

MARGE (*Feebly*): I was looking for a place for the typewriter. (*She points to typewriter.*) I'm terribly sorry. I didn't know that these dolls belonged to anyone.

MRS. PEET: They are my special friends. It gets very lonesome in this house, even for an old woman. (*Gestures*) These dolls are my companions.

MARGE: I — we — didn't know that anyone lived here. My husband and I are visiting the place for a day or two. He's on assignment.

MRS. PEET (*Suspiciously*): Who sent you here?

MARGE: My husband's a newspaper writer, and he's covering an assignment for the London *Times*.

MRS. PEET: This is Cedric Johnson's home. No one has any right to be here!

MARGE: Oh, we know that Cedric Johnson lived here, but he's been dead for two hundred years!

MRS. PEET: Why must everyone disturb his final resting place? (*Animal howls again.* MRS. PEET *points to the window.*) Out there you hear the creatures of the night. I am alone in here with my dolls.

MARGE: Who are you?

MRS. PEET: I am Mrs. Peet, the housekeeper. This has always been my home.

MARGE (*Relieved*): Oh, then you were hired by Cedric Johnson's heirs to take care of this place.

MRS. PEET: I am Cedric Johnson's housekeeper. (*In weird tones*) Strangers have no right to come to Devonshire Downs. You must leave tonight!

MARGE (*Anxious to change subject*): Your dolls are lovely — so skillfully made. Where did you get them?

MRS. PEET: I made them.

MARGE: Ah, you're a dollmaker. And a real artist! I've never seen such lifelike dolls before. (MARGE *picks up doll in modern dress. She touches doll's face.*) The skin is amazing. Is it plastic? How did you make it?

MRS. PEET: That is my own little secret. (*She takes doll from* MARGE, *returns it to table. She walks to left exit, turns.*) You must leave Devonshire Downs tonight!

MARGE: But my husband's assignment —

MRS. PEET: Leave tonight! (*Exits.* MARGE *gives a stifled scream, turns, runs right, and collides with* BOB *as he enters.*)

BOB (*Entering*): There's a bedroom upstairs with a fireplace and — Marge! What happened?

MARGE (*Pointing left*): Oh, that terrible woman! Please, Bob! Get our suitcases. We must leave!

BOB: What are you talking about?

MARGE: A woman — the housekeeper — told me to leave Devonshire Downs tonight!

BOB: What do you mean? No one lives in this place.

MARGE (*Hysterically*): I saw her! She spoke to me! Please believe me. She said she was Cedric Johnson's housekeeper.

(*She leads him to table, points to dolls.*) Look, she made all those dolls!

BOB: What's so terrifying about that? (MARGE *hands him male doll.*)

MARGE: Feel the skin. (BOB *gingerly examines doll.*)

BOB (*Slowly*): It certainly feels real, but I don't see —

MARGE (*Quickly*): When I touched the skin, it tingled under my fingers. There's something horrible about the doll. And look at that face! Doesn't it remind you of someone?

BOB: It looks like any other doll — stiff, wax-like . . . . (*Slowly*) Yes, there is something familiar about it.

MARGE: And those clothes! That sport shirt and trousers. The last time I saw Tom Trevor he was wearing an outfit like that.

BOB: Impossible!

MARGE: That doll is a dead ringer for Tom Trevor! (BOB *drops doll.*)

BOB: These dolls — your mythical housekeeper — I don't believe a word of it. But if you wish, we'll leave now. I have enough feeling for this atmosphere to write my article in London.

MARGE (*Gleefully*): Oh, yes, Bob! Please get our suitcases. I want to leave now. (*He gives her a gesture of confidence, exits.* MARGE *picks up typewriter.* MRS. PEET *re-enters. She carries a small crystal globe.* MARGE *drops typewriter, backs away.*) We're leaving now. We're going back to London.

MRS. PEET (*Kindly*): My dear, you must forgive a bothersome old woman. I've been alone so many years that I was not mindful of my manners.

MARGE: But we don't want to stay here tonight.

MRS. PEET (*Strangely*): There are so many wondrous things in this house. So many things Cedric Johnson discovered. Each room bears his handiwork. Look! Your husband wanted material for a newspaper article. (*She holds up crystal globe.*) Here is one of the wonders of Cedric Johnson's world. (*She hands globe to* MARGE, *who stares at it in fascination.*)

MARGE (*Slowly*): I had one of these when I was a little girl. When you shake it, there is a shower of flower petals.

MRS. PEET: This is different, my dear. It contains something else. Look into the crystal, and tell me what you see.

MARGE (*Hesitantly*): It's — it's cloudy. I can't see anything.

MRS. PEET (*Nodding*): Those are the shadows of the moor. But they will dissipate. Look deeply, my dear.

MARGE (*Excited*): Yes, I can see more clearly now. There is an old house — such a desolate place! I think it is this house — Cedric Johnson's house.

MRS. PEET: What else do you see?

MARGE: The house is a place of evil, of dark, frightening secrets. (*Raises head*) I — I don't want to look at it anymore.

MRS. PEET: Don't be frightened. There is nothing to be afraid of here, my dear. Look into the crystal. (MARGE *reluctantly lowers head and stares at globe.*)

MARGE: There is someone — something hovering above the house. There is a great cloak of darkness, but wait — eyes! There is a face peering from the darkness. It is a gloating — a menacing face. The eyes are opening, staring at me. They are burning into me! (*She screams, drops globe on table, and runs from room. She screams again from offstage — then there is silence.* MRS. PEET *pockets globe and exits after* MARGE. *In a moment* MRS. PEET *returns with doll dressed similarly to* MARGE. *She looks at it affectionately.*)

MRS. PEET: My foolish little friend! (*She puts doll on table.* BOB *enters, carrying suitcases, and sees* MRS. PEET. *Startled, he drops suitcases.*)

BOB: Who are you?

MRS. PEET (*Proudly*): I am the housekeeper.

BOB: The housekeeper? Then Marge was right. (*He glances around.*) My wife! Where is she? What have you done to her?

MRS. PEET: She is here, waiting for you to join her. (*She holds up crystal globe and hands it to* BOB.) But first, I have something interesting to show you — something that belonged to Cedric Johnson. You want to know all about him, don't you? (BOB *stares into globe.*) It holds many wondrous secrets.

BOB: I don't see — no, wait. (*Excited*) I see a house, a great dark cloud.

MRS. PEET (*Nodding*): That is Cedric Johnson's house. Stare into the globe, my friend. Take your time. You have all the time in the world. (BOB *continues to stare at globe.* MRS. PEET *reaches over to touch her dolls affectionately as curtains slowly close.*)

* * * * *

SCENE 2: THE SNAKE PLANT

TIME: *Two weeks later. Daytime.*

SETTING: *Same as Scene 1. Dolls have been removed from table. There is a folding screen up left.*

AT RISE: FRED LAMMERSON *sits at table, excitedly leafing through an old book.* BLANCHE *enters.*

BLANCHE (*In exasperation*): Fred! (*He continues to read.*) Fred! (FRED *looks up.*) You simply must do something about that housekeeper.

FRED (*Distracted*): Not now, Blanche. (*He taps book.*) This book is a real find!

BLANCHE: Always at your books! I'm trying to get this house in order — and I can't do it with Mrs. Peet always following me around.

FRED: Can't you two try to get along?

BLANCHE (*Bitterly*): Get along with her! She's impossible! She acts as though the house belongs to her.

FRED: She's lived here for years. I guess she feels that Cedric Johnson's house belongs to her.

BLANCHE (*Haughtily*): I'll change all that. I want it to be our home, Fred. Not a moldy museum.

FRED (*Standing*): I'm sorry, Blanche. I know I haven't been much help, but (*Holding up book*) I've found a book written by old Cedric himself, on plant propagation. He was an expert on the origin of plant species, and he discusses some forms of plant life unknown to modern botanists.

BLANCHE: That's hard to believe.

FRED (*Excitedly*): He writes about one species — six feet tall — a carnivorous plant that can devour a full-grown man!

BLANCHE (*Softly*): The old faker probably made it up.

FRED: No, I believe he's telling the truth. He says this particular plant is found only in tropical countries.

BLANCHE: So we won't encounter any man-eating plants at Devonshire Downs. Well, this house still frightens me. And what about that telephone call from the editor of the London *Times*? He sounded so worried.

FRED: He said he sent two reporters here on assignment, and they both disappeared. One of the men's wives disappeared, too.

BLANCHE (*Frightened*): What could have happened to those people?

FRED (*Shrugging*): Who knows? At any rate, I'm not responsible for the personnel problems of the London *Times*. (*He walks to French window.*) I want to get a good look at the grounds before sunset. Who knows what rare species I may find?

BLANCHE (*Shaking head*): Can't stop you, I guess! (*Sighs*) I'd better get back to work. Your cousin Adele is coming in another week and I want to fix everything up for her. (FRED *exits.* BLANCHE *returns to table, stares at book, cringes.*) A man-eating plant! Ugh! (*She slams book shut.* MRS. PEET *enters left.*)

MRS. PEET: Would you like to work on the upstairs rooms, Mrs. Lammerson?

BLANCHE (*Gratefully*): Yes, Mrs. Peet, let's do that!

MRS. PEET (*Bowing slightly*): As you wish. (*She turns to leave. BLANCHE touches her arm. She turns.*) Yes, Mrs. Lammerson?

BLANCHE (*Hesitantly*): Where do you live, Mrs. Peet?

MRS. PEET: In this house, of course.

BLANCHE: But we only see you at dusk.

MRS. PEET (*Defensively*): I have other duties in the daytime. I hope my habits don't disrupt your schedule.

BLANCHE: But what did you do — before you worked at the Johnson estate?

MRS. PEET (*Proudly*): I was always Cedric Johnson's housekeeper.

BLANCHE (*Puzzled*): Cedric Johnson was my husband's ancestor. Why, he's been dead for two hundred years.

MRS. PEET: Two hundred and twelve years.

BLANCHE (*Brightly*): I understand. You mean your family has been in service here all that time. But why are you so unfriendly to Fred — Mr. Lammerson — and me?

MRS. PEET: Strangers don't belong in Devonshire Downs.

BLANCHE (*Protesting*): But we're *not* strangers, Mrs. Peet. This is my husband's property. He is co-owner with Adele Johnson, his cousin. This is our house. And now that we're here, why can't we be friends?

MRS. PEET (*Dully*): I have no friends. (*She walks to window, points outside.*) No one but Cedric Johnson. He understands — and he will help me. (*BLANCHE joins her, looks out.*)

BLANCHE (*Nervously*): But there is nothing out there — nothing!

MRS. PEET: There are some things no one can see. (*Turning*) What do you know about Cedric Johnson?

BLANCHE: Nothing, really. I've heard some rumors, but I can't believe those horrible tales.

MRS. PEET: Did you know that he was a student of the occult?

BLANCHE: The occult? Witchcraft — devil worship?

MRS. PEET (*Disdainfully*): Some people call it that.

BLANCHE: My husband told me that Cedric experimented with many forms of plant life. (*With distaste*) They sound like dangerous species.

MRS. PEET (*Proudly*): That is true. Deadly plants were his specialty.

BLANCHE: Fred is a botanist. He'd like to study all of Cedric's books. Maybe you can tell me something about his experiments.

MRS. PEET (*Proudly*): The result of one of them is here now. Would you like to see a rare plant that has flourished in this house since the days of Cedric Johnson? (*Goes to screen up left*) This is Cedric Johnson's greatest gift to the world of botany. *Sanservieria trifasciata!* Do you know the species?

BLANCHE: I know nothing about plants.

MRS. PEET: It is commonly called the snake plant. (*She moves screen aside, revealing six-foot plant covered with long, thin green leaves and vines. Concealed in center of plant is* PLANT MAN, *a grotesque figure wrapped in shiny leaves and vines.* BLANCHE *screams at sight of plant.*)

BLANCHE: It's horrible!

MRS. PEET (*Proudly*): A snake plant, as tall as a man!

BLANCHE: It — it's not the average house plant, is it? (PLANT MAN *moves one arm slightly. She gasps and points.*) There! One of those vines moved. The plant is alive.

MRS. PEET (*Proudly*): Why not — all plants are living things. Cedric nurtured this plant from a tiny root. I have always tended it with loving care.

BLANCHE: Please, I don't want to look at it anymore.

MRS. PEET: Why not? Don't you find it beautiful? It has survived for two centuries. It is as old as this house — it is part of the house . . . .

BLANCHE (*Hoarsely*): It can't remain here. I want it destroyed!

(PLANT MAN *trembles violently.* BLANCHE *screams, grabs screen, quickly covers plant. She screams at* MRS. PEET.) You're — you're insane! I want you out of this house tonight!

MRS. PEET (*Simply*): As you wish. (*Crosses to exit, turns*) There is much about this house that you do not know. The house will decide who is to stay here. (*Exits*)

BLANCHE (*To herself*): The house, indeed! The sooner she leaves here, the better. (*Paces nervously; as she passes screen, arm of* PLANT MAN *reaches out from behind screen. She moves away and arm withdraws. She goes to French window, opens it and calls.*) Fred! Fred! (*Pauses*) Fred! (*Frantically*) Where are you? Why don't you answer me? (*She turns from window, crosses left, passing in front of screen. Arm of* PLANT MAN *reaches out and wraps around her. She screams.*) Help! Help! Fred! Help me! (PLANT MAN *pulls* BLANCHE *behind screen. She screams in terror. There is silence, then gurgling sound is heard.* MRS. PEET *re-enters. She looks behind screen, nods in satisfaction.*)

MRS. PEET: My lovely plant! No one will ever threaten you again. (FRED *enters through window.*)

FRED: Oh, Mrs. Peet — have you seen Mrs. Lammerson?

MRS. PEET: She was here a few minutes ago.

FRED: I was following a trail on the moor, when I thought I heard her calling.

MRS. PEET: It was probably the wind. There are many strange sounds on the moor.

FRED (*Excitedly*): And such wonderful specimens! I found a *Digitalis purpurea* and an excellent specimen of hemlock. I must tell Blanche about them. Where can she be?

MRS. PEET: She is in the house, I assure you. Perhaps you would like me to prepare tea?

FRED: I could do with something. But Blanche —

MRS. PEET (*Reassuringly*): She will join you in a little while. (FRED *sits at table.* MRS. PEET *nods.*) You are so much like Cedric Johnson.

FRED: I have a lot to learn before I can follow in his footsteps. (FRED *opens book, reads.* MRS. PEET *exits. Rustling sound comes from behind screen.* FRED *turns in his chair, frowns. He stands, walks slowly to screen.*) Who's behind that screen? (BLANCHE *steps from behind screen, holding her right hand behind her back.*) Blanche! You gave me quite a start.

BLANCHE: I'm sorry, Fred.

FRED: What were you doing behind that screen, anyway?

BLANCHE (*Slowly*): I've found something . . . interesting. I'll show it to you if you like — soon.

FRED: Fine, but let's have tea first. Mrs. Peet will bring it right in.

BLANCHE: Yes, I would like that very much. (FRED *sits at table, opens book.*)

FRED: Listen to this, Blanche. (BLANCHE *crosses to stand behind him, as* FRED *reads enthusiastically.*) "Although many plants may be propagated by root division or by taking cuttings, there are some plants that are able to absorb living animal tissue . . . ." (BLANCHE *lifts her right arm. It is covered with green leaves and long green vines. She reaches toward* FRED *with it. Quick curtain.*)

*   *   *   *   *

SCENE 3: THE VAMPIRE

TIME: *A week later, at dusk.*

SETTING: *Same as Scene 1. Screen, plant, and book have been removed. Painting of bright countryside scene hangs on left wall. Gay drapes hang at French windows. There is a vase of flowers on table.*

AT RISE: ADELE JOHNSON *stands at table, arranging flowers.* JIM STODDARD *enters right.* ADELE *smiles, leaves flowers. They embrace.*

ADELE (*Mildly rebuking*): And where have you been all afternoon, Jim? There's so much work to be done in this old place, and you choose to roam the moor with Dr. Braintree.

JIM: I'm sorry, Adele. Braintree is having a field day on the moor. You know, he's pretty important — the head of the London psychic research board, and all. He's finding traces of all sorts of strange phenomena on Cedric Johnson's estate.

ADELE: Former estate, you mean. One-half of it is mine, or it will be on my twenty-fifth birthday.

JIM (*Glancing around*): Well, you've certainly done wonders with this place in three days.

ADELE (*Pleased*): Thanks. (*Worried*) There's one thing that bothers me. What could have happened to Fred and Blanche?

JIM: Search me. You told me your cousin was batty about rare plants. (*Lightly*) Maybe they took off for Sumatra or Africa in search of new specimens.

ADELE (*Stubbornly*): But they promised to meet me here.

JIM: The Lammersons will turn up soon, I'm sure. (*Frowning*) What I'm worried about is that old housekeeper.

ADELE: Mrs. Peet? She *is* a strange woman — she frightens me.

JIM: Do you realize that we never see her until nightfall?

ADELE: Maybe she works somewhere else during the day.

JIM: Where else could she work, out here on the moor? No, I don't think that's the explanation. (DR. BRAINTREE *enters through French window. He carries a small plant.*)

BRAINTREE (*Genially*): Ah, here you are, my young friends! It is good to come in from the dampness of the moor.

ADELE: Good evening, Dr. Braintree.

JIM (*Pointing to plant*): What have you found? (BRAINTREE *places plant on table.*)

BRAINTREE: Most unusual. *Aconitum lycoctonum*!

JIM: Hold on, Doctor! I never got past freshman Latin.

BRAINTREE (*Pointing*): It is a perfect specimen of wolfsbane. I never imagined I'd find it growing on the moor.

ADELE: Wolfsbane?

BRAINTREE (*Nodding*): A common plant that has enjoyed a strange history throughout the ages. It is believed that wolfsbane will ward off the spirits of evil — especially werewolves and vampires! (*Baying is heard from offstage.*)

ADELE (*Nervously*): What's that?

JIM: A lost dog, probably, roaming on the moor. (ADELE *grins weakly.*)

ADELE: I'm sorry I was so foolish — but — wolfsbane, vampires, that terrible howling —

BRAINTREE: I understand, my dear. That is the purpose of my visit to Devonshire Downs — to investigate these things.

JIM: You don't believe the rumors about this place, do you?

BRAINTREE: As a psychic researcher, I believe nothing until it is scientifically proven. But there are indications. (*He tugs goatee.*)

ADELE: Yes?

BRAINTREE: I have found many signs of strange events that must have occurred a few centuries ago — in Cedric Johnson's lifetime.

JIM (*Skeptically*): We've all heard weird tales about the estate, but they're nonsense.

BRAINTREE: Johnson was a diabolically clever man — years ahead of his time in his interest in the occult. It is entirely possible that he made many amazing discoveries. Perhaps many of the phenomena he investigated continue to exist. (*Howling is heard again.* BRAINTREE *grimaces.*) Werewolves are immortal, you know.

JIM (*Angrily*): I'm not going to start believing in werewolves and vampires — and all that rubbish! (*Howling, growing louder, is heard again.*) Let's go find out what that noise is. We'll probably find some poor animal caught in a hunter's trap.

ADELE (*Terrified*): Please, Jim! Don't go out there!

JIM: Adele, if this is going to be our home, we'd better learn the truth about this place.

BRAINTREE: I think it is wise to be cautious. (*Breaks wolfsbane into three pieces.*) Here — each of us can carry a piece of the wolfsbane, to ward off evil. (ADELE *stretches out her hand, touches wolfsbane, and pulls hand away as if burned.*)

ADELE: I can't touch it — it seems to burn my hand!

JIM: I don't want any wolfsbane, either. I refuse to believe in these old wives' tales! Come on — let's investigate that howling. (JIM *opens French window, exits.* BRAINTREE *shrugs, drops wolfsbane on table, and follows him off.* ADELE *looks around fearfully, then timidly exits after them, leaving window open. After a minute,* MRS. PEET *enters, wearing long black cape which she removes and puts on chair near window. She crosses to table, looks at wolfsbane, touches a piece and jerks hand away as though burned.*)

MRS. PEET: Fools! Those headstrong fools! (*She looks at bowl of flowers and turns it, revealing withered and dead flowers.*) The flowers! Who has touched them? (*Scream is heard from offstage.* MRS. PEET *whirls.* ADELE *staggers in through window.*)

ADELE: Out there (*Pointing outside*) — something — something terrible has happened to Dr. Braintree! (JIM *enters, his coat dirty and his tie awry.* ADELE *rushes to him hysterically.*) What happened to Dr. Braintree? (*She starts toward window. He grabs her arm.*)

JIM (*Hoarsely*): Don't look out there, Adele, It's — awful! Terrible! Something flew at us. Something black — horrible! It killed Dr. Braintree!

MRS. PEET (*Ominously*): A creature of the night. (JIM *grabs* MRS. PEET*'s shoulders, shakes her roughly.*)

JIM (*Suspiciously*): What do you know about this? Where have you been? Why do we see you only at night? (*Wildly*) Who — what are you?

MRS. PEET (*Coldly*): I am Cedric Johnson's housekeeper — nothing more. I wanted to protect his experiments, his discoveries, but there were always intruders.

JIM (*Enraged*): You're a fiend! A demon! (*He clutches her again, but* ADELE *separates them.*)

ADELE: Jim, stop! There has to be a logical explanation for this.

JIM (*Bitterly*): What explanation can there be for vampires? I saw the thing that killed Braintree. It wasn't human — it was nothing of this earth. It hovered against the sky, and then it attacked. It was a vampire! (*He covers his eyes.*)

ADELE: I want to leave this place tonight. I'll give instructions to have the house demolished, stone by stone, if necessary, but I want Cedric Johnson's evil memory destroyed!

JIM (*With sudden realization*): His memory . . . there's more than just a memory at work here. (*He turns to* MRS. PEET.) He's still alive — after all these years — isn't he? (ADELE *gasps.* MRS. PEET *smiles mysteriously, folds her arms.*) Well, there's only one way to destroy a vampire. (*He exits left.* ADELE *starts to follow.* MRS. PEET *grabs her arm.*)

MRS. PEET: Wait! There is nothing he can do against the forces of the undead. (*Stares closely at* ADELE, *who tries to pull away*) There have been many intruders in Cedric Johnson's house, but you are different. You belong . . . yes, you belong in this house.

ADELE: Don't say that! I don't want to stay here.

MRS. PEET: Cedric Johnson has been waiting for his rightful heir for two centuries. (*Cautiously*) That young man — for his own sake you must not follow him to the moor tonight! You must remain in the house.

ADELE (*Wildly*): No! No! (*She pulls away.* JIM *returns, carrying a mallet and wooden stake. He moves toward window.*) Jim! What are you going to do?

JIM (*Boldly*): I won't be driven away by any force of evil! A vampire must have a place to find refuge during the daylight hours. I'm going to find Cedric's tomb, and I'm going to wait for him all night, if necessary. (*He brandishes stake.*) When he returns, I'll drive a wooden stake through his heart.

MRS. PEET: Do you realize you are dealing with the undead, young man? The forces of the night are powerful. Beware!

ADELE: Listen to her, Jim! Let's go away from this place tonight!

JIM (*Coldly*): No! I cannot leave until I have destroyed Cedric Johnson.

ADELE: Then I'm going with you.

MRS. PEET (*Quickly*): No! I told you not to go out on the moor with this young man tonight!

ADELE: If anything happens to Jim, there's nothing left for me. I must go with him.

MRS. PEET (*To* JIM): If you value your life, you must not take her with you!

JIM: Perhaps we'll be safer out there than in here with you! (ADELE *and* JIM *exit through French window.* MRS. PEET *walks to table, sits, buries her head in her hands. Howling is heard from offstage. She looks up.*)

MRS. PEET: Why did it have to end this way? I warned them . . . . (*Scream is heard from offstage.* ADELE *re-enters through window. She stares at her hand, rubs it against her dress.*)

ADELE (*Numbly*): Blood. There's blood on my hand.

MRS. PEET: You must rest, my child. (ADELE *joins* MRS. PEET *at table.*)

ADELE (*In shock*): Jim's dead! Something — something killed him.

MRS. PEET (*Nodding*): I know.

ADELE: It — it was so swift, so sudden. I can't remember what happened. I was walking beside him and then, in a moment, he was on the ground. I — I touched his throat and — he was dead! (*She stares at her hand.*)

MRS. PEET: Don't think about it. The night will soon be over, and then you will be able to rest.

ADELE: I am so tired. (MRS. PEET *points at vase of flowers.*)

MRS. PEET: Did you arrange the flowers?

ADELE (*Smiling*): Yes. They were so lovely. I wanted everything to be right — for Jim. (*She picks up several withered flowers from vase.*) The flowers are dead!

MRS. PEET: They were fresh flowers an hour ago, but now they are all dead. (*She looks meaningfully at* ADELE.) A flower dies when it is touched by a vampire.

ADELE: A vampire? (*She shakes her head.*) I can't remember . . . Jim . . . Dr. Braintree. (*Frowns*) I think . . . (*Suddenly*) They were killed by a vampire! I saw it! I was there! (*Sound of mournful howling is heard.*)

MRS. PEET: He is calling you. You must go now — go to him.

ADELE (*Slowly*): Yes . . . yes, I hear him. (*She goes to chair near window, picks up* MRS. PEET*'s black cape and puts it on.*) Devonshire Downs has waited two hundred years — and I am home at last. (*She spreads her arms and flaps cape as she exits through window.* MRS. PEET *nods contentedly as curtains close.*)

THE END

Production Notes

The Devonshire Demons

Characters: 4 male; 4 female; 1 male or female.

Playing Time: 40 minutes.

Costumes: Modern, everyday dress, for all except Mrs. Peet and Plant Man. Mrs. Peet wears long, dark gown, and apron. Plant Man wears green leotard covered with shiny green leaves, headpiece with green leaves and vines fastened to it, and green gloves with vines and tendrils. Dr. Braintree has moustache and goatee.

Properties: Several small dolls, in period costume and modern dress; doll dressed in sports shirt and slacks; doll dressed in costume similar to Marge's; glass globe with "snow" in it; suitcases; portable typewriter case; bowl of flowers, some withered and dead; branch of plant ("wolfsbane"); hammer and wooden stake; black cape.

Setting: Gloomy drawing room in Devonshire Downs, old English manor house. There are French windows up center leading outside to moor. There is a heavy wooden library table downstage, holding dolls covered with cloth in Scene 1. Several chairs are arranged at right. Scene 2, folding screen up left conceals plant and Plant Man. Scene 3, brightly-colored draperies and cushions are added; vase of flowers is on table; painting is on wall.

Lighting: Lighting is dim to create gloomy effect, brightening in Scene 2.

Sound: Sound of animal's mournful baying.

The Woman Who Owned the West

The nation's capital is in an uproar when a sweet but firm old lady turns up with a deed that shows she owns almost half of the United States!

Characters

SENATOR WILBUR FAIRCHILD
MISS WATSON, *his secretary*
HATTIE BATES
BETTY COSGROVE, *21, her niece*
TOM HAINES, *24*
FRANK ⎫ *reporters*
SUE ⎭
ED MALONE, *television newscaster*
DR. CLATTER, *psychiatrist*
PORTER, *attorney*
IRENE DONALDSON
EMILY WILLIAMS
MS. TWIDDLE ⎫
MS. THOMPSON ⎬ *members of Liberated Women of America*
MS. LONGFELLOW ⎭

BEFORE RISE: MISS WATSON *sits at desk, down left, talking into phone. Jar of jam and vase of goldenrod are on desk.*
MISS WATSON (*Into phone*): Senator Fairchild's office . . . .
No, the Senator hasn't arrived yet. It's impossible to see him

today without an appointment . . . . You represent the committee to change the state flower to goldenrod. Yes — yes,
we received the goldenrod. (*Waves hand at vase of goldenrod on desk*) The Senator will give the matter his immediate attention . . . . He'll be wild about it. (*Dryly*) As a matter of fact, it will probably bring tears to his eyes . . . . (*She
hangs up phone, writes on pad on desk.*) He has hay fever
that won't quit. (*Phone rings again and she answers it.*) Senator Fairchild's office . . . . The Society for the Preservation
of the Chicken Hawk? We've already given you ten thousand
dollars in federal funds . . . . What? A mistake in the
check? . . . It's for ten *million* dollars? (*Shrugs*) It would
just be too complicated for you to send it back, and it would
cost us more to correct the mistake — red tape, you know.
(*In bored tone*) Why don't you just keep it . . . . All in a
good cause, the Senator always says. (*She hangs up, starts
writing note on pad again.* SENATOR FAIRCHILD *enters.*)

FAIRCHILD (*Briskly*): Morning, Miss Watson.

MISS WATSON: Good morning, Senator.

FAIRCHILD: Did the Vice-President call? I'm expecting (*Suddenly sneezes*) — achoo! (*He is seized with a fit of sneezing.
He recovers, points to goldenrod.*) Where did you get that
confounded goldenrod?

MISS WATSON: The committee to change your state flower sent
it.

FAIRCHILD (*Bellowing*): What? You know I'm allergic to goldenrod! Get rid of it! (*He sneezes again, and she throws
vase with goldenrod into basket under desk.*)

MISS WATSON: I guess all that glitters isn't goldenrod.

FAIRCHILD: Goldenrod — hoot owls — coyotes — everyone
has a cause these days. Why, only yesterday I was approached by a group that wants to move the Dry Gulch
River to a new riverbed.

MISS WATSON: Sounds like a sensible idea. Where do they want to put it?

FAIRCHILD (*Shouting*): Smack in the middle of Denver! (*Quickly*) Any other calls?

MISS WATSON: The Chicken Hawk Society called. There's been a ten-million-dollar mistake . . . .

FAIRCHILD (*Absent-mindedly*): It doesn't sound too important. Probably just one of those minor bookkeeping errors. Anything else?

MISS WATSON: Oh, yes! (*Holds up jar of strawberry jam*) Someone named Hattie Bates sent you a jar of homemade strawberry jam.

FAIRCHILD: Hattie Bates? Strawberry jam?

MISS WATSON: I told you about her last week. She's the one who telephoned from Buffalo Hollow and said something about owning the West.

FAIRCHILD: Oh. Send her a note of thanks for the jam, and tell her I'm up for re-election in November. (*Suddenly*) Owning the West? What West?

MISS WATSON: The entire western territory of the United States. (*Deadpan*) When you look at the map, it's everything to the left of Pennsylvania.

FAIRCHILD (*In disbelief*): The entire West!

MISS WATSON: Including your home state, Senator. The story broke in her hometown paper, and the wire services have taken it up.

FAIRCHILD (*Scoffing*): Another crackpot!

MISS WATSON: Quite a few people are taking her seriously. There's been a lot of publicity . . . . She's staying at the Hotel Wellington. Perhaps you'd better see her (*Dryly*) — before she helps elect your replacement!

FAIRCHILD (*Booming*): Replacement? Bah! Cancel my appointments! I'm going to the Wellington and send Miss Hattie

Bates packing! (*He waves arms wildly.*) Chicken hawks! Goldenrod! And now, a woman who owns the West! (*Rises; begins to orate*) If I weren't a dedicated public servant, I might lose my temper! (*Exits. Blackout*)

*   *   *   *

TIME: *Morning, the present.*

SETTING: *Living room of suite in Hotel Wellington, Washington, D.C.*

AT RISE: *Telephone up right rings.* BETTY *runs in left.*

BETTY (*Calling over shoulder*): I'll get the phone, Aunt Hattie. (*She answers phone.*) Hello. . . . The hotel manager? . . . Some people to see Miss Bates? How many? . . . Newspaper reporters, TV commentators, and a senator? I don't believe it! . . . Tell them to wait. I'll call you back. (*She hangs up as* HATTIE BATES *enters left, carrying dustcloth. Her hair is unkempt. She dusts chairs and tables during following dialogue.*)

HATTIE: This hotel needs a good cleaning! Dust everywhere! But I suppose Washington, D.C., has its share of pollution, just like all other big cities.

BETTY (*Nervously*): Aunt Hattie, please forget the dusting. There are people downstairs waiting to see you.

HATTIE: Visitors? How nice! Tell that young man at the desk to send them up, Betty. We mustn't forget our manners, even though we are in Washington.

BETTY: You don't understand. There are reporters, television people, and a United States Senator! (HATTIE *makes a desperate sweep at her hair.*)

HATTIE: Then I must do something about my hair. It was always on the frizzy side, just like great-grandmother Amelia's. Tell them I'll be ready in a minute, Betty. (*She exits left.*)

BETTY (*Calling after her*): But, Auntie! (*There is a knock on door, right.* BETTY *opens door and* TOM HAINES *enters. He is dressed in work clothes. He carries a pail of water and a window squeegee.*)

TOM: Window washer.

BETTY: Forget the windows today. My aunt — I — we're terribly busy.

TOM: Can't help it. Orders are orders. (*He walks to window up center and begins to rub squeegee against pane.*)

BETTY: But everyone will be here in a few minutes! (*She looks at him suspiciously.*) Say — you aren't even using water.

TOM (*Quickly*): Oh — that? It's a — a new system. We have to conserve water . . . . Ecology . . . . Energy crisis, and all that. (*He dips squeegee into water and accidentally splashes* BETTY. *She jumps back.*)

BETTY: I wish you'd leave the windows for some other time! Oh, what's the use? Just finish them and leave. (*She exits left. Quickly,* TOM *drops squeegee into pail, takes walkie-talkie out of jacket pocket, adjusts antenna.*)

TOM (*Into walkie-talkie*): Haines calling. . . . Hello, F.A.? It's me — Tom . . . . I'm in the Bates's hotel suite now. The old window washer disguise . . . . No, they don't suspect a thing. (BETTY *re-enters and unobserved, watches* TOM. TOM *continues to talk enthusiastically.*) Yes, our paper will have an exclusive interview. (*He turns, sees* BETTY, *who stands with arms folded, tapping her foot impatiently.* TOM *smiles, cringes, begins to rub window with walkie-talkie.* BETTY *crosses to him, taps his shoulder. He turns. She points to right entrance.*)

BETTY: Out!

TOM: Have a heart, Miss Bates.

BETTY: I am not Miss Bates. Hattie Bates is my aunt. My name is Betty Cosgrove, and — why am I telling you all this? Please leave at once!

TOM: This is my big chance. If I could only interview Miss Bates —

BETTY: My aunt is indisposed.

TOM: She'd better get un-indisposed. There are a lot of people in the lobby, waiting for her. Do you realize what's happening?

BETTY (*Coolly*): I realize that my aunt is news.

TOM: News? Isn't it true that she is the direct descendant of Chief Running Wild and Amelia Bates?

BETTY: Yes, it's true.

TOM: Running Wild is only the son of Chief Sitting Bull!

BETTY: I never met the gentleman.

TOM: Don't make jokes. Sitting Bull gave his son and the son's new wife a certain deed — to the entire territory owned by the Wapanacki Indians.

BETTY: I'm aware of that.

TOM (*Exploding*): That territory is now known as Wyoming, Montana, Utah, Nevada, Arizona, and California! (*He collapses on sofa.*) Why, I can't even visualize it! (BETTY *grabs his collar, pulls him to his feet.*)

BETTY: Please do your visualizing somewhere else.

TOM: Your aunt owns the Great Salt Lake.

BETTY: Naturally.

TOM: The Rocky Mountains!

BETTY: Of course.

TOM: And the Golden Gate Bridge!

BETTY: And Reno — and Lake Tahoe — and Death Valley. (*She escorts him to door.*) You can read all about it in the newspapers. (*She opens door.* FRANK, SUE, ED MALONE, *and* SENATOR FAIRCHILD *surge in, pushing* TOM *and* BETTY *aside.* TOM *falls over back of sofa.* FRANK *and* SUE *hold pencils and notebooks poised.* MALONE *sets up television lights.*)

FRANK (*To* BETTY): How about an interview? Our readers want to hear about the woman who owns the West.

SUE (*Nodding*): My readers want to know what you are going to do with all those western states.

BETTY: You're making a mistake. I don't own the West — my aunt does. (FAIRCHILD *pushes forward.*)

FAIRCHILD: That's an outrageous lie! I am Senator Wilbur Fairchild, and I represent one of those fair western states.

FRANK: We'll get to you a little later, Senator Fairchild. We want to hear from Hattie Bates.

MALONE: My name is Malone, and I'm with Channel 3. My cameramen will be here in a little while. We're giving Hattie Bates two hours of prime time on television!

BETTY: My aunt is not prepared to make a statement. All this has been too much for her. She's getting old, and — (TOM *stands.*)

TOM: Miss Cosgrove is right. As personal physician for Hattie Bates, I will not permit her to get excited.

FRANK: A doctor?

SUE: He doesn't look like a doctor to me. Look at those clothes.

TOM: My patient likes informality. We must do nothing to upset Miss Bates. (HATTIE *enters left. She is checking off items on a list.*)

HATTIE (*To* BETTY): I think I have the perfect wedding present for Cousin Alice. She always loved hiking and the great outdoors. What do you think of the Grand Canyon as a gift?

BETTY: Please, Auntie —

HATTIE: It does seem a bit pretentious. Do you think the Grand Coulee Dam would be more suitable?

BETTY (*Uncomfortably*): We'll talk about it later. (*Gesturing*) I'd like you to meet some people. (*To others*) This is my aunt, Miss Hattie Bates. (FRANK, SUE *and* MALONE *rush forward.*)

FRANK: Do you really own the West?

SUE: What are your plans?

MALONE: Will you consent to an exclusive television interview? (FAIRCHILD *waves angrily.* TOM *steps in front of* HATTIE.)

TOM: I'm terribly sorry. No interviews today. As Miss Bates's personal physician, I order an immediate rest.

HATTIE (*Puzzled*): A physician? I don't believe I know you. (*She looks intently at* TOM.) Are you Caleb Frump's boy? He went away to be a doctor.

TOM: Yes, yes — I'm Caleb Frump's boy.

HATTIE: Well, he's a horse doctor! Young man, I think you've made a mistake. (FAIRCHILD *pushes forward.*)

FAIRCHILD: This man is no doctor. He's Tom Haines, a reporter for the *Post.* He has opposed every one of my environmental committees. Why, he's even opposing my re-election!

MALONE (*Shrugging*): He can't be all bad.

FAIRCHILD: I — Senator Fairchild — will see that justice is done!

HATTIE (*Delighted*): Senator Fairchild! (*Shakes his hand*) How nice to meet you. I hope you liked my strawberry jam!

FAIRCHILD: I didn't touch your strawberry jam!

HATTIE: Oh, that's too bad. My jam is the pride of Buffalo Hollow.

FRANK: Strawberry jam? Did you send Fairchild a gift?

HATTIE (*Nodding*): When I decided to come to Washington, I sent a little token of my good intentions.

SUE: What a headline! "Senator takes bribe from woman who owns the West!"

FAIRCHILD (*Sputtering, angrily*): You print that, and I'll sue you for libel! (*To* HATTIE) I — I — I'll fix you, Miss Bates. (*He shakes his fist, walks to phone, and makes several calls in pantomime.*)

FRANK: Miss Bates, are you prepared to substantiate your claim to ownership of the Western United States?

HATTIE: My, how formal you sound. I have the deed, if that's what you mean.

SUE: The deed?

HATTIE: Of course — the legal papers. It's quite simple, really. I'm the only survivor of Running Wild's family, so the territory belongs to me. (*Proudly*) I'm part Wapanacki. Gracious, I don't see why everyone's making such a fuss! I don't own the buildings or the cities — just the land. (FRANK *whistles in awe.* FAIRCHILD *hangs up phone, joins group.*)

FAIRCHILD: I've called the Attorney General's office. He's sending his assistant immediately. And I called Dr. Clatter, one of the most eminent men in his field.

HATTIE (*Beaming*): More visitors! Is Dr. Clatter a cow doctor, too?

SUE: No, a head doctor.

HATTIE: I simply must do something about my hair. It's frizzled again. (*She exits left.*)

TOM (*Angrily*): I've heard of Dr. Clatter. He's a psychiatrist.

BETTY: Oh, no! (*To* FAIRCHILD) Are you implying that my aunt needs psychiatric help?

FAIRCHILD (*Tapping forehead*): She's definitely a bit confused.

BETTY: Senator Fairchild, you're being terribly unfair. You stormed in here making all sorts of ridiculous accusations. I think you're a hateful, deceitful old windbag!

SUE: That's telling him!

FRANK: Hear! Hear!

FAIRCHILD: Young lady, I'll bring suit against you for your part in trying to steal the Western United States.

TOM: Hold on, Senator! If Hattie Bates really has the deed to the West, you'll look sillier than the time you allocated fifty million dollars for homeless homing pigeons!

MALONE: That's right, Senator. I think one of the homing pigeons was your brother-in-law.

SUE: You certainly feathered his nest.

FAIRCHILD: That's a lie. It was only five million dollars! One of the pigeons flew home with the rest of the money. (HATTIE *returns. She fluffs her hair.*)

HATTIE: There! My hair is a little better. Oh, I'm so anxious to meet your friend, Dr. Clatter.

FAIRCHILD (*Smugly*): He'll take care of your head, all right. I suppose you have the deed for the western territory?

HATTIE: Well, of course. Oh, I realize it's an important document, and I chose a particularly safe hiding place. (*She waves finger at* FAIRCHILD *admonishingly.*) Turn your head.

FAIRCHILD: I demand to see the deed.

HATTIE: No peeking! (*He covers his eyes with his hands.* HAT-TIE *half turns, unpins deed from hem of dress, and hands deed to* TOM.) You may read it, young man. You have an honest face. (FAIRCHILD *uncovers his eyes and stamps angrily.*)

TOM (*Reading*): "And let it be known to all men that I grant and bequeath to my son, Running Wild and his bride, Amelia Bates, all land bounded by the natural borders and inhabited solely by the Wapanacki Tribe, from the great Rocky Mountains to the shores of the Pacific Ocean. Duly sworn and notarized before me on this last day of February, 1872." (TOM *looks up.*) It's signed William Travers, notary. Sounds like the real McCoy to me. (FAIRCHILD *grabs deed from* TOM, *scans it quickly.*)

FAIRCHILD: This is preposterous! How could Sitting Bull give the entire West to anyone?

TOM: Sitting Bull owned the West at that time.

FRANK: Sure, that was before we decided to protect the American Indians and push them onto some obscure reservation.

FAIRCHILD: I — I never did that to the Indians. Why, I love Indians. I'm sure this document is a forgery!

FRANK: It sounds authentic to me.

TOM (*Nodding*): The paper looks at least one hundred years

old. You'll have to do a lot of fast talking this time, Senator Fairchild. (*He takes deed from* FAIRCHILD, *hands it to* HATTIE.) I'd say that Miss Hattie Bates really does own the West!

FRANK (*Excitedly*): I have to make the final edition.

SUE: Out of my way! (*She nudges past him, rushes for door, right.*) If you break this story first, I'll break your head! (*They exit.*)

MALONE: I'd better get the TV crew. I'll have them here — pronto! (*He exits.*)

FAIRCHILD: The Attorney General will take care of you, Miss Bates. Owning the West, indeed! They won't be easy on you. (TOM *takes* FAIRCHILD, *leads him to door.*)

TOM: I'd like to speak to Miss Bates privately.

FAIRCHILD: Young man, I'll have your hide!

TOM: Remember the homeless homing pigeons, Senator. (*He slams door in* FAIRCHILD's *face, dusts off his hands, returns to* HATTIE *and* BETTY.)

BETTY (*Bewildered*): Now you sound like a lawyer. A window washer — a doctor — a reporter? You've had quite a career in one morning.

TOM: I am a reporter — and I just graduated from law school.

BETTY: You've been very nice. I — we don't know what we would have done without you. (HATTIE *pins deed inside hem of dress again.*)

HATTIE: He is a kind young man. And I have the perfect gift for him, too.

TOM (*Defensively*): I don't want Old Faithful or Sequoia National Park!

HATTIE: Oh, nothing like that. But I'm sure you'll like my strawberry jam. (*She exits left.*)

BETTY: What about the psychiatrist? Do you think he'll make trouble for Aunt Hattie?

Tom: I don't know. Senator Fairchild is a pretty important figure in Washington. He'll stop at nothing to discredit Aunt Hattie.

Betty: I tried to convince her to forget the whole thing. Oh, I should never have let her leave Buffalo Hollow.

Tom: Why didn't she present the deed a long time ago?

Betty: She didn't know anything about it. She found the deed in an old trunk during last year's spring cleaning. One of the local papers got hold of the story from the cleaning lady, the deed was authenticated by the county courthouse, and — here we are!

Tom: If the claim holds, it will change the entire social and economic structure of the United States.

Betty: I know it's important — but I'm more concerned about hurting Aunt Hattie.

Tom: I'm willing to help if you'll let me — so why don't we discuss this over a cup of coffee downstairs?

Betty: Do you think I should leave Aunt Hattie alone?

Tom (*Smiling*): Hattie Bates is a very capable woman! (*They exit right. In a moment, DR. CLATTER enters right. He has horn-rimmed glasses and black beard, which he tugs at throughout scene. He carries black bag. He walks around room, nods several times, places bag on table by sofa. HATTIE enters left. She carries jar of strawberry jam which she places on table near sofa.*)

Hattie (*Surprised*): Oh, where did he go?

Clatter (*Suspiciously*): Where did *who* go?

Hattie (*Turning and noticing CLATTER*): That nice young man. I believe his name is Tom Haines. He's a reporter (*Dryly*), also a window washer and a lawyer. Confidentially, he's a horse doctor, too. My name is Hattie Bates, by the way.

Clatter (*Tugging on beard*): Madam, you seem confused.

Hattie (*Sighing*): Mercy, yes. Who isn't confused these days?

Rising prices, shortages, power crises — it's not easy to keep a level head.

CLATTER: Ah, then you admit you suffer from depression?

HATTIE: We had a depression once, and I hope those days will never return. There's no reason to want for anything in a land of plenty — if you're willing to work.

CLATTER (*Musing*): Very interesting.

HATTIE: I don't believe I know your name.

CLATTER: I am Dr. Alexander Clatter.

HATTIE: Oh — the head doctor. We were expecting you. (*She touches hair.*) I don't think you'll be able to do a thing with my hair today. Frizzy, you know. Tell me, do you like strawberry jam?

CLATTER (*Perplexed*): I don't understand.

HATTIE: It's very good, really. And I find it so relaxing.

CLATTER (*Frowning*): Strawberry jam — relaxing?

HATTIE (*Nodding*): Whenever I have a serious problem, I drop everything and make a batch of strawberry jam. I forget about my problems — and they manage to work themselves out.

CLATTER: Very, very interesting. (*Abruptly*) But I mustn't forget my purpose for coming here.

HATTIE: I suppose you'll suggest one of those severe hairdos for me.

CLATTER: Hairdo? Madam, I'm confused — er — you're confused — well, I guess we're both confused. (*Tugs at beard*)

HATTIE (*Clucking disapproval*): You're very nervous, pulling at your beard like that. (*He drops his hand quickly.*) Young man, you must learn to relax. (*She leads him to sofa. They sit.*) There! Now, inhale deeply. (*He inhales.*) Now, exhale slowly. (*He exhales.*) Don't you feel better already?

CLATTER: Yes, but — (HATTIE *rises and pulls* CLATTER *up.*)

HATTIE: Now, here's a little game that always settles me down.

An old Indian tribeswoman taught it to me when I was a little girl. It's called Wapanacki Hopscotch. (*She places her left hand on her head and hops on her right leg five times. Then she places her right hand on her head and hops on her left leg five times.*) See how easy? Five times right leg — five times left leg.

CLATTER: Wapanacki Hopscotch? (HATTIE *continues hopping.*)

HATTIE: Why don't you try it? (*He begins to hop. They hop around sofa several times.*) Isn't it fun? And don't you feel more relaxed?

CLATTER (*As he hops*): I like it! I like it! (*Game continues. FAIRCHILD enters right, followed by PORTER. They pause and watch HATTIE and CLATTER in bewilderment.*)

PORTER (*Angrily*): Fairchild, did you call me from the Attorney General's office to play games?

FAIRCHILD: I — I don't understand, Mr. Porter. (*Pointing*) That's Dr. Clatter, one of Washington's greatest minds. (FAIRCHILD *tugs at* CLATTER'*s arm.* HATTIE *and* CLATTER *stop hopping.*)

CLATTER: Now, why did you do that? I was just getting the hang of Wapanacki Hopscotch!

FAIRCHILD: Dr. Clatter, what has this woman done to you?

CLATTER: She has given me one of the most pleasant visits I've ever had!

HATTIE: Senator Fairchild, would you like to play Wapanacki Hopscotch, too?

FAIRCHILD: Enough of this nonsense, Miss Bates. (*Gesturing*) This is Mr. Porter, the Assistant Attorney General of the United States.

PORTER: If I may examine the deed, Miss Bates —

HATTIE: Yes, of course — you sound formal! Everyone in Washington is so fussy. I'm surprised you make so many mistakes.

PORTER: We do not make mistakes in the Attorney General's office! (*Pauses*) Not too many, anyway.

HATTIE: Nonsense, young man. To err is human.

FAIRCHILD: Don't let her double-talk you, Porter. She's a clever one, all right.

HATTIE (*Proudly*): Oh, thank you, Senator Fairchild.

FAIRCHILD (*Turning*): Dr. Clatter, what is your professional opinion of this woman?

CLATTER: I think she is probably the finest — and certainly the sanest — person I've met in the Washington rat race!

FAIRCHILD: What? Impossible! (CLATTER *picks up his black bag.*) What do you intend to do?

CLATTER: I intend to go home and make a batch of strawberry jam! (*He exits right.* FAIRCHILD *slaps his forehead, turns to* PORTER.)

FAIRCHILD: Porter, do something about this woman!

PORTER: We must find the facts first, Senator. (*To* HATTIE) Miss Bates, if I may examine the deed . . . .

HATTIE: Yes, Mr. Porter. (*She touches hem of her dress.*) I'll step inside and get it for you. (*Quickly*) Of course, I trust you — but Senator Fairchild peeks! (*She exits left.*)

FAIRCHILD (*Huffily*): That woman acts as though I were dishonest.

PORTER: Maybe she remembers the homeless homing pigeons.

FAIRCHILD (*Angrily*): Porter, I'll cite you for contempt!

PORTER: Oh, come off it, Fairchild. I'll examine the deed — but I almost hope Miss Bates is right! (FAIRCHILD *gestures helplessly, as* TOM *and* BETTY *enter right.*)

BETTY (*To* FAIRCHILD): What have you done to Aunt Hattie?

TOM: We just met Dr. Clatter outside. He had no right to examine Miss Bates without the presence of her attorney!

BETTY: He kept muttering something about Wapanacki Hopscotch — and strawberry jam. I know he's done something terrible to — (*Stops as* HATTIE *re-enters with deed and hands it to* PORTER.) Aunt Hattie! Are you all right?

HATTIE: Why, of course. Please handle the deed carefully, Mr. Porter. (PORTER *nods, crosses to table up right, where he examines deed during following dialogue. There is knock at door.* TOM *goes to door, opens it.* FRANK, SUE, MALONE, MRS. DONALDSON, *and* MRS. WILLIAMS *enter.*)

FRANK: My editor is holding the front page of the final edition for an exclusive interview.

SUE: My editor is devoting the entire Sunday supplement to Miss Bates.

MALONE: Move aside, kids. The TV studio is canceling *The Merv Griffin Show* and *The Waltons* for Miss Bates's exclusive appearance.

HATTIE: Oh, that's a shame. I love those programs.

FAIRCHILD: That's unfair! I can't get fifteen minutes of prime time.

MALONE (*To* FAIRCHILD): We'll be glad to give you prime time — when you produce a deed for the Western United States! (HATTIE *crosses to* MRS. DONALDSON *and* MRS. WILLIAMS.)

HATTIE: We're forgetting our manners. I don't believe I've met these nice people. (*Beaming*) I always enjoy visitors.

MRS. DONALDSON: Miss Bates, we've heard so much about you.

HATTIE: Some good things, I hope.

MRS. DONALDSON: Very good things — and I need your help. My name is Irene Donaldson and I represent a home for the elderly in Rippling Falls, Nevada.

HATTIE: That's lovely, my dear. It's so nice to know that some people have time to devote to the elderly.

MRS. DONALDSON: I'm afraid there is no time for the elderly any longer. Our home is being threatened.

TOM: Threatened?

MRS. DONALDSON (*Nodding*): The City Planning Commission wants to put up a new federal office building. There's no place for these sick and elderly people to live.

BETTY: How terrible!

HATTIE: Isn't there any other place to put a new office building?

FAIRCHILD: I'm fully acquainted with the case, Miss Bates. It is imperative that we secure this site for our new facilities.

HATTIE: But all those poor people without a place to live! What kind of building do you need?

FAIRCHILD (*Nervously*): We — er — it's a new administrative building to secure housing facilities for the elderly.

HATTIE: Isn't that foolish? These elderly people already have a home, and yet you want to tear it down. Senator Fairchild, I'm surprised!

FAIRCHILD: We mustn't stand in the way of progress!

HATTIE: We mustn't prevent Mrs. Donaldson and her friends from having a place to live. (*To* MRS. DONALDSON) I'll do everything I can to see that you keep your home. Let them build their offices somewhere else. (*She shakes her head at* FAIRCHILD.) The very idea!

FAIRCHILD (*Sputtering*): But the new administrative building — the elderly — Miss Bates, you make it sound so simple! Things aren't done that way in Washington!

HATTIE: I'm sure I don't know why not.

MRS. DONALDSON: Oh, thank you, Miss Bates. I knew you'd help us! The people in Rippling Falls will be so happy.

HATTIE: Tell them I'll send over some strawberry jam. We'll have tea together the next time I'm in Nevada. (*She turns to* MRS. WILLIAMS.) I don't believe I know your name.

MRS. WILLIAMS: I am Emily Williams, and I'm looking for a favor, too.

HATTIE: That's what people are for — to help each other.

MRS. WILLIAMS: I represent the Committee for American Summer Camps. Camps for needy children. We have a fine place in Utah for the youngsters — a great lake, cabins, fields for sports and recreation. The kids love it.

HATTIE: How nice! Utah is such a lovely place. (*Proudly*) I own it, you know! But how can I help you? If you need money, I'm afraid there's not much I can do. I only own the West — and money is scarce today. Of course, if it's a small contribution, there's always my pension.

MRS. WILLIAMS: No, it's more than money. Our summer camp is being taken away. We won't have the facility this year.

FAIRCHILD: Summer camp, indeed! As chairman for Improved Highways in America I say that the camp site must go. One of my major projects is the highway through Utah.

HATTIE: That's a shame. (*To* MRS. WILLIAMS) After all, highway improvements are necessary. (*To* FAIRCHILD) Where will this new highway lead?

FAIRCHILD: Well — er — the destination is uncertain at this time. (*He gestures.*) We need a new highway, that's all!

HATTIE: Fiddle! What's the use of a new highway, if we don't know where we're going? (*To* MRS. WILLIAMS) I'll see that your summer camp will remain at its present site. Senator Fairchild can look for another unknown destination for his highway.

FRANK: What a human-interest story! Woman who owns the West saves children's summer camp!

SUE: Hattie Bates is a philanthropist!

HATTIE: Religion has nothing to do with it, young woman. So many problems in America could be settled with a little application of common sense. (Ms. TWIDDLE, Ms. THOMPSON *and* Ms. LONGFELLOW *enter right, carrying signs that read:* LIBERATED WOMEN OF AMERICA; RIGHT ON, HATTIE BATES!; *and* HATTIE BATES FOR PRESIDENT. LONGFELLOW *also carries drum.*)

Ms. TWIDDLE: We are looking for Hattie Bates.

BETTY (*Indicating* HATTIE): This is Miss Bates.

Ms. THOMPSON: Hattie Bates, the Liberated Women of America salute you!

Ms. TWIDDLE: We will help you free the government from male domination.

Ms. LONGFELLOW: You and your ancestor Amelia Bates have

added another chapter to the glorious history of American women.

HATTIE: Why, thank you!

FAIRCHILD (*Impatiently*): Enough of this nonsense. I demand that this room be cleared immediately.

TOM: You're overstepping your bounds, Senator. The hotel suite belongs to Miss Bates and you have no right to order her guests away.

MS. TWIDDLE (*Looking closely at* FAIRCHILD): Hah! I know you. Old Frog-Face Fairchild!

MS. THOMPSON: You voted against our bill to liberate the women of America!

MS. LONGFELLOW: Let me at him! (*She picks up jar of strawberry jam from table, waves it threateningly.* FAIRCHILD *backs away.*)

HATTIE: Please, ladies! I appreciate your interest, but Senator Fairchild is only doing his job. After all, it isn't every day that someone claims to own the West. (*She sits on sofa.*) This is all too much for me. All I ever wanted was to pay off the mortgage on my house in Buffalo Hollow and do a little side business selling strawberry jam. But owning the West! (*She shakes her head in bewilderment, stands up.*) No one person can possibly own a whole territory of the United States.

BETTY: Aunt Hattie, you don't know what you're saying.

HATTIE: No, dear, it's very clear for the first time. America belongs to all the people.

MS. TWIDDLE: Hattie Bates for President! (LONGFELLOW *beats drum. Everyone but* FAIRCHILD *cheers. He kicks at floor, sheepishly, and thrusts hands into pockets.*)

HATTIE: You're very kind, but I'm sure you can find a more capable leader. (*Turning to* BETTY) Let's pack our things, Betty. I want to go home.

MALONE (*Dismayed*): But the TV show —

FRANK: The interview on the front page —

SUE: And the Sunday supplement —

HATTIE (*Nodding*): You'll find more important things to write about. People are always doing great things in America and that's the truth. (PORTER *stands suddenly, overturning chair. He rushes forward, waving deed excitedly.*)

PORTER (*Loudly*): Listen to this! (*Reads from deed*) "Duly sworn and notarized before me on this last day of February, 1872. Signed, William Travers, Notary."

TOM: Let me see that. (*Snatches deed from* PORTER *and scans it; reading*) "Before me on this last day of February, 1872." (*Slowly*) "My commission expires on February 28, 1872." (TOM *shrugs.*) The notary's commission expired on the last day of February, and the deed was signed that last day. What's the problem, Porter?

PORTER: 1872 was a Leap Year.

SUE: I don't see what difference that makes.

PORTER (*Excitedly*): It makes *all* the difference! 1872 was a Leap Year, so the last day of February was February 29 . . . .

TOM: And since the deed was notarized the last day of February 1872, it was on the 29th. . . .

SUE (*Nodding*): And that was the day *after* the notary's commission expired.

MALONE: The deed is worthless! (*Slaps forehead*)

BETTY: And — and Aunt Hattie has no right to the West at all.

FRANK (*Shrugging*): There goes the story of the year.

SUE: Wait until my editor gets his hands on me.

MALONE: Now we'll have to re-run "King Kong" on prime time tonight!

PORTER (*Kindly*): Wait a minute, everyone. Miss Bates's deed may be invalid, but she taught us a very important lesson about common sense. The Attorney General's office is going to see that her wishes are carried out. (*To* MRS. DONALDSON) We'll fight to keep the present site of the home for the elderly people. (*To* Mrs. Williams) And there'll be no highway running through the summer camp.

Hattie: Will you really do that for us, Mr. Porter?

Porter: Of course!

Hattie: And you won't forget the women and equal rights?

Porter (*Smiling*): Equal rights for everyone.

Hattie: That's a relief! (Ms. Longfellow *examines jar of strawberry jam. She dips her finger into jam, tastes it, registers delight. During following dialogue, she offers jam to* Ms. Twiddle *and* Ms. Thompson, *who sample it. They talk in pantomime. Meanwhile,* Hattie *extends her hand to* Fairchild.) Senator Fairchild, I know you're a busy man. I've caused so much trouble — I must have wasted your time.

Fairchild (*Slowly*): Wasted my time? (*He drops his head.*) Miss Bates, there's one thing I'll never forget. You relinquished your claim to the West, even before you knew the deed was invalid. You're a fine person, Miss Bates. A very fine person.

Hattie: Why — thank you.

Fairchild: And I'll try to use more of that common sense you spoke about.

Ms. Twiddle (*Suddenly*): This jam is delicious!

Ms. Thompson: Absolutely yummy!

Ms. Longfellow: Miss Bates, did you make this jam?

Hattie: Oh, yes. The recipe has been in the family for years.

Ms. Twiddle: The Liberated Women of American have a splendid idea.

Ms. Thompson (*Nodding*): We want to sell this jam commercially. We'll be able to use it to raise funds.

Ms. Longfellow (*Enthusiastically*): Like Girl Scout Cookies.

Hattie: Mercy, that's a big order! I suppose it's possible, but I'd need a large kitchen.

Ms. Twiddle: The Liberated Women of America will attend to all those details.

Ms. THOMPSON: You'll be able to pay off that mortgage in Buffalo Hollow!

Ms. TWIDDLE (*To* THOMPSON *and* LONGFELLOW): Forward for women's liberation!

Ms. THOMPSON: And Aunt Hattie's strawberry jam! (Ms. LONGFELLOW, Ms. TWIDDLE *and* Ms. THOMPSON *shoulder signs and lead way out right.* FRANK, SUE, MALONE, MRS. DONALDSON, MRS. WILLIAMS *and* PORTER *follow. They all exit right.*)

TOM (*Smiling at* BETTY): I'd like to visit you in Buffalo Hollow, someday soon — if you could stand to have a male chauvinist around. You know, I'm looking for a place to practice law when I pass the bar, and suddenly the West seems very inviting to me, pardner! (*He walks around, thumbs hitched into belt, in bow-legged cowboy fashion.*)

BETTY: It would be a pleasure!

FAIRCHILD: It's been quite a day. Guess I'll be getting back —

HATTIE (*Interrupting*): Why, Senator Fairchild, not until you join me in a game of Wapanacki Hopscotch! (*She begins the hopping game.* FAIRCHILD *looks around uneasily.* BETTY *and* TOM *smile and gesture to him to join* HATTIE. *He begins to hop, awkwardly at first, then with enthusiasm.* BETTY *and* TOM *laugh and join in as curtains close.*)

THE END

Production Notes

THE WOMAN WHO OWNED THE WEST

Characters: 6 male; 9 female.

Playing Time: 35 minutes.

Costumes: Modern, everyday dress. Clatter has black beard, horn-rimmed glasses. Fairchild may wear Stetson when he enters. Tom is wearing work clothes.

Properties: Jars of strawberry jam, television light, dust cloth, pail of water, squeegee, walkie-talkie, paper, pencil, deed, signs as indicated in text, drum.

Setting: Before Rise, Senator Fairchild's office. Desk, chair are onstage. There are a telephone, jar of jam, vase containing goldenrod, papers, pencils, etc., on desk. Main set, living room of hotel suite. A sofa with tables at either end is down center. There are a desk, telephone and chair up right. Large window up center overlooks Capitol. Other chairs, tables, lamps, paintings, etc., complete the furnishings. Right exit leads to corridor; left exit leads to bedroom.

Lighting: No special effects.

The Big Top Murders

The mysterious death of an aerial artist creates a crisis under the Big Top . . . .

Characters

TOM KELLY, *a young man, ringmaster and owner of Imperial Circus*
BOB KELLY, *his brother*
DONNA, *business manager*
SNAVELY, *barker*
BELLINI, *knife thrower*
ARMAND, *strong man*
LOLA, *snake charmer*
ASTRID, *aerialist*
DOC BARNES, *circus physician*
BUBBLES MASON
DENNY, *clown*
MISS HERMIONE FINCH, *middle-aged schoolteacher*

SCENE 1

BEFORE RISE: *Traditional circus music is heard from offstage. TOM KELLY, in ringmaster's costume, enters right with flourish. Spotlight follows his entrance. He waves riding crop, gestures to audience.*

TOM: Ladies and gentlemen — and children of all ages. Imperial Circus, the greatest show in the universe, invites you to focus your attention on the center ring. (*He gestures off-*

stage right.) You will be astounded, amazed, as Miss Genevieve, the world's greatest high wire performer, attempts her
death-defying walk across the arena, fifty feet above ground
— without the benefit of a net! That's right, ladies and gentlemen, Miss Genevieve laughs at death as she ascends to the
roof of the big top! (*Drum roll is heard from offstage.*)
I give you Miss Genevieve, Queen of the High Wire! (*Offstage applause and circus music are heard.* DONNA *enters
left. Spotlight leaves* TOM, *moves into right wings, as if following Genevieve's ascent.* DONNA *quickly crosses to* TOM,
grabs his arm.)

DONNA (*Breathlessly*): Tom! Tom! I must talk to you.

TOM: Donna, what are you doing out here? Genevieve's act
has just begun.

DONNA: It's about Lola. Something terrible happened.

TOM: Not now. (*He gestures right, addresses audience.*) Miss
Genevieve has reached the high wire platform. She will now
begin her death-defying walk. (DONNA *tugs at his arm.*)

DONNA: Tom, this is important! (*Suddenly she stares upward
into right wings. She points.*) Something's wrong with Genevieve!

TOM: She's slipping — she's going to fall! (*Sound of screams is
heard from offstage.* DONNA *turns away, covers eyes.* TOM
addresses audience.) Ladies and gentlemen, please keep your
seats. Everything is under control. (*Calls off right*) Bring up
the music! Clear the arena! Start the next act! (*Offstage
music rises to crescendo. Blackout.*)

* * *

TIME: *Evening, the present.*

SETTING: *Dressing room in tent on Imperial Circus lot. Entrance through canvas is at right. Posters and colorful costumes hang on walls. There are a dressing table and bench*

down left. Up right is a large clothes cabinet, door facing audience, with LOLA *concealed inside it. There is another entrance up center. Next to opening is wooden board mounted with knives of various sizes. Large sign reading* THE GREAT BELLINI *is at top of board. There are several straight chairs down center.*

AT RISE: BOB KELLY *sits down center, head in hands.* TOM *and* DONNA *enter right and join him.*

TOM (*In comforting tone*): Bob, what can I say? (BOB *raises head slowly.*)

BOB: Have they taken her away? (TOM *nods.*)

TOM: She died instantly. (TOM *punches left hand with right fist.*) Why did this have to happen to Genevieve?

BOB (*Bitterly*): If only we had closed the show after the first couple of accidents — if we had sold Imperial to the Ames Brothers — it wouldn't have happened. I'm the co-owner of the show. I'm to blame for Genevieve's death.

DONNA: Don't say that, Bob. You and Tom have a wonderful show. You're the best troupers in the business. Your dad wouldn't want you to sell the show.

BOB: But all those warnings. (*Stands*) The fire in St. Louis, the lion that escaped in Houston, the elephant stampede in Miami. Accidents! (*He turns to* TOM, *snaps bitterly.*) Genevieve is dead. We were going to get married in two weeks — and now she's dead. I don't suppose that means anything to you!

DONNA: Please, Bob, you're upset. Gen was a great trouper. She wouldn't want you to say such things. (SNAVELY *enters right.*)

SNAVELY (*To* TOM): We've cleared everyone out of the Big Top, Mr. Kelly.

TOM: Thanks, Snavely. The police and Doc Barnes will be here soon. (*To* DONNA) We've got to keep the publicity down.

SNAVELY: The roustabouts are searching the grounds now.

TOM: Searching?

SNAVELY (*To* DONNA): Didn't you tell him?

DONNA: Snavely, I tried, but there wasn't time. (*To* TOM) That's what I was trying to tell you before Genevieve's act. It was about Lola.

BOB: Lola, the snake charmer? What's she got to do with this?

SNAVELY: One of her snakes is missing. The fer-de-lance.

TOM (*Excited*): The fer-de-lance? That's the most dangerous snake in the exhibit.

BOB: I warned you, Tom. I told you that snake was too risky.

TOM: The snake never left its glass case. It was used for exhibition purposes only.

BOB: Yes, but the fer-de-lance is one of the world's deadliest snakes. One bite can cause death — instantly!

TOM: When did the snake escape?

SNAVELY: Just before the show started. I was going into my barker act outside the Big Top when Lola ran out of her tent and told me the snake was missing.

DONNA: That's impossible. Lola had the only key for the snake case in the menagerie.

SNAVELY: She said the key was missing. She couldn't explain how she lost it.

TOM: Unless it was taken deliberately.

SNAVELY: Doc Barnes has alerted the local hospital. They're trying to come up with some special serum, just in case anyone's bitten. (*He glances around warily.*) Who knows? That snake might be in this dressing room now.

DONNA: I hope it's not in the Big Top. If anyone gets hurt, the show will be ruined.

BOB: That's all you ever worry about — this precious show!

DONNA: Why not? I'm the business manager. The interests of the Imperial Circus are my job.

BOB (*Bitterly*): Does that include my brother's interests, too?

SNAVELY (*Uneasily*): I'm going outside. Maybe I can help the roustabouts. (*He exits quickly.*)

TOM: That wasn't necessary, Bob. Donna and I feel bad about

Gen, too, but it was an accident. (DOC BARNES *enters, unobserved. He carries a circus performer's costume and a pair of acrobat's slippers which he places on chair near entrance.*)

BOB: For some reason, I felt something was going to happen. I asked Genevieve to meet me after her act. I wanted to see her. (*Brokenly*) We were going away together.

DONNA: Bob, I think Tom is right. It must have been an accident.

BARNES (*Interrupting*): No, Donna, it was more than that. I've just returned from the coroner's office. (*He points to chair.*) I brought back Genevieve's costume.

TOM (*Slowly*): Not an accident, Dr. Barnes? What happened to Genevieve?

BARNES: She suffered only a broken arm and minor contusions in the fall.

BOB: But that wouldn't be enough to kill her.

BARNES: I'm afraid you're right, Bob. Genevieve died because she was bitten by a poisonous snake. The venom acted on her blood stream and muscles — it caused almost instantaneous death.

TOM: The fer-de-lance!

BARNES (*Nodding*): Yes, I've heard about the missing snake. It must have bitten her when she climbed to the high wire platform.

DONNA: It couldn't have happened that way. Gen couldn't have been bitten by a snake and then calmly started to perform her wire walk.

TOM: That's right. Someone would have seen the snake if it had entered the arena.

DONNA: And the snake couldn't have climbed the slippery pole support to the platform.

TOM (*Recollecting*): Gen took a step onto the wire, faltered for a moment, then screamed, and fell. (*He shakes his head.*)

There was so much confusion — so many people running around.

DONNA: We all rushed to her aid.

TOM: We were on the far side of the arena. There were other people with Gen when we reached her.

DONNA (*Nodding*): One of the performers — a clown, I think.

BARNES: I was there, too. I was standing in the wings, and it took me only a minute or two to reach her.

TOM (*Slowly*): There was someone else. One of the spectators left the box seats. I think it was a woman.

BARNES: A mature-looking woman with a ridiculous hat.

BOB: Where is that woman now? Maybe she can tell us something.

BARNES: I don't know. I left with the coroner as soon as he arrived.

DONNA: We must find that woman. She might have seen something important to us. (*Confusion is heard from offstage. BELLINI and ARMAND enter. They hold MISS HERMIONE FINCH by either arm and escort her to center, roughly. MISS FINCH carries large, old-fashioned purse. Her only mark of frivolity is a large flowered hat, perched precariously over one eye.*)

MISS FINCH (*Struggling; indignant*): Unhand me, you ruffians! (*She shakes loose, adjusts her hat.*)

BELLINI: We found this woman snooping around outside your tent, Tom.

ARMAND: Then she tried to run to another tent, probably to steal something.

MISS FINCH: I've never stolen anything in my life. (*She glances around.*) Who's in charge here?

TOM: I'm Tom Kelly, co-owner of Imperial. (*Gestures toward BOB*) This is my brother, Bob. We're partners. (*BOB snaps to attention.*)

BOB (*Pointing to* MISS FINCH): That's the one! That's the woman who came into the ring after Gen fell!

MISS FINCH: Of course I went to the unfortunate woman. Do you think I would have stayed in my seat when I might have helped her?

DONNA: What are you doing here?

MISS FINCH: I am the guest of Miss Marigold Mason. I believe she goes by the name of Bubbles Mason now.

TOM: Bubbles? She has our trained seal act.

MISS FINCH: Precisely! I was head-mistress at the Hartridge Finishing School for many years and Marigold — er — Bubbles was my favorite pupil. Of course, I never taught her anything about handling seals. (*Distastefully*) Always eating fish — and things. The seals, I mean. I was trying to locate her tent when these two nincompoops jumped on me.

TOM (*Indicating* BELLINI): This is Bellini. He does a knife-throwing act.

MISS FINCH: Definitely the criminal type!

TOM (*Introducing* ARMAND): And this is Armand, our strong man.

MISS FINCH: I'll bend a bar over his head, if he puts another finger on me. (ARMAND *retreats defensively.*)

BARNES: I don't believe we know your name.

MISS FINCH: The name is Finch. Miss Hermione Finch. (*Staring at* BARNES) You look fairly intelligent. Who are you?

BARNES: I am Dr. Barnes, the circus physician.

MISS FINCH: An animal doctor, eh?

BARNES (*Smiling*): I treat other patients, too.

DONNA: Miss Finch, all the spectators have gone home. You must leave now.

MISS FINCH: Nonsense, young lady. I'm determined to see that justice is done. Especially when there's been a murder!

TOM: Murder?

MISS FINCH: It must have been. There are police milling all

over the place. (*Points at* BARNES) He has been in consultation with the police and the coroner. And what about those trumped-up accidents that have been plaguing your show? Of course it's murder. (*Slyly*) And I know about the missing snake, too.

TOM (*Suspiciously*): How could you know that?

MISS FINCH: I overheard your conversation while I was outside this tent. (*Proudly*) I never miss a detail. Now, there's one thing more I must know. (*She looks closely at everyone's face.*) Does "clover" mean anything to you?

TOM (*Puzzled*): Clover?

DONNA: There's no one in the show named Clover.

MISS FINCH: I'm sure it was clover. (*Thoughtfully*) And yet —

BARNES: What are you talking about, madam?

MISS FINCH (*Indignantly*): Miss Finch, if you please — and don't disturb my train of thought. (*She closes her eyes.*) The young lady fell. Then Dr. Barnes — no, it was someone else — rushed to help her. I think a clown reached her first. I was the second person.

BARNES: I reached her immediately after she fell. I tried to administer first aid, but it was useless.

MISS FINCH: She had enough mental faculty to whisper the word "clover" to me before she lost consciousness. (*She muses.*) "Clover" — "clover" — no, that doesn't seem quite right. (*Quickly*) Where are the clowns now?

TOM: We have two clowns with the show. Denny and David. They're probably in their dressing room. (MISS FINCH *suddenly snaps her fingers.*)

MISS FINCH: Of course! I understand now. When I was a little girl my grandmother taught me to remember events by word association. In this instance, "clover" was the first thing to come to my mind. But it wasn't "clover" at all. The young woman whispered "shamrock" before she died! (*Brightly*) Yes, she said "shamrock."

DONNA: That doesn't make any sense either.

MISS FINCH (*Impatiently*): That young woman wouldn't have said a senseless thing with her dying breath. She identified her murderer. She called him "shamrock."

BOB: I won't listen to such nonsense. A missing snake — murder — a garrulous old woman. It's too much for me. (MISS FINCH *opens her purse, takes out a handkerchief.*)

MISS FINCH: If you must be arrogant, young man, at least do it with a clean face. (*She dabs his face with her handkerchief. He stands, surprised.*) There! You had something on your chin. It looks like powder — or flour. (*Sympathetically*) I understand that you were attached to the young woman who died, and I know you want to see justice done — but you're handling it the wrong way.

BOB: What do you propose?

MISS FINCH: Right now, I'd like to see the clowns.

BOB: The clowns?

ARMAND: I told you she was balmy.

MISS FINCH: Yes, clowns. Don't forget — a clown was the first person to reach Genevieve.

TOM (*Gesturing*): Armand, get the clowns in here.

ARMAND: But, boss!

TOM (*Smiling*): Just do as I say. Miss Finch, I think you're a very sensible woman.

MISS FINCH (*Flustered*): Why, thank you, young man. (AR-MAND *and* BELLINI *exit, muttering to themselves.*) Now, I have a few questions. How long has Miss Genevieve been with Imperial Circus?

TOM: About six months. She joined our troupe in Houston.

MISS FINCH: I remember when the circus was quartered there. Isn't that the place where the lion escaped?

DONNA: That's right. Gen's act was an instant success. In a few weeks we gave her top billing and the prime spot.

MISS FINCH: The prime spot?

TOM: That's the main act in the center ring.

MISS FINCH: Very interesting. Who had this — er — prime spot before Genevieve's appearance?

TOM: Another aerialist. Her name is Astrid.

DONNA: She's still with the show. We moved her performance into another ring.

MISS FINCH: I remember that young lady. I saw her act. (*Points to costume*) Is that her costume?

BARNES: No, it belonged to Gen. It's just been released by the coroner. (*He points to chair. MISS FINCH walks to chair, examines costume, especially shoes.*) It's an old circus tradition. The costume of a deceased person is always retired with her other belongings.

MISS FINCH (*Nodding*): A circus hall of fame. (*She drops costume and shoes onto chair, returns to center.*)

BARNES: I must remind you, Miss Finch, that you have no authority to ask these questions.

MISS FINCH: Authority, my foot! I paid good money to see the circus, and I'm going to get my money's worth. Why are you afraid of my questions?

BARNES: Er — I — this is outrageous!

MISS FINCH: You were one of the first ones to reach Miss Genevieve.

BARNES: I'm a doctor. It was my professional duty to help.

MISS FINCH: To be sure. (*Slowly*) Doctor Barnes, would it be possible to inject snake venom into a victim with a hypodermic syringe?

BARNES: A hypodermic? Yes, it's possible.

MISS FINCH (*Nodding*): That's what came to my mind. You're a doctor, and you would have access to hypodermics.

BARNES: I won't tolerate these accusations!

MISS FINCH: Nobody accused you, but it's always a possibility. While there is a murderer loose, everyone is under suspicion — including myself. Anyone could operate a hypodermic syringe. (*Impatiently*) By the way, where are those clowns? (BUBBLES MASON *enters right. She wears costume with plumes, elaborate makeup. She throws her arms around* MISS FINCH *affectionately.*)

BUBBLES: Miss Finch! It's good to see you after all these years.

MISS FINCH: Marigold Mason. I'd hardly recognize you with all that paint — and fluff — and things.

BUBBLES: I'm Bubbles Mason now, and I'm a circus performer.

MISS FINCH (*Nodding*): Trained seals! Just think! Back at school you were voted the girl most likely to succeed.

BUBBLES (*Defensively*): There's nothing wrong with seals.

MISS FINCH: Now, now, Marigold. I'm just an envious old woman. (*Twinkling*) Why, I wanted to join the circus when I was a girl.

BARNES (*Angrily*): This is enough of Old-Home-Week business! We must remember there's a poisonous reptile loose!

MISS FINCH: Yes, and there's a murderer loose!

TOM: There's no need for an argument. Miss Finch, I'd like you to stay until this is settled. After all, you are a key witness.

BARNES (*Angrily*): She has no right to interfere.

TOM: I'm co-owner of the show, and I have every right to ask for her opinion. Until the official investigation begins, at least.

DONNA: That's right. Miss Finch told us about the "shamrock" business.

BOB (*Sarcastically*): That made a lot of sense! (BARNES *gestures helplessly.*)

BARNES: Let her stay! The police will put her in her place.

MISS FINCH: Police? I am not interested in police methods. The small, insignificant details — they will put me on the trail of our murderer. (ASTRID, *an aerialist in appropriate costume, enters.*)

ASTRID: Where's Bob? (*She looks around, sees Genevieve's costume on chair, stiffens.* MISS FINCH *watches her closely.*) It's terrible! (ASTRID *rushes to* BOB.) Bob, I'm so sorry.

BOB (*Comfortingly*): I know, Astrid.

ASTRID: When Genevieve took my spot in the show I was angry, but I knew that she was a better performer.

MISS FINCH: You must be Astrid. (ASTRID *nods.*) I caught your performance and I thought it was outstanding.

TOM: You can have the prime spot now, Astrid.

ASTRID: No, thank you, Tom. I'm leaving the show.

DONNA: But your contract!

ASTRID: I'll finish the season out. (*She looks at Genevieve's costume, shivers.*) Some day it might happen to me. Anything can happen on the high wire.

MISS FINCH: Miss Genevieve wasn't killed in the fall. She died from snake venom.

ASTRID: Snake venom? That's impossible! (*Dazed*) Then that means it wasn't the high wire. I didn't know.

MISS FINCH: You couldn't know. We just received the coroner's report. Genevieve's death was part of a well-calculated plan to ruin the Imperial Circus.

TOM: I don't follow you, Miss Finch.

MISS FINCH: It's rather obvious. The escaped lion — the elephant stampede — the mysterious fire. All those near casualties were perpetrated by someone who traveled with the circus throughout the country.

TOM (*Angrily*): If I get my hands on him, I'll —

MISS FINCH: What makes you so certain it's a "him"? A person trained in the handling of snakes — someone who knew how to extract venom from a deadly viper — could have administered the lethal dose. (*Thoughtfully*) Yes, a snake handler would fill the bill. (*Suddenly*) Where's Miss Lola? (*Others look at each other, shrug.*)

BUBBLES: I saw her when the show began. She told me that she was going to this tent.

BARNES: The police have searched the circus grounds. Evidently they didn't find her.

MISS FINCH (*Excited*): Then it might be too late!

TOM: What do you mean?

MISS FINCH: If Bubbles saw her come into this tent, and no one saw her on the grounds after that — well, she may still be in this tent. Tell me, does a performer have his own dressing room?

DONNA: There are lean-tos used as dressing rooms by the prime performers. (*Gestures*) Generally, makeup is applied and last-minute changes are made here, before the performers enter the Big Top.

MISS FINCH: Where are Lola's things?

DONNA: Her dressing room is in the menagerie tent. (*She points to large cabinet, right.*) She keeps some costumes and supplies in that cabinet. (MISS FINCH *steps cautiously to cabinet. She throws door open quickly.* LOLA, *in circus costume is inside, standing rigid.* BUBBLES *screams. As* TOM *and* BARNES *rush forward,* LOLA *falls. There is general confusion.* BARNES *kneels beside* LOLA.)

BARNES: It's Lola! She's dead! She's been strangled. (*He points to* LOLA's *throat.*)

ALL (*Ad lib*): Oh, no! I can't believe it! Who would do such a horrible thing? (*Etc.* MISS FINCH *looks into bottom of cabinet, motions everyone to silence. She picks up long pole next to cabinet, prods bottom of cabinet. She raises stick. On the end of stick is long "snake."* NOTE: *Snake is made of papier-mâché or cloth.*)

DONNA: The snake!

BUBBLES (*Hysterically*): It's the fer-de-lance! Miss Finch, be careful. (MISS FINCH *drops pole and snake on ground.*)

MISS FINCH (*Weakly*): It's all right. This snake won't hurt anyone again. It's quite dead, I assure you. (*She looks soberly at others.*) The fer-de-lance is another victim of our Big Top murderer! (*Quick curtain*)

* * * * *

SCENE 2

TIME: *Short time later.*

SETTING: *Same as Scene 1.* LOLA *and "snake" have been removed.*

AT RISE: MISS FINCH *sits down center, lost in thought.* DOC BARNES *paces.*

BARNES: I won't have it, do you hear? It's impossible.

MISS FINCH (*Casually*): I think my proposal is perfectly reasonable, under the circumstances.

BARNES (*Outraged*): Reasonable! You're asking me to sanction a performance of the circus now — tonight! Why, it's almost midnight!

MISS FINCH: I want everyone to be in the same places they were for this afternoon's performance when Miss Genevieve fell. I think a reenactment will tell us many things. (*She stands, walks to chair on which Genevieve's costume is placed. She picks up slippers.*) For one thing, it might tell us who put wax on the soles of Genevieve's slippers. (BARNES *quickly joins her, examines slippers, gives slow whistle.*)

BARNES: There *is* wax on the sole of the right slipper.

MISS FINCH: And a high-wire walker usually puts the right foot forward when first approaching the wire. Someone wanted Genevieve to slip after she took her first step from the platform.

BARNES: I'm an idiot for not noticing this slipper at the

coroner's office. (*Angrily*) And why didn't the police make the discovery?

MISS FINCH: We can't blame anyone. It must have been an oversight.

BARNES: How did you discover the wax?

MISS FINCH: Merely an observation. When I spoke to members of the troupe a short time ago, one in particular was actually terrified when she saw Genevieve's things in the chair. I wondered why the costume should cause such panic. Someone put the wax on the slipper — deliberately.

BARNES: Who?

MISS FINCH: In good time, Dr. Barnes. I think the person who put wax on the slipper wanted to frighten Genevieve and force her to leave the Big Top — but I don't think that person wanted to commit murder.

BARNES (*Bitterly*): A fifty-foot fall would kill anyone!

MISS FINCH: That is true, but the method leaves entirely too much to chance for murder to have been intended and, remember, Genevieve died from toxic venom. No, putting the wax on the slipper was a mean, impulsive — perhaps vengeful — act. The fer-de-lance was cold, deliberate, well-planned. Crimes with two different characteristics — two different motives.

BARNES (*Musing*): That's a possibility. (*Suddenly*) If your theory is correct, there are *two* murderers under the Big Top. (DENNY, *young man in clown's outfit and heavy makeup, enters.*)

DENNY: I understand we're having a midnight performance, Doc Barnes. (BARNES *nods.*) I'm all ready.

MISS FINCH (*Brightly*): Just the young man I wanted to meet.

BARNES: Miss Finch, this is Denny. He and David, his partner, are always favorites with our audience.

MISS FINCH (*To* DENNY): I believe you were the first person to reach Genevieve after her fall.

DENNY: No, I was in the wings. My performance was scheduled to start after Genevieve's act.

MISS FINCH: Then it must have been your partner, David. I saw a clown kneeling beside her when I left my seat. I joined him in the ring.

DENNY: David? Oh, no. That's impossible.

MISS FINCH (*Haughtily*): Young man, I know a clown when I see one.

DENNY: But you must be mistaken. David wasn't scheduled to appear tonight. He left town this morning.

BARNES: Has David left the show? I didn't know that.

DENNY: His sister is seriously ill. He got permission to be away for two days, starting tonight.

MISS FINCH (*Slowly*): Just a minute. If you were in the wings, and David wasn't scheduled to perform tonight, then someone else must have put on a clown costume and appeared in the ring.

BARNES: And that person was the first one to reach Genevieve after her fall.

MISS FINCH: The murderer! (*To* DENNY) How many people knew that David wouldn't perform tonight?

DENNY: It was common knowledge, I guess. David told Snavely and most of the performers. And Bob Kelly gave him permission to leave. I suppose it was discussed with Donna. (*He shrugs.*) Everyone knew about it.

MISS FINCH: One person took advantage of that knowledge. Someone who wanted to kill Miss Genevieve. The same person who carefully prepared the hypo after extracting the snake venom. Perhaps our murderer intended to kill Genevieve after her performance.

BARNES: It's a possibility.

MISS FINCH: When Genevieve fell, the murderer saw an unexpected opportunity. In the confusion, he ran forward in the pretense of helping her, but instead he injected her with the deadly venom. Yes, a clown's costume was a fine disguise for the murderer.

DENNY (*Quickly*): I was in my clown costume. But, if you think I killed Genevieve, you're crazy!

MISS FINCH: No one is accusing you. (*Slowly*) Not yet!

DENNY (*Nervously*): I'd better get ready for my performance. (*He exits quickly.*)

BARNES: Do you think he's telling us the truth?

MISS FINCH: Wait and see, Doctor. The reenactment of the murder will tell us many things. (BUBBLES *enters. She carries school yearbook.*)

BUBBLES: Oh, Miss Finch, you'll never guess what I found.

MISS FINCH: Marigold — er — Bubbles, you should get ready for your performance.

BUBBLES: My seals and I are always ready. (*She grins.*)

BARNES: I'd better get under the Big Top. The performance will start in ten minutes. (*Exits.*)

BUBBLES: Look at this! (BUBBLES *hands yearbook to* MISS FINCH. *She leafs through pages.*)

MISS FINCH: My word! It's our old yearbook. The class of '67. (BUBBLES *points to specific page.*) And here are the individual pictures of all my old students.

BUBBLES: Not that old, Miss Finch. Look! (*She points.*) There's my picture. (*Reads*) "Marigold Mason. Likes horseback riding, animals, volleyball, and Latin."

MISS FINCH: Latin? You were a terrible Latin student. You never got past Caesar's Gallic wars.

BUBBLES (*Nodding*): I only put it in to sound academic. (MISS FINCH *continues to examine page.*)

MISS FINCH (*Reading*): "Is popular with all the class. Answers to the nickname Bubbles." (MISS FINCH *closes book.*) So, that's where the nickname started.

BUBBLES: The girls knew I was interested in show business.

I got stuck with the nickname after my first month at school. (*Mechanically,* MISS FINCH *returns book to* BUBBLES. *She stares into space, bewildered.*) What's the matter, Miss Finch?

MISS FINCH: A nickname! "Shamrock"! But, of course. That's what Genevieve tried to tell me.

BUBBLES: I — I don't understand.

MISS FINCH: What are some of the first names of people associated with the circus?

BUBBLES (*Puzzled*): They have all kinds of names. There are Tom and Bob Kelly. Armand is just Armand. There's Robert Bellini, the knife thrower. And John Snavely, the barker, and Dr. Robert Barnes. (*She shakes her head.*) What a crazy question!

MISS FINCH: Please get ready for your performance. I must have time to think this thing out. (BUBBLES *shakes her head, exits.* MISS FINCH *muses.*) If I'm right — if I can believe my own senses — then there's only one solution. Shamrock . . . . (TOM *and* DONNA *enter.*)

TOM: I'm against this performance tonight, Miss Finch. The publicity is going to ruin the show.

MISS FINCH (*Quickly*): How long have you and your brother controlled Imperial?

TOM: Bob and I took over shortly after Dad's death. That was five years ago.

DONNA (*Nodding*): I've been the business manager for three years. Before that, I was a performer for several years. Not a very good one, I'm afraid.

MISS FINCH (*To* TOM): I suppose you and your brother always loved circus life.

TOM: We both did as kids. Bob's interests changed during college.

MISS FINCH: Did you both attend college at the same time?

TOM: That's right. I'm only two years older than Bob. I got a
B.S. in business administration, and Bob studied marine life
and herpetology.

MISS FINCH: Very interesting. How strongly did Bob feel about
his new pursuits?

TOM: He wanted to unload the circus, but I was determined to
keep it at any cost.

MISS FINCH: Sometimes we have to pay a high price for the
things we want. Sometimes even murder.

TOM: Look here, Miss Finch, if you think I had anything to do
with these murders, you're wrong.

DONNA: It's ridiculous! Tom loves Imperial. We lost money
for the first few years, and he worked hard to make it
profitable.

MISS FINCH: I made no accusation — merely an observation.

TOM (*Nervously*): I'd better get ready for my performance.
You'd better come along, Miss Finch. After all, we're doing
the show for your benefit! (*He clenches his fists, exits.*)

DONNA: You mustn't mind Tom. He's terribly upset.

MISS FINCH (*Warmly*): I know, my dear. And I know you're
very much in love with the young man.

DONNA (*Flustered*): In love with Blarney Stone? Yes, I'd do
anything for him.

MISS FINCH: Blarney Stone? How appropriate! An Irish nickname for a young, Irish circus manager.

DONNA: He's been called Blarney Stone for years. It started
back in school, I guess.

MISS FINCH (*Musing*): That fits in very neatly. (*Suddenly*)
Take your place in the wings, Donna. I'll join you shortly.
(*DONNA prepares to exit. MISS FINCH calls.*) And, Donna
(*DONNA turns.*) — Tom is very fortunate to have a young
lady who would do anything to insure his happiness. (*MISS
FINCH smiles. DONNA looks at her, puzzled, then exits. MISS
FINCH rushes quickly to LOLA's cabinet, picks up an object
from the floor. Object is not seen by audience. She drops it*

into purse, snaps purse closed, pats it reassuringly.) And now, to observe an old circus tradition, I'll have a bottle of soda pop! (*She cocks her head warily, as though listening to something offstage.*) Wait . . . . (*She picks up acrobat's slippers from chair, hides behind clothes cabinet.* ASTRID *enters cautiously. She glances around to make certain she is unobserved. She quickly searches Genevieve's costume in chair, drops it in disappointment. She bends, searches under chair, rises slowly.* MISS FINCH *emerges from hiding place. She dangles slippers before* ASTRID.) Are you looking for these slippers, Astrid?

ASTRID (*Flustered*): Why, I — er — no. I — I lost something, that's all. (*She turns to leave, but* MISS FINCH *grabs her arm.*)

MISS FINCH: Attempted murder is a serious charge, young lady.

ASTRID (*Nervously*): I don't know what you're talking about.

MISS FINCH: I think you do. You were enraged when Genevieve got the Big Top prime spot. You wanted revenge — you wanted to do something that would frighten her away. Isn't that true?

ASTRID: No!

MISS FINCH: You put wax on her slipper. Did you think that she'd discover it in time, before she mounted the high wire platform? She would be terrified. She would leave the show.

ASTRID (*Terrified*): Miss Finch, please!

MISS FINCH: But Genevieve didn't notice the wax. The floor of the Big Top is covered with sawdust. She didn't slip as she walked to the high wire ladder. She took that first step on the high wire — and she fell into the arena. You are a would-be murderess!

ASTRID: I didn't mean to kill her! (*Hysterically*) You must believe that! (*More calmly*) I wanted her to leave the show — but, murder, never. I only meant to frighten her.

MISS FINCH (*Slowly*): Someone else wanted to murder Genevieve. Someone who planned to inject her with snake venom, probably after the show — someone disguised as a clown. You gave that murderer his opportunity. You're as guilty as Genevieve's killer!

ASTRID: What are you going to do?

MISS FINCH: I am going to present Dr. Barnes with the evidence. He can turn you over to the police. (*She tightens her grip on* ASTRID*'s arm.*) Come. We'll find him now.

ASTRID: I'm sorry. I didn't think.

MISS FINCH (*Tight-lipped*): Murderers never do! (*They exit. Entrance in up center flat is opened slightly. Hand appears, fumbles and slaps curtain noisily, then removes knife from* BELLINI*'s display.* NOTE: *Spotlight shines on knife blade. Hand and knife slowly retreat. Quick curtain.*)

* * * * *

SCENE 3

TIME: *Immediately following.*

SETTING: *The wings of the Big Top. Main ring is off right. Several flats are lowered showing section of empty bleachers, animals' cages, etc. Circus props such as animal trainer's hoops, balls, and so forth are placed around set. Iron bars, weights and chains are at center. Scene may be played before curtain.*

AT RISE: ARMAND *is at center. He is engaged in bending "iron" bars, lifting weights, and breaking "chains," and continues to do so during following dialogue.* TOM *is standing at right.* DONNA *enters right, in aerialist's costume.* TOM *stares at her in surprise.*

TOM: Donna! What do you think you're doing? (*Circus music is heard faintly from offstage.*)

DONNA: If we're going to reenact the crime, someone has to play Genevieve's part.

TOM: I'm not going to let you go up there. (*He points right, upward.* MISS FINCH *enters left and joins them.* ARMAND *continues his performance. He breaks a "chain" in half, takes a bow to an imaginary audience, right, then strides angrily toward others.*)

ARMAND: Bah! I, the great Armand, performing before an empty house. It is an insult!

TOM (*Patiently*): Please, Armand, everyone is doing his part. It's Miss Finch's suggestion.

ARMAND: Troublesome old woman! (*He exits quickly.*)

MISS FINCH: I don't think I stand in favor with the strong man.

DONNA (*Slyly*): Well, we appreciate your efforts. Schoolteacher indeed. You're a born detective.

MISS FINCH (*Defensively*): I am a schoolteacher.

DONNA: That's true — and you're also the sister of the local chief of police. Criminal investigation must run in the family.

MISS FINCH (*Surprised*): You're a good detective yourself. How did you know that?

DONNA: You seemed to know the right questions to ask the right people. I made a telephone call to the local police headquarters, and I found out your secret.

MISS FINCH: Splendid, my dear. I'll solicit your aid on my next case — if I survive this one. (MISS FINCH *rubs her hands together.*) Everyone is in place, I see. (*To* DONNA) And you are going to play the part of Genevieve.

TOM: She's performing against my wishes. (*To* DONNA) If anything happens to you, I'll never forgive myself.

DONNA (*Frightened*): Do you think anyone will try to kill me? (*Circus music swells.* MISS FINCH *squeezes* DONNA'*s arm confidently.*)

MISS FINCH: We'll protect you, Donna. Don't worry. (DONNA *smiles, exits right.*) Tom, the main act is about to begin. (*She gestures left.*) I'll wait here while you introduce Donna's performance. (TOM *exits right as* MISS FINCH *quickly walks left. She looks off, right, as though watching performance.* BOB *enters left, stands behind her.*)

BOB: Everything is on schedule, Miss Finch. (*She turns quickly.*)

MISS FINCH: Bob, you startled me. Why, yes, the show is on schedule.

BOB (*Staring right*): Isn't that Donna ascending the high wire platform?

MISS FINCH: Yes, she's reenacting Miss Genevieve's performance. (BOB *rubs his hands together nervously.*)

BOB: Isn't that dangerous? Something might happen to her.

MISS FINCH: No, that's highly unlikely. The murderer will not strike again.

BOB: How can you be sure? (*He attempts a smile.*)

MISS FINCH (*Coldly*): Because I know the murderer — Shamrock!

BOB (*Quickly*): You know? (*Startled*) Shamrock! You called me Shamrock!

MISS FINCH: Yes, I did. My former pupil, Bubbles Mason, furnished me with the missing clue. A nickname acquired in school often stays with the person for the rest of his life. Your brother, Tom, was known as Blarney Stone. What was more natural than a nickname for his brother, an Irish counterpart, the nickname — Shamrock?

BOB (*Heatedly*): That's ridiculous!

MISS FINCH: I think not. Genevieve knew your nickname. She was closer to you than any other member of the circus. She thought you were going to marry her in a few weeks, but then, somehow, she discovered you were responsible for all those accidents. She realized that you wanted to force Tom to sell the circus — and she threatened to expose you. Genevieve knew that you were a sick young man.

BOB (*Emotionally*): That's not true. That's not . . . .

MISS FINCH (*Interrupting*): She was probably going to tell Tom everything after the performance tonight. You had to silence her — and silence her fast.

BOB: You have no proof!

MISS FINCH: Of course there's proof. Examine the method of the crime. Someone stole the key to the fer-de-lance case. Someone had to hold the serpent skillfully, extract the venom, and, after killing the snake, fill the hypodermic with the toxic venom. Not every murderer could carry out such a crime. It took someone with a great knowledge of snakes, someone who knew that the venom would kill instantly. Someone who had studied and practiced herpetology!

BOB: Herpetology?

MISS FINCH (*Nodding*): The branch of zoology that concerns reptiles. In short, the study of snakes. Tom told me you studied herpetology in college. It was that knowledge which helped me identify a murderer.

BOB: How was I to know that Genevieve would fall? I couldn't have planned it.

MISS FINCH: That point puzzled me, until I discovered that Astrid had put wax on Genevieve's slipper. Her act of revenge gave you the opportunity. You probably planned to kill Genevieve after the show, disguised in the clown's outfit you wore in the wings tonight. When Genevieve fell, you rushed forward and injected her with the serum. In that moment of truth, she knew that you were her murderer. That's why she whispered "Shamrock" to me.

BOB: If she wanted to identify me with this — this crime, why didn't she merely use my name?

MISS FINCH: The name "Bob" would have implicated too many people. I found out that Dr. Barnes' first name is Robert — as well as Bellini's. "Shamrock" could only mean one person. Sooner or later, Tom would have recognized your old college nickname.

BOB: And how can you be sure that I wore a clown costume tonight? How do you know I was the first one to reach Genevieve?

MISS FINCH: You knew that David wouldn't be here tonight. You gave him permission to leave. Lola probably saw you putting on the clown's outfit in the dressing tent. That's why she had to be silenced. Remember, Lola was last seen as she entered the tent. And I know that you wore a clown's make-up. (*She pats her purse.*) I removed a smudge of powder from your face when I first met you. That smudge is still on my handkerchief. I think that a lab test will prove that it's the same powder Denny and David use for their clown makeup.

BOB (*Viciously*): There's one thing you don't know, Miss Finch. (*He pulls knife from pocket.* NOTE: *"Knife" has rubber blade.*) I took one of Bellini's knives from the dressing room, and I'll use it if you try to prevent my escape! (MISS FINCH *slowly opens her purse, takes out hypodermic syringe.*)

MISS FINCH (*Steadily*): I'd say that we're both adequately armed. You see, I found the hypodermic needle in Lola's cabinet where you had discarded it after the murder. I tried to retrieve it when I first opened the cabinet, but came up with the dead snake, instead. (*She slowly raises syringe.* BOB *watches her arm.*) There's some venom left. A fatal dose, I'm sure. One scratch is usually fatal, isn't it, Bob? (*He backs away, drops knife.*)

BOB: No! No! (*He shouts hysterically.*) You haven't won! You haven't beaten me! (*He points upward into right wings.*) Look, Donna is on the platform now. (*He laughs hoarsely.*) I cut the support wire. She's going to fall. Then my brother will have to close the show! (*He breaks down, covers his face, sobs. Scream is heard off right.* MISS FINCH *quickly returns hypodermic to purse.* TOM, *supporting* DONNA, *enters right. They are followed by* BARNES, SNAVELY, BELLINI, ARMAND, BUBBLES *and* DENNY.)

TOM: Donna! Thank goodness you're safe.

DONNA: I don't know what happened. I stepped onto the wire and it suddenly snapped. I — I fell.

BOB (*Muttering*): She's safe! Safe!

MISS FINCH (*To* BOB): Do you think I would risk Donna's life, knowing that a murderer was under the Big Top? I had Dr. Barnes and his staff, ready and waiting in the wings, with a life net!

BARNES (*To* MISS FINCH): It was a close one, but you saved the day. (MISS FINCH *gestures at* BOB.)

MISS FINCH: Take Bob to the police. He's our murderer. (*Everyone registers surprise.*) I'll explain everything later. (BARNES, SNAVELY, ARMAND, BELLINI *take* BOB *off left.*)

TOM (*In disbelief*): Bob — my own brother — a murderer?

MISS FINCH: Yes. Bob is a sick young man who would let nothing stand in his way. He wanted to kill me, too, but I threatened him with the hypodermic of snake venom.

BUBBLES: You handled that dreadful thing? Why, you might have been killed.

MISS FINCH: I took precautions, my dear. The syringe was quite empty, but I filled it with a small quantity of — soda pop! (MISS FINCH *places her arm around* DONNA.) You're a brave young woman. You'll make a perfect partner for Tom Kelly and the Imperial Circus, the greatest show in the universe!

BUBBLES (*Solicitously*): Poor Miss Finch! I'm sure you must be exhausted. Why don't you come to the dressing room, and I'll make you a nice cup of tea. (MISS FINCH *waves impatiently.*)

MISS FINCH: Nonsense! I came to see the circus and, by Lord

Harry, I'm going to see the circus! (*She gestures dramatically.*) Places, everyone — the show must go on! (*Circus music rises in crescendo, as curtain falls, or there is a blackout.*)

THE END

Production Notes

THE BIG TOP MURDERS

Characters: 7 male; 5 female.

Playing Time: 35 minutes.

Costumes: Everyday dress. Casual, everyday clothes for Bob, Snavely, Doc Barnes, and Donna. Miss Finch wears outsized, flowered hat. Donna changes to aerialist's costume in Scene 3. Tom wears ringmaster's costume — red coat, white breeches, black boots, top hat. He carries riding crop. Denny wears clown costume and makeup. Armand wears leopardskin tunic. Bellini wears colorful shirt and dark trousers. Lola, Astrid, and Bubbles wear tights, colorful swimsuits or similar costumes of shiny fabric, decorated with plumes and sequins. They have long cloaks and ballet slippers.

Properties: Purse, handkerchief, yearbook, circus costume and ballet slippers, hypodermic syringe, long-handled knife with rubber blade, "snake" made of papier mâché or cloth.

Setting: Scenes 1 and 2, dressing room in tent on Imperial Circus lot. There are a dressing table and bench down left. There is a large clothes cabinet up right, with door facing audience (Lola is concealed inside cabinet during Scene 1). Syringe and "snake" are on floor of cabinet. Long pole rests beside cabinet. There is a wooden board attached to wall up center, with knives of various sizes mounted on it. Sign reading THE GREAT BELLINI is at top of board. Several straight chairs are down center. Walls of tent are made of canvas. Flaps in canvas serving as entrances are at

right and up center. Circus posters and colorful costumes
hang on walls. Scene 3, in the wings of the Big Top, may
be played before curtain if desired. Flats with paintings of
empty bleachers, animal cages, etc., may be lowered onto
set. There are animal trainers' hoops, balls, stands, and so
forth, placed around set. Fake iron bars, chains, and weights
reading 500 POUNDS are at center. Entrance to Big Top
and main ring is at right.

Lighting: Spotlight effects, as indicated in text.

Sound: Appropriate circus music, drum roll, crowd noises, as
indicated in text.

The Bermuda Triangle Mystery

A pleasure cruise becomes a nightmare when the yacht
Enchantress *sails into the Bermuda Triangle. . . .*

Characters

CAPTAIN MAYBERRY, *captain of "Enchantress"*
GLOVER, *first mate*
TURNER, *radioman*
BILL ARMSTRONG, *owner of "Enchantress"*
MADGE, *his wife*
LEE, *his teen-age daughter*
MRS. AGNES BELLAMY, *his aunt*
PROFESSOR JANE SAMSON, *expert on psychic phenomena*
AUDREY KENT, *a young widow*
DAN PARSONS, *newspaperman*

TIME: *An evening in January.*
SETTING: *The foredeck and wheel room of "Enchantress," an
ocean-going yacht. The deck is a triangular area downstage,
with apex of triangle down center. A rail borders foredeck.
The wheel room is at center on a raised platform. It is
reached from deck by a short ladder. Wheel room has large
spoked wheel, compass on a waist-high stand, and table
with radio equipment.*
AT RISE: CAPTAIN MAYBERRY *stands in wheel room, at wheel.*
TURNER, *wearing headphones, sits at radio table up left.*
GLOVER *enters deck area from up right and climbs ladder to
wheel room.*

MAYBERRY: How's our course, Glover?

GLOVER (*Going to compass at right of wheel*): We're directly on course for Miami, Captain. We should arrive an hour from now, at twenty-two hundred.

MAYBERRY (*Looking out over audience, as if studying ocean*): If we make it through the Bermuda Triangle, you mean.

TURNER (*Pushing back earphones*): Are you superstitious, Captain?

MAYBERRY: I'm cautious. These waters can be treacherous. The sea is so calm . . . it's unusual for January. I don't like it.

GLOVER (*Shaking his head*): All the passengers are asking questions about these waters — the Bermuda Triangle. Captain, do you ever wonder about what's really out there?

MAYBERRY: I don't speculate, Glover. I'm a practical man. Whatever the stories, ships have sailed these waters for centuries and for millions of miles without incident. I only accept things I see and understand.

GLOVER: I wonder how much we really understand about the sea. (MRS. BELLAMY *enters up right, carrying knitting bag, and calls to wheel room.*)

MRS. BELLAMY (*Waving bag*): Oh, Admiral!

MAYBERRY: It's Captain Mayberry, ma'am.

MRS. BELLAMY: Whatever it is, when will we reach Miami?

MAYBERRY: Very shortly, Mrs. Bellamy.

MRS. BELLAMY: I certainly hope so. I haven't had a moment's rest since I climbed onto this dreadful yacht.

MAYBERRY (*Smiling*): Boarded, Mrs. Bellamy.

MRS. BELLAMY (*Sighing*): Why is everyone so technical about boats?

MAYBERRY: The *Enchantress* is a ship.

MRS. BELLAMY: Boat — ship — what's the difference?

MAYBERRY: Technically, a boat is a vessel that can be placed upon a ship.

MRS. BELLAMY: I see. Well, I wish my nephew Bill had never

persuaded me to get onto this ship. He should find more important things to do than sail around this — this Devil's Triangle.

MAYBERRY: The Devil's Triangle is off the coast of Japan. We're off the coast of Florida, in the area called the Bermuda Triangle.

GLOVER: It's a triangle-shaped area between Bermuda, Miami, and Puerto Rico . . . .

MRS. BELLAMY: That means nothing to me, I'm afraid. All I know about this Triangle business is what I've read. (AUDREY KENT *enters left, unnoticed.*) People have disappeared here — without a trace.

MAYBERRY: That's right. The records go back a long time. Aaron Burr's daughter and her sailing party vanished more than a hundred and fifty years ago.

MRS. BELLAMY: And there have been many disappearances in modern times. (*Confidentially*) Take poor Audrey Kent, for instance. Her husband vanished on that freighter five years ago — disappeared without a trace, as though the sea had swallowed him. (AUDREY *steps forward.*)

AUDREY: Yes, Mrs. Bellamy. My husband and his crew of seventy men.

MRS. BELLAMY: Oh, Audrey . . . Mrs. Kent . . . I didn't see you. (*Flustered*) I — I never would have mentioned it . . .

AUDREY: I can talk freely about it now. (*Looking out over audience*) I don't know what happened to Jim and his ship — no one does — but someday, I'll find the answer. That's why I came on this cruise. (*Pointing off right*) Why, look, that glow on the horizon must be Miami. (AUDREY *walks to railing, right.* GLOVER *joins her.* BILL ARMSTRONG, MADGE, *and* LEE *enter up left.*)

LEE: Hi, Aunt Agnes!

MRS. BELLAMY: Good evening, Lee. Bill, I won't breathe easily until this wretched boat reaches Miami.

BILL: Relax, Aunt Agnes. Enjoy the cruise. And the calm seas!

MRS. BELLAMY: Cruise, indeed! I know what I know, and if you ask me, we shouldn't be here. There's something threatening about the Bermuda Triangle. (BILL *laughs.*)

MADGE: Now, Aunt Agnes, calm down. (*She and* BILL *sit.*)

LEE: I think it's romantic. (*She points.*) Look at that moon — and those stars.

MRS. BELLAMY (*Grudgingly*): If I were sixteen, I'd find it romantic, too. (*Sits*)

LEE: It's so peaceful and calm. Everything is so still . . . . It's like waiting for the curtain to rise on a play. Waiting for something to happen.

GLOVER (*Joining them*): The calm before the storm?

LEE (*Nodding*): That's right, Mr. Glover. There's something all around us, and although I can't see it, I can feel its presence.

MRS. BELLAMY (*Sharply*): Stop talking like that! You'd frighten a person to death.

BILL: Don't be frightened, Aunt Agnes. The *Enchantress* is unsinkable. (GLOVER *ascends ladder, relieves* MAYBERRY *at wheel.* MAYBERRY *stretches, descends ladder, joins group on deck.*)

MRS. BELLAMY: Rubbish!

BILL (*Getting up*): It's true enough. (*Looking out*) She has real stay-afloat insurance. The *Enchantress* is sink-proof.

MRS. BELLAMY: I suppose all those missing ships were sink-proof, too. (*To* MAYBERRY) I simply cannot understand how you keep on course, Captain. The sea is so vast — and yet you claim we're headed directly for Miami.

MAYBERRY: There are many ways of finding our position. The navigator can get an accurate reading from the stars. (*He points to wheel room.*) We have radio and radar. And I showed you the magnetic compass the other day.

MRS. BELLAMY: That thing with all the numerals and symbols?

MAYBERRY (*Nodding*): The compass needle points almost at a reading of the magnetic North Pole.

LEE: Almost? I thought the compass always pointed North.

MAYBERRY: Not really. Compasses are never at a direct reading of true North. When a pilot charts a flight, he must make allowances of almost 20 degrees for an off-course reading.

MADGE: Imagine that.

MAYBERRY: There are only two places in the world where the compass points directly North. The Devil's Triangle off Japan — and here, in the Bermuda Triangle!

LEE: Why is that, Captain Mayberry?

MAYBERRY: No one has ever been able to explain it. If we knew the answer, we might be able to solve the mystery of the Bermuda Triangle.

MRS. BELLAMY: I'll be glad when we set foot on dry land.

MAYBERRY (*Smiling*): The technical term is disembark, Mrs. Bellamy. (*He smiles, ascends ladder, as* DAN PARSONS *and* PROFESSOR JANE SAMSON *enter up left.*)

DAN (*To* JANE, *as they enter*): And I tell you, Professor Samson, I can't accept your theory about the Bermuda Triangle. (*As dialogue continues,* MAYBERRY *relieves* GLOVER *at wheel.* GLOVER *rejoins* AUDREY *at railing, talking in pantomime.* TURNER *adjusts radio, studies charts on table up center.*) I can't believe that there are hidden pockets in the atmosphere over the ocean where ships actually disappear. (*They walk toward group on deck.*)

JANE: It's possible, Dan. In a few short years we've learned more about space than we know about the sea. (DAN *shakes his head.*)

DAN: Time pockets — a twilight zone. It's too much for me. (*To others*) Hello, everyone.

BILL: Hello, Dan, Professor Samson. It sounds as though you're in the midst of a heated scientific argument.

DAN (*Laughing*): I wasn't arguing with Professor Samson.

JANE: Just a friendly discussion, and you can call me Jane. Forget the "professor," please, Dan.

DAN (*To others*): My paper has wanted an interview with the eminent Professor Samson for years. Her Bermuda Triangle theory is news.

LEE (*To* JANE): Jane, I'll never forget what you told us about people who disappeared beyond a time barrier. Is it really possible?

JANE: I believe numerous funnels or tunnels exist that are invisible, but can act as imprisoning sleeves. (DAN *starts to interrupt, but* JANE *holds up her hand.*) Please listen, Dan. These sleeves can suck up people and vessels and whirl them on a course from North to South, finally depositing them in the vicinity of Antarctica — or beyond.

MRS. BELLAMY: I've never heard such nonsense, Jane.

BILL (*Nodding*): It's far-fetched. Dan is right, I'm afraid. His readers will never buy that.

LEE: I don't know, Dad. Something happened to all those people lost in the Bermuda Triangle. Why, in 1945 five Army planes with thirteen people vanished around here without a trace. And not only that. Another plane went out searching for the missing planes, and it was never heard from again.

MADGE (*Gesturing*): It's incredible that six planes disappeared at once, but I can't believe in a time tunnel, either.

BILL: I suppose a sudden storm might have destroyed those six planes.

LEE: The planes were equipped with life rafts and jackets. Nothing was found — not even an oil slick, although the Navy searched these very waters for a month.

MRS. BELLAMY: This part of the ocean?

LEE (*Nodding*): Right off shore from Miami.

MRS. BELLAMY (*Fearfully*): You're terrifying me! (BILL *puts his arm around her.*)

BILL: It was a sudden storm, Aunt Agnes. A violent, tropical storm. (LEE *shakes her head.*)

LEE: No way, Dad. The missing planes — all the ships that

have disappeared — radioed that the waters were calm. They always specified calm conditions, just like tonight.

JANE: The disappearances strengthen my theory. After all, Einstein taught us that time travels in a straight line. We all know that the Earth is shaped more like a pear than a globe, with indentations and grooves. Has time really compensated for the shape of the Earth? Can time actually pass over these spaces without having its effect?

MADGE: These stories frighten me, too.

JANE: Listen to this: In 1941, a young pilot pulled out of a cloud bank, and found himself on a collision course with another plane.

MRS. BELLAMY: Gracious!

JANE: The young pilot banked, but not before the other plane scraped his own craft. And the other plane was like a nightmare! The frightened pilot later described it as World War One vintage, constructed of wood and canvas. Its pilot was wearing a leather flying helmet and goggles.

LEE: It sounds like the Red Baron.

JANE: When the young pilot landed, he reported the incident to the Civil Aeronautics Board. No such plane was on record anywhere as flying in the area.

MADGE: It might have been an unlicensed plane, flying illegally.

JANE: I don't think so. A few months after the incident, an ancient plane just like the one the young pilot described was found not far away in a barn.

DAN: That explains it! Somebody was having a good time in an unlicensed plane.

JANE: There's more to it. It was established by the CAB that the old plane had been in the same position, untouched, for many years.

MRS. BELLAMY: Fancy!

JANE: And in the old plane was a log book. In the last entry its pilot noted coming upon a strange-looking silver aircraft that almost collided with him. Well, the log underwent a series of tests — and its age was authenticated. The entry was nearly fifty years old!

MADGE: That's incredible.

JANE: There's still more. On the ancient plane, investigators found a long scrape along the side. Traces of the substance were put through extensive tests and found to match up perfectly with the material used in the modern plane!

MADGE: There has to be an explanation.

JANE (*Slowly*): I believe that the two planes met beyond the time barrier, two planes flying fifty years apart in time, but not in space.

DAN (*Smirking*): And where did all this take place — somewhere over Tibet?

JANE: No, Dan. The planes met in a near-collision course over Ohio!

MRS. BELLAMY (*Standing*): I've had enough of your ghost stories! I'm retiring to my cabin until we reach Miami — and a luxury hotel! (*She exits.*)

TURNER (*Standing suddenly, knocking over his chair, and waving a sheet of paper*): Captain! Captain! What do you make of this?

MAYBERRY (*Taking paper and reading aloud*): "May Day. May Day. Caught in a whirlpool. Sinking fast. Intense fog. Location 80 degrees west longitude . . . ." (*Looking up*) Is that all, Turner?

TURNER: I lost contact, Captain. I'll try the distress frequency.

MAYBERRY: She didn't give her latitude reading. See if you can locate her on radar. (TURNER *nods.*) And call the Coast Guard at Miami. (TURNER *sets chair erect, adjusts earphones and radio, pantomimes sending a message.*) Glover, take the wheel. (GLOVER *steps to wheel.*)

BILL: What's going on, Captain? Is it serious?

MAYBERRY (*Moving to center*): Afraid so. We've received word of a vessel in distress. We must stand by for further instructions.

JANE: Did the ship give identification?

MAYBERRY (*Looking at paper*): It's a vessel called the *Marie North*. (AUDREY, *in great agitation, rushes up ladder, shouting.*)

AUDREY: No! Someone is playing a cruel, senseless trick on me. It can't be the *Marie North*! The *Marie North* was my husband's ship. It disappeared five years ago! (*Others move center.*)

BILL: Calm down, Audrey. It's a coincidence. It must be a vessel with the same name.

AUDREY (*Frantic*): There couldn't be another ship named the *Marie North*. (*Hysterically*) It's Jim's ship, I tell you!

TURNER (*At radio*): The Miami Coast Guard ordered us to stand by for further instructions. So far, there's no sign of the ship on radar. (TURNER *operates radio during following dialogue.*)

MAYBERRY (*Grimly*): We don't have enough fuel for an extensive search.

GLOVER: But the *Marie North* must be nearby. We received a clear, direct signal.

AUDREY: Yes, I know Jim is near. I felt his presence all day.

MAYBERRY (*Pounding his fist into his hand*): There must be an explanation! We'll follow the Coast Guard's instructions and stand by.

DAN: How can we help a ship that disappeared five years ago?

BILL: Stay calm, Dan. We all must stay calm. (*Gesturing*) Madge, Lee, you'd better go to Aunt Agnes's cabin and keep her company. I don't know how long we'll be delayed. (MADGE *and* LEE *exit.*)

DAN: I guess I havc quite a story.

BILL: You'd better wait until we're certain of the facts.

JANE: Will we ever be certain?

MAYBERRY: One thing puzzles me. The *Marie North* mentioned "intense fog." (*He gestures.*) Yet we can see Miami. There's no fog within miles of the *Enchantress.*

GLOVER (*Frightened*): Captain Mayberry! Captain Mayberry! (*Everyone turns.*) Look at the compass! (*As* MAYBERRY *crosses to compass*) I've never seen anything like that.

MAYBERRY: The needle is spinning clockwise. It's gone crazy! (*Everyone looks at compass.*)

DAN (*Whistling softly*): Look at that needle travel. It's ready to jump off the compass.

GLOVER: I've heard of such a thing. It happened in the St. Lawrence River when a vessel passed over a big deposit of iron ore on the river bottom.

MAYBERRY: That's hardly likely out here. (*He looks at compass again.*) It's impossible to get a reading. (*Suddenly,* GLOVER*'s hands tremble. He struggles to maintain control of the wheel.*)

GLOVER: Captain!

MAYBERRY: What's wrong, Glover?

GLOVER (*Straining*): There's something pulling at the *Enchantress.* I — I can't control the wheel. (*MAYBERRY quickly joins him. They struggle to control wheel.*)

MAYBERRY (*Straining*): It — It seems as though we're being pulled backward! (*BILL studies compass.*)

BILL: The needle is moving faster than ever.

JANE (*Nodding*): There is no reading at all.

AUDREY (*Distracted*): It's Jim. He is trying to find me. He wants me to join him on the *Marie North.*

DAN (*Roughly*): Stop it, Audrey! Pull yourself together. We're sailing through ocean turbulence, that's all. (*MAYBERRRY and* GLOVER *continue to strain at wheel.*)

MAYBERRY (*Tense*): I can hold it now, Glover. (GLOVER *relaxes, wipes brow.* MAYBERRY *takes wheel alone.*) Whatever it was, it's over.

GLOVER: We must have passed through some kind of strong crosscurrent. The ship was uncontrollable.

BILL: The compass is still spinning. (*To* AUDREY *and* JANE) It may not be safe here. Shouldn't you go below?

JANE: Bill, I'm a scientist. Something is happening to the *Enchantress*, and I must know what it is.

MAYBERRY: She's O.K. now. I rammed the throttles full ahead to get out of that turbulence. It seemed that something wanted to pull us back, but couldn't make it.

BILL (*Proudly*): I told you the *Enchantress* is a seaworthy vessel.

AUDREY: The *Marie North* was seaworthy, too.

TURNER (*Calling*): Captain, I still can't make contact with the *Marie North*.

MAYBERRY: Keep trying. Radio that help is on the way. Ask for a new fix on their position. (TURNER *nods, returns to radio.* GLOVER *sways, grips compass for support.*)

GLOVER: Help! (*Hoarsely*) Something is pulling at me. (*His hands hold compass.*) I can barely stand up. (BILL *and* DAN *grab* GLOVER.)

DAN (*Struggling*): I feel it, too.

BILL: It's as though something is pulling my arms in opposite directions. Captain, can you manage the wheel?

MAYBERRY (*Nodding*): It's under control.

DAN: Then it must be a force from the compass. Try to let go, Glover. Let go! (*Straining,* GLOVER *finally pulls hands from compass. He sags against table, breathing heavily.*)

GLOVER: I know it sounds crazy, but I was being pulled into the compass. It seemed as if it were alive!

BILL: Nonsense! It must have been an atmospheric disturbance.

DAN (*Shaking his head*): No, the compass has become highly magnetized. Don't touch it. (AUDREY *points right.*)

AUDREY: Look! The shoreline is gone. The lights of Miami have disappeared. (*Everyone looks right.*)

DAN: They haven't disappeared. There's a heavy fog on the coast, that's all. We can't see through it.

BILL: There wasn't any fog a few minutes ago.

DAN: But the ship that called itself the *Marie North* signaled about the fog. It must have swept in from the ocean.

MAYBERRY (*Sharply*): Mr. Glover! What's wrong with the generator? The *Enchantress* is losing power.

GLOVER: That's impossible. I checked the generators before I came on deck. They were in working order.

MAYBERRY: Go below to the generator room. (GLOVER *dashes down ladder, exits up right.*)

TURNER: Sir, I can't reach Miami anymore. There's something wrong with the radio and the radar equipment.

MAYBERRY: It must be the generator. (*He glances at compass.*) The compass needle is still spinning. (MAYBERRY *stares straight ahead.*) I don't know the direction. We're drifting and I don't know where.

AUDREY (*Excited*): I see something in the distance.

DAN (*Squinting*): I don't see anything.

BILL (*Looking*): I think it's a fog bank. A great wave of mist. (*Suddenly*) Audrey's right. Something is moving beyond that fog.

JANE: Yes, I see it too. It looks like a large ship. (*Frightened*) It seems to be bearing down on us.

BILL: If it hits the *Enchantress*, we'll be crushed. Captain, the vessel is moving to starboard. (MAYBERRY *swings wheel sharply to left.*)

MAYBERRY: Turner, did you receive a signal from another vessel in these waters? What's on the radar?

TURNER: The radio equipment is still dead, Captain. There's nothing on radar. (TURNER *adjusts headphones.*)

BILL: The ship is still headed in our direction.

DAN: It's much closer now. (*He gasps*) I think it's a freighter. A large freighter. (AUDREY *descends ladder, rushes to right railing.*)

MAYBERRY: Stop her!

DAN: Come back, Audrey. Don't be a fool! (DAN *descends quickly, pulls* AUDREY *back.*)

BILL (*Suddenly*): The life raft and jackets. I must have them ready. (*He descends, rushes off up right.* AUDREY *struggles with* DAN.)

AUDREY (*Frantically*): Let me go! I recognize that ship.

DAN: We're not certain there is a ship. It might be only the fog.

AUDREY: I know it's a ship. Jim's ship.

DAN: The *Marie North*?

AUDREY: Yes, it's the *Marie North.*

DAN: You know that's impossible, Audrey. Your husband's ship was lost at sea. You must accept that.

AUDREY: What about the distress call we received?

DAN: It must have been a mistake.

JANE (*Descending and crossing to them*): Let me take you to your cabin, Audrey.

AUDREY: No, I must stay here. (*She points right.*) I can see the ship clearly now. I can almost touch it. I can read the name on the hull. (DAN *turns right, shades his eyes.*)

DAN (*In disbelief*): The *Marie North*!

AUDREY (*Screaming*): Jim! (AUDREY *presses against railing, extends her arms.*) Jim! Jim, please, come back! (JANE *draws* AUDREY *away from railing.*)

JANE: It's gone, Audrey. The ship has vanished into the mist.

DAN: It seems as though it passed right through the *Enchantress*! Now there's nothing out there but the fog.

AUDREY (*Sobbing*): Jim's gone. The *Marie North* isn't there.

DAN: It was never there. We imagined the whole thing.

JANE (*Nodding*): We mistook a fog bank for the freighter. It was a case of mass hysteria.

AUDREY (*Insistently*): No. No. Jim is out there. He wants me to come to him. (BILL *re-enters.*)

BILL: The raft and life jackets are ready.

DAN: We won't need them.

BILL: What about the ship you saw?

JANE: Whatever we saw is gone. Maybe it was only fog.

BILL: That's impossible. We saw it. (DAN *indicates* AUDREY, *and motions* BILL *to silence.*) Yes, I suppose we could have made a mistake.

AUDREY (*Slowly*): I'm tired. I'd like to go to my cabin now.

JANE: May I help you?

AUDREY (*Shaking her head*): I'd rather be alone. (AUDREY *exits left, walking as if in a trance.*)

JANE: This has been a terrible ordeal for her.

DAN: That message from the *Marie North.* . . . (*He shrugs.*) It was a mistake, of course.

JANE: Do you really believe that?

DAN: No. I guess not. I saw a ship there, about to collide with us.

BILL: I don't know what to believe.

DAN (*Musing*): The time tunnel theory . . . . Do you think we could have seen a ship that disappeared five years ago?

JANE: Yes, it's possible. An atmospheric funnel may throw a ship into another time dimension.

BILL: Incredible!

JANE: Our compass has gone crazy. The generator has broken down for no apparent reason. The radio and radar have failed. These things have happened before to ships in the Bermuda Triangle. Consider many of the ships that have disappeared here. Their last messages have invariably been the same: "Everything seems wrong." No one has found an explanation. (JANE *sighs, walks to rail, turns.*) We must concern ourselves with more than crosscurrents and tides, longitude and latitude. We must consider time. (BILL *and* DAN *join her at rail. They talk in pantomime.* GLOVER *re-enters, right, and joins* MAYBERRY *and* TURNER.)

GLOVER: The generators are working now, Captain.

MAYBERRY (*Nodding*): Thank you, Glover. The water is calm now — there is no pull against the boat. (*He gestures.*) Only the fog. (GLOVER *studies compass.*)

GLOVER: The compass is steady again. It's pointing true North.

MAYBERRY (*Nodding*): Turner, have you been able to reach Miami?

TURNER: No, sir. The radio seems to be O.K., but I can't get a response.

GLOVER: Have there been any other messages from the distressed ship?

TURNER: Nothing. It's like sailing in a vacuum.

MAYBERRY (*To* GLOVER): The *Marie North* passed our course a few minutes ago.

GLOVER: I can't believe it.

MAYBERRY: It's true, but no one wants to admit it. It appeared at the starboard bow and disappeared into the fog. It was on a direct collision course with the *Enchantress*. (*As they talk, a series of red lights blink offstage right, reflected across the deck.* JANE, BILL *and* DAN *look up.* MAYBERRY *and* GLOVER *stand transfixed as lights grow brighter.* TURN-ER *stands, joins* MAYBERRY *at helm.*)

DAN: What's going on out there, Captain?

MAYBERRY: I've never seen anything like it.

JANE: It's like fireworks. (*Pointing*) Why, there are red rockets bursting in the sky.

DAN: Whatever those lights are, they are not earthly. Why, there's no noise — nothing but silence.

BILL: Is it possible that it's an electrical disturbance like St. Elmo's Fire or Northern Lights?

JANE: I don't think so. St. Elmo's Fire doesn't act that way. (*She shields her eyes.*) Those lights are blinding. (*DAN ascends ladder.* JANE *and* BILL *follow quickly.*)

TURNER: Captain, the compass is spinning again. (*GLOVER joins him, nods.*)

GLOVER: The needle is turning slowly and steadily. (*MAYBERRY grips wheel tightly.*)

MAYBERRY: There's that pull again! (*GLOVER glances around.*)

GLOVER: The generators are still working. (*Gradually, offstage red lights fade.* JANE *points upward.*)

JANE: Look at the sky.

DAN (*Looking up*): There seems to be a huge dark shape directly overhead.

BILL: It's descending! It's trying to land on us! (*BILL throws his arms upward as though to protect his head. He retreats, backs into radio table.*)

JANE: Something is hovering behind that cloud. I think it's trying to reach us. (*TURNER points up.*)

TURNER: The lights are disappearing behind the cloud, but I can still see them. They seem to be dancing in space!

GLOVER: The cloud is fading. The darkness is melting away. (*GLOVER sighs.*) It's gone. (*He points.*) There's nothing but the stars — and the night. (*BILL rushes forward, tugs at* MAYBERRY*'s sleeve.*)

BILL: What's happening to us?

MAYBERRY (*Soberly*): I've heard of these things before. Glowing lights, a descending dark cloud. This has happened many times in the Bermuda Triangle. Mariners are hesitant to speak about it. They think no one will believe them.

DAN: But this is an important discovery. Perhaps that cloud was an electromagnetic field, something that can literally disintegrate a ship or an aircraft.

MAYBERRY: Who can tell? Navigation is my business, Mr. Parsons. It's not my job to speculate. (*MAYBERRY grips wheel.*)

Right now, I have to get the *Enchantress* and its passengers to port. (*He gestures.*) Turner, get our position. Make every effort to contact Miami. We must be near port.

GLOVER (*Looking right*): There's nothing out there. Not even a trace of light. (LEE *screams offstage and rushes in. She climbs ladder and throws herself into* BILL's *arms.*)

LEE: Dad, it was terrible — terrible!

BILL: Lee, what's the matter?

LEE: It's Audrey. I saw her disappear!

BILL: I don't understand. Maybe she went to her cabin.

LEE (*Hysterically*): No — no! I saw her standing on the after-deck. She looked so strange. Suddenly I saw flashing red lights that frightened me terribly. I shielded my eyes. When I opened them, Audrey was fading into the lights. She became part of them.

DAN: You must have been dreaming, Lee.

LEE (*Sobbing*): I tell you it happened. I rushed to the after-deck, but she was gone. Vanished!

Glover: She might have fallen overboard.

LEE: No. She wasn't near the rail. The lights took her away, but she didn't seem to mind. She wanted to go with them. (*She sobs.*) Dad, I'm frightened!

BILL: We'll be in port soon.

LEE: We'll never reach port. (*She laughs hysterically.*) We'll be another statistic. We'll be lost in the Bermuda Triangle, and they'll never find us. (*Her wild laughter continues.* BILL *shakes her. Gradually, her laughter fades to a whimper.*) I'm sorry, Dad.

BILL: I'll take you to the cabin. Is your mother still with Aunt Agnes?

LEE: Aren't they here? (LEE *glances around wildly.*) They left the cabin to come up on deck.

JANE: We haven't seen them.

BILL: Madge — Agnes — gone? No, they must be below. (*He*

takes LEE*'s arm.*) We'll find them. (*They descend ladder, exit up left.*)

DAN (*In disbelief*): Audrey can't be gone. She was here a few minutes ago.

JANE: Those lights and that cloud had a purpose. I think I know what happened to Audrey. (JANE *walks to radio table, turns.*) Everyone on earth has a counterpart in another system of time. She's gone there.

DAN: I won't buy that.

JANE: Do you have a better explanation? And what happened to Mrs. Armstrong and Mrs. Bellamy?

DAN: They're in the cabin below.

JANE: I'd like to believe that, but it seems inconceivable that they'd remain below when the generator failed. No, we'll never see them again. They're gone, too.

DAN: Don't talk like that!

JANE: Each person aboard the *Enchantress* will disappear — one by one!

MAYBERRY (*To* JANE): These people are my responsibility, Professor. I hope you're mistaken!

JANE: Captain, I think the Bermuda Triangle disappearances are due to a parallel world in another universe that has come close to our world, causing people and craft to jump from this world into the other. That could explain the sudden appearance of the *Marie North.*

DAN: But the disappearing passengers — that's crazy.

JANE: Hardly. In the nineteenth century, a French vessel was found afloat with sails set, cargo intact, all hands missing. The *Marie Celeste.*

GLOVER: That's a remote case.

JANE (*Insistently*): The German bark *Freya*; the *John and Mary*; the *Gloria Colite*; the Cuban freighter *Rubicon*; the yacht *Connemara IV* — are these remote cases, Mr. Glover? All of those vessels were found intact without a single person aboard.

MAYBERRY: Turner, please tell Mr. Armstrong and his family I want to see them at once. (TURNER *exits.*)

JANE (*Absently*): We'll never see them again. We'll never see Turner again. Something is out there waiting for us.

DAN: Stop it, Jane! (*Suddenly, offstage drone of airplane motors is heard. Happily*) Listen! Airplanes! It must be a search party. The Coast Guard has reported the *Enchantress* missing and planes are looking for us. (GLOVER *points right.*)

GLOVER: And the fog is lifting. I can see the shoreline. (*Everyone stares right.*)

JANE: Yes, there is land ahead. But what land? (*Airplane motor sounds increase.*)

DAN (*Happily*): We're heading for Miami! We're safe — that's the important thing.

TURNER (*Offstage*): Mr. Armstrong! Mrs. Bellamy! Where are you? The Captain wants — (*His voice trails off, fades.* JANE *nods thoughtfully.*)

JANE: One by one.

DAN (*Pointing upward*): Those planes are real enough. I can see them now. There are five planes in perfect flight formation.

MAYBERRY: And there is a sixth plane bringing up the rear. (MAYBERRY *grips wheel tighter.*) Five of those planes are TBM Avengers.

DAN: Who cares? The planes are here to rescue us.

GLOVER (*Slowly*): TBM Avengers haven't been used by the Air Force in thirty years. They were World War Two bombers.

DAN: What are you talking about? (JANE *places her hand on* DAN*'s arm.*)

JANE (*Calmly*): I think I know what Mr. Glover means. In 1945 five Avengers took off from Fort Lauderdale on a routine training mission. They disappeared from the face of the earth.

DAN: Yes, yes, we went over that before. (*Panicky*) Do you mean that those planes overhead are the same ones? (*He shakes his head.*) No, Jane — don't tell me that! Those planes up there are real. Look! (*He points.*) They're circling over the *Enchantress.* (*To* JANE) You're all crazy! I won't believe that we're anywhere but in the Atlantic Ocean, about to reach Miami. (MAYBERRY *looks up.*)

MAYBERRY: The planes are disappearing over the horizon. (*Offstage motors fade, then are silent.*) They're gone now. (DAN *raises his arms, shakes his fists violently.*)

DAN: No, no! We're down here. You mustn't stop searching. Come back! Come back! (MAYBERRY *leaves wheel, walks to ladder, beckons to* GLOVER.)

Mayberry: Come, Mr. Glover. We must search for Armstrong and the others.

DAN: You can't leave your post, Mayberry. What will happen to the *Enchantress*?

MAYBERRY: The boat is on automatic pilot. My first responsibility lies with our missing passengers. (MAYBERRY *and* GLOVER *descend ladder. They look up, nod to each other, exit up left.*)

DAN: What got into Mayberry? How can he take all this so calmly?

JANE: Don't question it, Dan. The Captain has accepted the inevitable. He knows the mystery of the Bermuda Triangle. (JANE *descends ladder, walks to right rail.* DAN *follows.*)

DAN: We're all alone, Jane. Everyone has gone . . . .

JANE: And they won't come back.

DAN: I wonder what the explanation is.

JANE: There are some things we'll never know. "There are more things in heaven and earth . . . than are dreamt of in your philosophy."

DAN (*Slowly*): Yes. Shakespeare was right — strange things. (*He points right.*) Look — the sky is bright as day. And there is the shore!

JANE: Daylight. We must have sailed all night.

DAN (*Nodding*): We foundered in the Bermuda Triangle but — (*He points again.*) There's land! (DAN *shields his eyes, squints.*) But I don't see any buildings or people. It's just land. (*He points.*) And there — in the harbor — Look!

JANE (*Excited*): Sailing vessels. Freighters, skiffs, two-masted schooners.

DAN: I've never seen such a display. They're all in clear view. I can read some of the names on the hulls.

JANE (*Reading*): *The Sea Venture* —

DAN : *The Patriot* —

JANE: *The Rosalie* — *The Atlanta.* Yes, Dan, they're all here in the harbor. The ships that have disappeared in the Bermuda Triangle!

DAN: I think we've reached our port-of-call. I'm not frightened any more, Jane. We're in a strange place, but I've never known such a sense of peace.

JANE: We've been in the time tunnel.

DAN: But we're alive. And I think we'll make it. Even in a new world — a world beyond time. (DAN *takes* JANE*'s hand. They continue to stare right. Curtain.*)

THE END

Production Notes

THE BERMUDA TRIANGLE MYSTERY

Characters: 4 male; 5 female; 1 male or female for Glover.

Playing Time: 30 minutes.

Costumes: Captain, Glover and Turner are in uniform. Others wear casual dress. Mrs. Bellamy has knitting bag.

Properties: Headphones, paper.

Setting: The foredeck and wheel room of the *Enchantress*. The deck is triangular, with apex (bow) at center. Deck widens to right and left to back of stage, and has a railing to suggest deck of a boat. Entrances to deck are up right and left. A pole with blinking green light is down right and pole with blinking red is down left. Wheel room is a raised platform above deck up center, and is reached by short ladder at right. In wheel room are large spoked wheel, compass on waist-high stand and at left, a table with radio and radar equipment and chair.

Lighting: Offstage red lights, as indicated in text.

Sound: Offstage airplane motors, as indicated in text.

Dig That Mastodon!

---

*An average American family becomes nationwide news
when the bones of a prehistoric monster are uncovered in
their backyard . . . .*

Characters

DWIGHT REED
RUTH, *his wife*
BILLY, *their son, 10*
SHARON, *their daughter, 15*
CHARLIE, *photographer*
SALLY, *a reporter*
GUIDE
MR. POPPER
MISS UPDYKE
DR. RIGBY
PROFESSOR SLOANE
MR. SMITHERS
MRS. STRINGER
MISS FELLOWS
MISS THROCKMORTON
WESTERN UNION MESSENGER
TOURISTS, *male and female*

SETTING: *The living room of the Reed home.*
AT RISE: RUTH REED *is nervously pacing floor, occasionally
brushing back lock of hair from her forehead. Telephone
rings. She jumps nervously, then hurries to answer it.*

RUTH (*Into phone*): Hello . . . . Yes, this is Mr. Reed's home.
. . Dwight Reed, that's right . . . . Yes, my husband dug
up some old bones in the front yard yesterday, and a museum curator is coming today to look at them, but —
NBC-TV? . . . What? . . . You want to interview us for
NBC News? (SHARON *enters left, carrying a telegram.*) Well,
I knew it was in the local paper, but . . . you say it made
the United Press . . . No, you may not have a television
interview with him, not now, anyway . . . . Because he's in
the shower! Goodbye! (*She hangs up receiver angrily.*)
That's the fourth call this morning, Sharon.

SHARON (*Nodding*): Well, wait till you hear this telegram!
(*Reads telegram*) "Come to New York immediately. Have
spot for you and your family on the *Tonight* show. America
is waiting to hear about the fabulous prehistoric find of the
Reed family. Signed, Johnny Carson." Isn't that great?

RUTH: I suppose so, but I wish they'd stop saying prehistoric.
It makes me feel terribly old. (*Doorbell rings.*) Not again!
(*She crosses to door, right, and opens it.* WESTERN UNION
MESSENGER *enters, holding telegram.*) Not another telegram!

MESSENGER: Are you Mrs. Reed?

RUTH: No — I mean, yes — oh, I don't know who I am! (*He
gives her telegram and holds out pad and pencil.*)

MESSENGER: May I have your autograph? (RUTH *quickly signs
pad.*) I'll always cherish this, Mrs. Reed.

RUTH: You can find it on a dozen overdue charge accounts
in town.

MESSENGER: Do you think I could have Mr. Reed's autograph?

RUTH (*Walking away*): No. He's in the shower.

MESSENGER: Wow! Wait till I tell the guys at the office that I
was in Dwight Reed's house while he was taking a shower!
(*He rushes out right, leaving door open.* RUTH *opens telegram.*)

RUTH (*Reading*): "Accept no other offer. I have prime-time
spot for you Thursday on coast-to-coast TV. Will await your
reply. Signed, Merv Griffin."

SHARON: Merv Griffin? Johnny Carson? Why all this fuss over some old bones?

RUTH: I don't understand it, either, dear. (*Phone rings.*) There's that phone again.

BILLY (*Offstage*): It's O.K., Mom. I'll pick it up in the kitchen!

RUTH (*Calling offstage*): Thank you, Billy! (SALLY *and* CHARLIE *rush in.* CHARLIE *carries large camera with flash attachment and bag of photographic equipment. He begins to take flash pictures, as* SALLY *takes out pad and pencil and makes notes.*)

RUTH: Young lady, if you're selling anything —

SALLY: Oh, hi. I'm Sally Atherton — Associated Press. We're doing a syndicated story about the discovery of prehistoric bones on your property. (*To* CHARLIE) Be sure to get all the angles, Charlie.

CHARLIE: Check! (*Continues to take pictures*)

SALLY (*Sadly, to* RUTH): It's a shame you don't have a white couch. That's the most popular style in the average American home this year.

SHARON (*Glumly*): Oh, Mother, I told you we needed new furniture!

RUTH (*To* SALLY): If you'll just tell me what you want —

SALLY (*Enthusiastically*): I want an exclusive interview with the family who found the mastodon bones.

RUTH (*Puzzled*): Mastodon bones? We're not even certain what kind of bones my husband found. (GUIDE *and group of* TOURISTS *enter, excited, pushing* RUTH *and* SALLY *back against wall.* CHARLIE *takes closeup photo of* SHARON. *She looks at her clothes self-consciously, hurries off.*)

GUIDE: Right this way! (TOURISTS *mill around room, picking up lamps, books.* SALLY *takes notes furiously.*)

RUTH (*Protesting feebly*): Now, just a minute — (BILLY *enters, carrying several shovels, and wearing sandwich board sign reading,* DO-IT-YOURSELF SOUVENIRS. DIG YOUR OWN MASTODON BONES! *He tugs at* RUTH's *arm.*)

BILLY (*Happily*): Isn't it great, Mom? The tourists are here! (*To* TOURISTS, *in carnival barker style*) Ladies and gentlemen, step this way to the great prehistoric dig! (*Gestures right*) Get your free souvenirs. I have shovels for rent. Dig your own mastodon bones! (*Several* TOURISTS *turn toward* BILLY *with interest.* CHARLIE *takes* BILLY*'s picture.* BILLY *turns to* RUTH.) How am I doing, Mom?

RUTH (*Angrily*): Billy! Who are these people?

BILLY (*Shrugging*): All I know is that Tottingham's Terrific Tours called and said that a bunch of tourists wanted to visit our house. I guess they read in the paper about the bones Dad found. Anyway, I told the guide to bring them over.

RUTH (*Upset*): Oh, Billy, how could you? They'll have to leave at once!

BILLY (*Shaking his head*): If you say so, Mom — but you'll be sorry that you destroyed your son's initiative. I was going to rent these shovels to the tourists, so they could dig for bones.

RUTH (*With spirit*): Not in my flower beds! Now, put those shovels back.

BILLY: All right. (*Starts off right, then pauses and calls mischievously*) This way to the prehistoric dig, folks! (*He exits quickly and several* TOURISTS *follow him off right.* RUTH *shakes head wearily. More* TOURISTS *enter and* GUIDE *crosses center.*)

GUIDE (*Clearing his throat*): Step over here, folks. (*As* TOURISTS *gather around him, pushing* RUTH *aside*) Good. Now, in just a few minutes we're going to step outside to the actual site of this amazing prehistoric find. But first, I want you to imagine what it must have been like 20,000 years ago — when the mighty mastodon, an elephant-like creature with tusks fifteen feet long, was lord of the prehistoric world. (*DWIGHT REED enters center, in stocking feet, carrying his tie. He sees* TOURISTS, *does a double take.*)

DWIGHT (*Frantically*): Ruth! Ruth! (*He crosses downstage.*) What's going on here?

RUTH: I'm over here, dear! (*She pushes through* TOURISTS.)

GUIDE (*Gesturing*): . . . through the swamps and rain forests, seeking food. Yes, ladies and gentlemen, paleontologists have established that this lovely development, Shadydale Acres, was once the site of a prehistoric rain forest where mastodons roamed free. (*Takes postcards from pocket*) You can purchase a full-color postcard of the mastodon for the nominal sum of fifty cents, as a memento of your tour. (TOURISTS *push forward, buying postcards.* CHARLIE *photographs scene.* RUTH *finally reaches* DWIGHT.)

RUTH (*Disapprovingly*): Dwight, look at you! Where are your shoes?

DWIGHT (*Sputtering*): Never mind my shoes. Who are these people?

RUTH (*Helplessly*): You know how things have been since you found those bones under the patio.

DWIGHT (*Sputtering*): No, I don't know how things have been, and I don't have a patio. Remember? I was only digging the foundation for the patio when I found those confounded bones, and (*Sighing*) I haven't had a minute's peace since. (*He glances at his wristwatch.*) I'm late for my sales meeting with Mr. Smithers. He'll be furious!

RUTH (*Sighing*): I can't do anything about these people. They're from Tottingham's Tours.

DWIGHT: Tourists? You've got to be kidding.

RUTH: It's the truth. Billy gave them permission to bring the tourists here. (DWIGHT *rolls up his sleeves.*)

DWIGHT: Where's that kid?

RUTH: He's outside — renting shovels to the tourists. Everyone wants souvenirs.

DWIGHT (*Angrily*): I'll give him a souvenir!

RUTH: Please, Dwight! It's not really Billy's fault. It's just that people want to have a hero — and we're it!

GUIDE (*Excitedly*): Just a minute, ladies and gentlemen. (*Pointing to* DWIGHT) This must be Mr. Reed, the actual discoverer of the mastodon bones! (TOURISTS *turn and applaud enthusiastically, rushing over to* DWIGHT. TOURIST *grabs* DWIGHT*'s tie, and he pulls it away, furious.*)

DWIGHT (*Angrily, to* GUIDE): Now, look here. You'll have to get all of these people out of our house, right away. I'm late for work already.

GUIDE: Work? Oh, come now, Mr. Reed. A celebrity like you doesn't need to work!

DWIGHT: It'll be hard to feed my family on mastodon bones. Look, I have an important appointment with my boss, Mr. Smithers, and he's a stickler for punctuality.

RUTH: You see, Mr. Smithers owns Shadydale Acres, and he doesn't understand about mastodons . . . .

DWIGHT: I'll say! He's a regular slave driver.

SALLY (*Making notes*): Wow! What a story! I can see the headlines now! (*Dramatically*) "Mastodon Hero Tormented by Slave Driver."

DWIGHT: Wait a minute! You can't print that!

SALLY (*To* CHARLIE): Come on — maybe we can make the afternoon edition. (*They exit right.*)

GUIDE (*To* TOURISTS): Now, ladies and gentlemen, if you will follow me, we will visit the site on which the historic bones were first unearthed. (*He exits right, followed by* TOURISTS.)

RUTH (*Sinking into chair*): I hope you put those bones in a safe place. (DWIGHT *points to desk up right.*)

DWIGHT: They're locked in the desk until the paleontologists get here. (*Musing*) You know, I guess we are pretty important, at that.

RUTH: Don't get carried away, dear. We still don't know whether you found real mastodon bones or not.

DWIGHT: Well, they certainly look like the mastodon bones in

the book from the library. (*With pride*) Who knows? Mr.
Smithers might be proud of me, at that.

RUTH (*Dryly*): He won't be proud when he finds tourists digging up Shadydale Acres.

DWIGHT (*Happily*): Oh, I don't know. I'm his star salesman.
Maybe I can sell one of them a house.

BILLY (*Running in*): There's a TV truck outside with a newscaster! They're filming a story about us for the six o'clock
news. (*Heading toward exit*) I'd better go find some more
shovels. (*Exits*)

DWIGHT: Maybe they'll want to interview me.

RUTH: If they don't, Johnny Carson will. We got a telegram
from him this morning, asking us to go on his show. And
Merv Griffin wants us, too.

DWIGHT (*Excitedly*): Griffin? Carson? Wonderful! Terrific!
(*Worried*) I already have stage fright! (*He flops on sofa.
MR. POPPER and MISS UPDYKE enter right.*)

POPPER: Oh, I hope I'm here in time!

MISS UPDYKE: I heard about the Reeds first. This is *my* contract, Popper.

POPPER (*Icily*): What would your little company know about a
big business contract, Miss Updyke?

MISS UPDYKE: Male chauvinist!

POPPER: Female opportunist! (*They glare at each other.*)

RUTH: Just a minute. Who are you?

POPPER (*Bowing*): Popper is my name. Dog food is my game.
I represent the Bow-Wow Dog Food Company, the largest
in the country.

MISS UPDYKE: You mean the second largest. I am Gladys Updyke, of Peppy Pup Dog Food — and do I have news for
you!

RUTH: Dog food? We're not interested.

DWIGHT (*Standing*): We don't even own a dog.

POPPER: Oh, I don't want to sell you dog food. I want your endorsement, for our product.

MISS UPDYKE (*Insistently*): Peppy Pup wants your endorsement, too. Remember our famous slogan:
"Peppy Pup Food for your pet,
Bestest dog-gone meal treat yet!"

POPPER (*Condescendingly*): How corny! It's almost as revolting as the dog food you make!

RUTH: We're really not interested.

POPPER: But you can't afford to miss this opportunity.

DWIGHT: Why should we endorse dog food?

MISS UPDYKE: Why, what better endorsement for dog food than a testimonial from the owners of the world's largest bones?

POPPER: Bow-Wow wants the endorsement, and we're prepared to pay you well! I've already created a slogan — "Treat your mastiff to a mastodon meal."

MISS UPDYKE: I have a better proposition, Mr. Reed. Your family's picture will appear on every package of Peppy Pup.

POPPER: Bow-Wow will do better than that. We'll have you on every billboard in the nation, surrounded by a litter of Bow-Wow dog products.

DWIGHT: No, I'm afraid we won't endorse any dog food.

POPPER: Do you mean to tell me that you're going to jeopardize the entire dog food industry?

MISS UPDYKE: The makers of Peppy Pup are depending on you!

DWIGHT: I tell you I'm not interested in dog food! I only want to get ready for work.

RUTH: Please don't get so upset.

DWIGHT (*Frantically*): Look, Ruth, I'm late for my appointment with Mr. Smithers. Strangers are digging up my front lawn. My house is a shambles, and I've ruined the future of the dog food industry. (*Exploding*) Why shouldn't I be upset? (DR. RIGBY *and* PROFESSOR SLOANE *enter right.*)

DR. RIGBY: Stop! Don't sign anything!

PROFESSOR SLOANE (*Glaring at* POPPER): Just as I suspected! You probably wanted a dog food endorsement from these poor, unsuspecting people.

RIGBY (*Accusingly*): You did the same thing when they unearthed a triceratops in Trenton.

SLOANE: And I met you, Miss Updyke, when a brontosaurus was uncovered in Brooklyn. (SLOANE *turns to* DWIGHT.) How do you do? I am John Sloane from the Natural History Museum.

RIGBY: I am Miles Rigby, from the university paleontology department.

SLOANE (*Anxiously*): You didn't sign anything, did you?

RUTH: No, and we don't intend to.

POPPER: Bow-Wow never gives up. I'll be back.

MISS UPDYKE: Neither does Peppy Pup! We'll be back! (*They exit.*)

SLOANE: Those people are a menace! And now, Mr. Reed, if we may examine the alleged prehistoric discovery . . . .

DWIGHT (*Excitedly*): I'll be glad to show you the mastodon bones!

SLOANE: Don't be too hasty.

RIGBY (*Nodding*): The last so-called mastodon discovered near here turned out to be soup bones buried by a neighbor's dog. There's a great possibility that your bones may not be those of a mastodon.

DWIGHT (*Soberly*): I suppose you're right. I'll get the bones. (*Goes to desk, takes key out of pocket, unlocks desk drawer and takes out sack. He pulls two large bones out of sack, hands them to* SLOANE *and* RIGBY.)

SLOANE (*Taking magnifying glass from pocket*): Amazing!

(*Peers at bone through magnifying glass*) I'd say it's from the Jurassic period. (RIGBY *takes magnifying glass from his own pocket, grabs bone.*)

RIGBY (*Looking at bone*): My dear Sloane, one can easily see that it's not Jurassic at all — it's Cretaceous.

SLOANE (*Offended*): Jurassic!

RIGBY (*Heatedly*): Cretaceous!

SLOANE: You're a stubborn man, Rigby!

RIGBY: Are you questioning my authority, Sloane?

DWIGHT: Gentlemen, please! (*They turn, surprised, then relax.*)

SLOANE: I — I apologize. We were carried away.

RIGBY: It's the excitement of the discovery. These are definitely mastodon bones! (*He shakes* DWIGHT'*s hand.*) Young man, this is the paleontological find of the century! (DWIGHT *sinks onto sofa.*)

SLOANE: Rigby, when can you begin the excavation?

DWIGHT (*Alarmed*): You're not planning to dig any more, are you? Mr. Smithers won't approve.

RUTH: Oh, Dwight, he'll be furious!

DWIGHT (*Impatiently*): Well, it was your idea to build a patio!

RUTH: Yes, but I didn't think it would become a national event! (POPPER *and* MISS UPDYKE *enter right.*)

POPPER: The suspense is killing me! (*To* SLOANE) Have you examined the find?

MISS UPDYKE (*Reverently*): Look! The bones!

RIGBY: Yes, you can both relax. They are authentic mastodon bones. (POPPER *rushes to doorway, right, and shouts outside.*)

POPPER: Listen, everyone! They really are mastodon bones! (*Sound of wild cheering is heard from offstage.* GUIDE *and* TOURISTS *rush in.* DWIGHT *quickly puts bones into sack and holds it tightly.* SALLY *and* CHARLIE *enter, and* CHARLIE *begins to take pictures.* TOURISTS *start to take pillows, lamp shades, etc.*)

RIGBY: Come, Sloane. We'll prepare for the dig. (RIGBY *and* SLOANE *exit.*)

TOURISTS (*Ad lib*): A dig! Wonderful! Where's that kid with the shovels? (*Etc. They exit, followed by* GUIDE.)

POPPER (*To* DWIGHT): Bow-Wow will pay any price for your endorsement!

DWIGHT (*Wearily*): I'm too confused to think about it now. (*To* RUTH) Let's have some coffee before I leave for work. (RUTH *nods, takes his arm. He puts down sack of bones. They exit center.*)

MISS UPDYKE: You'd better be careful, Popper, or I'll report you to the Better Business Bureau for unethical business practices! (*They glare at each other, then exit right.*)

SALLY (*To* CHARLIE): You'd better get outside with the camera and photograph the dig. (*He exits.* SALLY *begins writing as* MR. SMITHERS *enters right.*)

SMITHERS (*Furiously*): What's going on here?

SALLY: You must be one of the tourists. (*Points right*) The dig's outside.

SMITHERS (*Indignantly*): I am not a tourist! I am Virgil E. Smithers, Mr. Reed's employer. My company, Merry Mortgage, owns Shadydale Acres. Where's Reed?

SALLY: Why, haven't you heard about the mastodon?

SMITHERS: Of course I've heard about the mastodon. Everybody's heard about it. It's been in all the papers.

SALLY: Then you must be very proud of Mr. Reed.

SMITHERS (*Exploding*): Proud? I'm ready to crown him. I worked for years to develop Shadydale Acres, and what happens? (*Points right*) Grown men and women groveling on the ground, muttering about old bones, digging unsightly pits. The Shadydale image has been ruined by Dwight Reed. (*Making a fist*) Wait till I get my hands on him!

SALLY: Mr. Reed is right about you. You're an overbearing old slave driver!

SMITHERS (*Shocked*): How dare you!

SALLY: Well, it's true, even though he didn't say it exactly like that.

SMITHERS (*Roaring*): I demand to see Dwight Reed at once!

SALLY (*Nervously*): I — I'd better get him. I'll be right back. (*She exits center. SMITHERS angrily paces floor. SLOANE and RIGBY re-enter. SLOANE rushes forward, picks up sack containing bones.*)

SLOANE (*Relieved*): Thank goodness it's safe! We left this priceless treasure unguarded.

RIGBY: You'd better give it to me, Sloane. The mastodon rightfully belongs to the state university. (*He takes sack from SLOANE.*)

SLOANE: It belongs to the museum! (*He grabs the sack from RIGBY.*)

RIGBY: The very idea! Give me that mastodon!

SLOANE: Over my dead body!

RIGBY: Thanks for the suggestion!

SMITHERS: Gentlemen!

SLOANE (*Seeing SMITHERS*): Oh-oh. Rigby, I knew we should have hired a guard.

RIGBY: You're right. This fellow looks like a criminal type to me.

SMITHERS: I'm Virgil Smithers, the owner of Shadydale Acres. You two are behaving more like criminals than I am! (*Curiously*) Tell me, why are you so interested in those foolish bones? Are they valuable?

SLOANE (*Surprised*): Valuable? Why, they're worth a fortune — this whole site is.

SMITHERS: Oh? I guess that Shadydale Acres will be worth a tidy amount, then.

RIGBY: Money couldn't buy this place.

SLOANE: Could you buy the Taj Mahal?

RIGBY: Or the Leaning Tower of Pisa?

SMITHERS (*Happily*): Wonderful! Why, thanks to Dwight Reed,

Shadydale Acres is priceless! (DWIGHT, RUTH *and* SALLY *enter center.* DWIGHT *now wears shoes, tie, jacket.*)

DWIGHT (*Nervously*): Mr. Smithers, if you'll only let me explain —

SMITHERS (*Beaming*): Dwight, my boy! (*He thumps* DWIGHT *on back.*) The Merry Mortgage Company is proud of you.

DWIGHT (*Quickly*): I knew you'd be angry, but I'll forget all about the mastodon, and (*He shakes head in disbelief.*) — You're proud of me? And you're not angry?

SMITHERS: Angry? Nonsense! I love mastodons! Those sweet, furry little creatures.

RIGBY: A full-grown mastodon weighed ten tons.

SMITHERS (*Quickly*): Oh, there's nothing like a big pet around the house! (*To* DWIGHT) Come, my boy! We'll begin our campaign at once. We'll double — triple — the asking price for Shadydale home sites. (*Gleefully*) Every site complete with its own mastodon! (*Sound of a drum is heard offstage.* MRS. STRINGER, MISS FELLOWS, *and* MISS THROCKMORTON *march in, right.* MISS FELLOWS *is beating a bass drum which hangs around her neck.* MRS. STRINGER *and* MISS THROCKMORTON *carry signs reading* ENVIRONMENT NOW! SALLY *takes notes.* MISS FELLOWS *stops drumming.*)

MRS. STRINGER (*Angrily*): Where is Dwight Reed?

DWIGHT: I'm Dwight Reed.

MRS. STRINGER: Destroyer of the environment!

MISS FELLOWS: Polluter of rivers!

MISS THROCKMORTON: Desecrator of the natural soil!

SMITHERS: Ladies — calm yourselves! I am Virgil Smithers, and I own Shadydale Acres.

MRS. STRINGER: Then you're the real culprit! (MISS FELLOWS *hits him on the head with a drumstick.*)

MISS FELLOWS: You are a discredit to the human race!

MISS THROCKMORTON: You have destroyed the natural beauty of nature.

MISS STRINGER: Think of all the children in India.

DWIGHT: There must be some mistake.

MRS. STRINGER: Mistake, indeed! I am Mrs. Stringer, head of the local chapter of Save the World!

MISS FELLOWS: And I am Miss Fellows, chairwoman of the S.P.C.M. — Society for the Prevention of Cruelty to Mastodons!

MISS THROCKMORTON (*Haughtily*): I am Miss Throckmorton — and we are here to save humanity.

MRS. STRINGER: Think of all these natural resources — being destroyed!

MISS FELLOWS: It wasn't bad enough that you built all these houses. Now you want to disturb the final resting place of our first citizen (*Solemnly*) — the mastodon!

MISS THROCKMORTON (*Valiantly*): We'll take our case to the Supreme Court!

RUTH: Ladies, I'm sure there's some misunderstanding. My husband only wanted to build a patio, a little place to relax with his family in the great outdoors, and he unearthed the mastodon bones by accident. We're firm believers in the environment. Didn't you see my garden?

MRS. STRINGER (*Softening*): Yes — it's lovely.

MISS FELLOWS: Marigolds are my favorite flower.

MISS THROCKMORTON: But what are you going to do about the mastodon? Those people are destroying the topsoil, digging for old bones.

DWIGHT (*Firmly*): That will end, Miss Throckmorton. There'll be no more digs in Shadydale Acres.

RIGBY: No more digs?

SLOANE: No more paleontological finds?

SALLY: What a story!

SMITHERS: Have you lost your mind, Reed?

DWIGHT: No, Mr. Smithers. I think I've regained my senses. I may have been a national celebrity for a day, but from now on I'll stick to selling homes to families who want to put roots in the ground. I guess that's all I'll ever contribute to humanity. (*Picks up sack, offers it to* RIGBY *and* SLOANE) There are several mastodon bones here. Divide them between the museum and the state university. I guess that'll make everybody happy. (POPPER *rushes in.*)

POPPER (*Pointing right*): Everyone's leaving! That confounded guide made an announcement, and all the tourists got on the bus and left. There's no one outside — no one! (BILLY *enters, dejectedly.*)

DWIGHT: What's the matter, Billy?

BILLY: Aw, it's that T.V. truck.

SALLY: The television truck?

BILLY (*Nodding*): Yes. The reporter got a message that a man building a garage over in Hector County uncovered some kind of skeleton. They said it might be a stegosaurus.

SLOANE (*Stunned*): A stegosaurus?

RIGBY (*Excited*): A stegosaurus is fifty million years old. It predates the mastodon!

SLOANE: We must get to Hector County at once! It's only twenty miles away.

RIGBY: To the dig! (*They exit.*)

SALLY: What a story! Stegosaurus, here I come! (*She exits right.*)

MRS. STRINGER: An outrage! Ladies, we will march on Hector County.

MISS THROCKMORTON: As chairwoman of the S.P.S.S. — Society for the Prevention of Cruelty to the Stegosaurus — I will stop this fiendish attack on the environment! (*The ladies march off,* MISS FELLOWS *beating the drum.*)

RUTH (*Shaking head*): Oh, Dwight! We're almost back to normal again.

DWIGHT: It's the best feeling I've had all day.

SMITHERS: We may not have national publicity anymore, but I still think we have the best property in the state. Dwight, thanks to you, everyone knows about Shadydale Acres. I'll see you in the office in half an hour — and you'd better have some good ideas for our new sales program! (*He exits.*)

RUTH: Mr. Popper, aren't you going to leave? I'm sure you're interested in stegosaurus bones.

POPPER: Oh, Miss Updyke can have that account. I like the sincerity of the Reed family. (*Grins*) Popper is the name. Dog food is my game. (*Takes contract out of pocket*) I'd still like your endorsement, and I have a contract to prove it. Bow-Wow will pay you five thousand dollars.

RUTH (*Happily*): Five thousand dollars? Oh, Dwight! We can finish the patio, after all.

DWIGHT: And maybe there'll be enough left over for a new workshop. (SHARON *re-enters, center. She has changed her clothes.*)

POPPER (*Delighted*): Oh, that young lady will look wonderful, simply wonderful, on a box of Bow-Wow Dog Biscuits! (*He exits.*)

SHARON: Where's the camera? The reporter? The TV crew?

BILLY: Everybody's gone.

DWIGHT: A stegosaurus just thundered into our lives, and the Reed family is happily forgotten.

RUTH (*Smiling*): It was fun while it lasted. New York! Hollywood! Johnny Carson — Merv Griffin! (WESTERN UNION MESSENGER *enters with telegram.*)

MESSENGER: Telegram for Mr. Dwight Reed. (MESSENGER *stifles a yawn.* DWIGHT *takes telegram, reads aloud.*)

DWIGHT: "Previous commitment will not permit your appearance on program. Stop. Mastodon show canceled. Stop. Entire Tonight show crew en route to Hector County. Stop. A stegosaurus is more important than a mastodon. Signed, Johnny Carson."

RUTH (*Happily*): Wonderful! (MESSENGER *hands* RUTH *a slip of paper.*)

MESSENGER: I just applied for a transfer to Hector County, Mrs. Reed. I guess I won't need your autograph, after all. (*He exits.*)

SHARON: Oh, Mother, how disappointing!

RUTH: Cheer up. After all, my autograph is still famous on the charge accounts, and they'll all be coming in the first of the month. (DWIGHT *raises his right hand.*)

DWIGHT: I'm taking an oath here and now. There'll be no more digs for this family.

RUTH: I don't agree.

DWIGHT (*Puzzled*): What?

RUTH (*Warmly*): I'll always dig (*Beaming*) the best husband in the world! (RUTH *gives* DWIGHT *quick hug as curtains close.*)

THE END

Production Notes

Dig That Mastodon!

Characters: 5 male; 7 female; 4 male or female for guide, Dr. Rigby, Professor Sloane, messenger; extras for Tourists.

Playing Time: 35 minutes.

Costumes: Modern, everyday dress. Dwight is in shirt, trousers, and stocking feet. He later changes to business suit, shoes, tie, etc. Sharon first wears casual skirt and sweater, re-enters later in a different outfit. Western Union Messenger wears a uniform.

Properties: Telegrams, pads and pencils, sandwich board sign reading DO-IT-YOURSELF SOUVENIRS, shovels, bag containing several large bones, flash camera and bag of photographic equipment, postcards, contract, keys, magnifying glasses, bass drum and drum stick, two signs reading ENVIRONMENT NOW.

Setting: The living room of the Dwight Reed home. There is a sofa downstage, with an end table beside it holding a telephone and lamp. Upstage there is a desk, with a locked drawer. There are other chairs, tables, lamps, etc., around the room. Exit up right leads outside; center exit leads to upstairs rooms; and left exit leads to kitchen.

Lighting: No special effects.

Sound: Telephone and doorbell, as indicated in text.

The Third Richest Man
in the World

---

*An eccentric billionaire with a mania for privacy be-
comes the target for two newspaper reporters, who are
after the story of a lifetime . . . .*

Characters

BOB HOLLAND
MARGE AMES
EFFINGHAM ELLSWORTH
TOM ALLISON, *his bodyguard*
TWO GUARDS
MISS DUDLEY, *secretary*
NURSE
DOCTOR
MISS FARRELL
MARY ELLSWORTH
ALICE BOND
MAID

TIME: *Morning, the present.*
SETTING: *Living room of a suite in a New York City hotel.*
AT RISE: TOM ALLISON, *a bodyguard, enters left. He wears
dark uniform and has gun in holster. He yawns, stretches,
walks up center and pulls open drapes. Light streams into
room, as if from sun. New York skyscrapers are seen*

through window. MISS DUDLEY *enters right, carrying steno pad and pencil. At sight of window she gasps, drops pad and pencil on desk, and rushes to window to close drapes.*

ALLISON (*Startled*): Who's there? Oh, it's you, Miss Dudley.

MISS DUDLEY (*Tartly*): It's evident that you've been in the employ of Effingham Ellsworth for only one week. I would have you dismissed immediately if it weren't for that!

ALLISON: Dismissed? What's wrong?

MISS DUDLEY: Mr. Ellsworth has a strong aversion to sunlight. (*As she speaks, she turns off several table lamps in room. She crosses to desk, right, pushes intercom button impatiently.* TWO GUARDS *rush in right, guns drawn.*)

1ST GUARD: Is something wrong, Miss Dudley?

2ND GUARD (*Glancing around*): What's the trouble?

MISS DUDLEY (*Crisply*): The trouble is that the newest member of our organization, one of Mr. Ellsworth's personal bodyguards, does not understand the standing orders against sunlight. It was your duty to acquaint Allison with Mr. Ellsworth's specific requests.

1ST GUARD (*Lamely*): Sorry, Miss Dudley.

2ND GUARD: We forgot.

MISS DUDLEY (*Storming*): You forgot! Mr. Ellsworth will not tolerate forgetfulness or insubordination by any member of his staff. (*She claps hands.*) Check every window on the floor immediately. Make certain that the blinds are closed.

1ST GUARD: Yes, Miss Dudley.

MISS DUDLEY: And it is especially important that no strangers are admitted to this suite. Is that perfectly clear?

2ND GUARD: Yes, Miss Dudley. (*She waves her hand.* GUARDS *rush off.*)

ALLISON: I'm sorry about the sunlight, Miss Dudley. This is my first trip to New York, and I wanted to see the city.

MISS DUDLEY: You were not hired to conduct a sightseeing tour. You were hired to be personal bodyguard for Effingham Ellsworth, the third richest man in the world!

ALLISON (*Shaking head*): I hope the first two richest men are happier.

MISS DUDLEY (*Shocked*): Mr. Allison! (*Counting on fingers*) Effingham Ellsworth controls the oil industry, the automobile industry, the motion picture empire, international airline and steamship companies, and many, many other interests.

ALLISON: All that money — and we have to make telephone calls from a phone booth!

MISS DUDLEY: That's only because Mr. Ellsworth is a fanatic on the subject of hygiene. No one ever uses his personal telephones — here at the Royal Arms Hotel or at his estate.

ALLISON: Why did we come here, anyway?

MISS DUDLEY: Such questions! If you must know, Mr. Ellsworth is leaving for Europe tomorrow on extremely important business. (*Scornfully*) Does that satisfy your curiosity?

ALLISON: I guess so. I understand he's been around the world many times. But drawn curtains — dim lamps — never leaving the hotel — this life is a prison!

MISS DUDLEY: Mr. Ellsworth demands complete seclusion, and he expects all members of his staff to cooperate. (*She glances at watch.*) It's ten o'clock. Mr. Ellsworth wishes to be awakened at precisely 10:04. You'd better attend to it.

ALLISON: Yes, Miss Dudley. (*He exits left.* MISS DUDLEY *crosses to door right, snaps fingers.*)

MISS DUDLEY (*Calling*): Come in at once, all of you! There's no time to waste. (BOB, MARGE *and* MAID *enter.*) Now, I believe that the hotel manager has outlined your duties. (*To* MAID) You are to be on duty continuously during Mr. Ellsworth's stay at the Royal Arms.

MAID: Yes, ma'am. It is an honor to serve Mr. Ellsworth.

MISS DUDLEY: The housekeeper has told you Mr. Ellsworth's requirements. Please see that they are followed without fail.

MAID: Yes, ma'am. (MISS DUDLEY *turns to* MARGE.)

MISS DUDLEY: You're new. I don't remember you from our last visit.

MARGE: The woman who acted as your secretarial assistant last year is ill. I've been assigned to take her place. My name is Marge Ames.

MISS DUDLEY: Have you been cleared by the E.I.C.?

MARGE (*Brightly*): The Ellsworth Investigating Committee? Oh, yes! (*She takes papers from pocket and hands them to* MISS DUDLEY, *who examines them and nods. She returns papers to* MARGE.)

MISS DUDLEY: Very well. Fortunately, I'll only require your services for the day. (*She turns to* BOB.) You will check all the telephones on this floor.

BOB: Yes, ma'am. The name's Bob Holland.

MISS DUDLEY: Very well, Mr. Holland. (*She takes paper from desk.*) Here is a blueprint of all the telephone lines in this suite. They must all be in perfect working order at all times. (*She hands paper to* BOB.) We are particularly interested in lines A, B and C at these points. Line A is Mr. Ellsworth's direct wire to Washington, D.C. Line B is a hot line to the U.S. Embassy in London. And Line C is — well, that is so confidential I can't disclose it, but the line must be ready for instant service.

BOB: Yes, ma'am.

MISS DUDLEY: Please study the blueprint carefully. There must be no margin for error in Mr. Ellsworth's communication system. (BOB *continues to study blueprint.* MISS DUDLEY *addresses* MAID.) Come with me, please. (*To* MARGE) Miss Ames, I will return shortly. I have a great deal of dictation for you. (MISS DUDLEY *and* MAID *exit right.*)

MARGE (*Turning to* BOB; *excitedly*): Bob, we made it! We really made it!

BOB (*Shaking head*): I can't believe it. A couple of City College seniors standing at a desk in Effingham Ellsworth's private hotel suite. Why, this place is surrounded by a small army of Ellsworth's guards.

MARGE: Imagine! We're going to get an exclusive story about

Effingham Ellsworth, the third richest man in the world! There isn't a newspaperman in the country who's been able to do it. (*Holding up pendant she is wearing*) My secret camera is ready for action. All I have to do is press this concealed shutter — and I'll have Ellsworth's picture!

BOB (*Glancing around*): The light is miserable in here. I hope you remembered to load the camera with infrared film for indoor shots.

MARGE (*Panicky*): I forgot about Ellsworth's light phobia! I brought regular film.

BOB (*Slapping forehead*): Great! There go our pictures for the exclusive college newspaper story. (*He indicates tool holster on his belt.*) At least the tape recorder is working perfectly. You know, I paid the regular lineman one hundred bucks to let me take his place today. (*Glumly*) And you forgot the infrared film!

MARGE: It's too late to do anything about it now. (*She crosses to window, opens drapes several inches.*) This light'll be better than nothing.

BOB: You can't do that! Ellsworth will see that light right away. Those guards have guns, you know!

MARGE: I know, I know! I'm so scared I'm shaking. But isn't getting the story of a lifetime worth the risk?

BOB: I guess so. But, Marge, you used forged credentials to get in here. What are you going to do if the real secretary turns up?

MARGE: I thought of that. I got her name from the telephone book and called her. I said that I was Mr. Ellsworth's private secretary and her services wouldn't be required until *tomorrow* morning.

BOB: You really thought of everything! Even reading up on Ellsworth to find out about that investigating committee.

MARGE (*Nodding*): If we're lucky, we'll have material for our article before we're discovered.

BOB (*Nervously*): And if we're unlucky . . .

MARGE: I wonder if Ellsworth is as terrible as all those stories we've heard?

BOB: That's what we're here to find out. (BOB *and* MARGE *jump to attention as* MISS DUDLEY, NURSE, DOCTOR *and* TWO GUARDS *enter right.* GUARDS *take stations at either side of entrance, hands poised above their holsters.* NURSE *carries an aerosol can.*)

MISS DUDLEY: Mr. Ellsworth will arrive in exactly one and one-half minutes. (*To* DOCTOR) Have you examined all the hotel personnel?

DOCTOR: Yes, Miss Dudley. Everyone has a clean bill of health.

MISS DUDLEY: Good! (*Turns*) Nurse, please disinfect the room. (NURSE *sprays room. To* BOB) Hygienic precautions are extremely important to Mr. Ellsworth. You will find disinfectant cans at strategic places throughout the suite. Spray every telephone with disinfectant as soon as you have ascertained that it is in working order. And remember not to cough or smoke in Mr. Ellsworth's presence.

BOB: I'll try not to breathe, ma'am. (*Door left opens. Everyone snaps to attention.* EFFINGHAM ELLSWORTH *enters. He wears dark glasses.* MARGE, *standing in his path, touches pendant.* ELLSWORTH *sidles away.*)

ELLSWORTH (*Coldly*): No bodily contact, please. (*To* MISS DUDLEY) Do these people have medical certificates?

MISS DUDLEY (*Nodding*): Yes. They were examined by the doctor before coming to the suite.

DOCTOR: Everything's in order, Mr. Ellsworth. (MISS DUDLEY *waves hand in dismissal.* NURSE, DOCTOR *and* GUARDS *exit right.*)

ELLSWORTH: Are the contracts ready for signature, Miss Dudley? (*She rushes to desk, holds up contracts.*)

MISS DUDLEY: Yes, Mr. Ellsworth. The Nu-Tire Amalgamation, the Lester Industries, and Hercules Farm Equipment.

It will take forty-three seconds to sign the contracts. (BOB *touches tool holster on belt.*)

ELLSWORTH (*Sharply*): Thirty-three seconds, Miss Dudley. (*He sits at desk, begins to sign contracts.*)

MISS DUDLEY: Thirty-three seconds. A time-conscious employee is a good employee. (*To* BOB) Did you check lines A, B, and C?

BOB (*Nodding*): All lines are A-O.K.

MISS DUDLEY: Very well. You must check Mr. Ellsworth's private hotel wire in a few minutes. (*She points to phone on desk.* ELLSWORTH *finishes signing contracts. He looks up, sees partially open drapes, gasps, and rises, covering his eyes.*)

ELLSWORTH (*Hoarsely*): That drapery! Close that drapery! (MISS DUDLEY *rushes upstage, closes drapes.*)

MISS DUDLEY: Such carelessness! (*To* MARGE) Did you open that drape?

MARGE (*Innocently*): Oh, no, Miss Dudley, but I might have brushed against it.

ELLSWORTH: Who is that girl? Dismiss her at once.

MISS DUDLEY: Her papers are in order, sir. She's highly recommended.

ELLSWORTH (*Angrily*): Silence! I must get a stronger pair of sunglasses. Miss Dudley, come with me. (ELLSWORTH *and* MISS DUDLEY *exit left.* BOB *sags weakly against desk.*)

BOB: You almost gave the show away that time.

MARGE (*Determined*): I don't care! I had to get my pictures! (*Pauses*) Everyone is right, Bob. Ellsworth is a strange man.

BOB: You can't be sure. A good reporter doesn't jump to conclusions, you know.

MARGE: You sound like my professor!

BOB: Well, you'd better make yourself scarce. Ellsworth will skin you alive when he returns.

MARGE (*Stubbornly*): I'm not leaving! This story might win

me a graduate scholarship. It means everything to me. (*She crosses to desk, picks up notepad.*) Miss Dudley's notepad. Ellsworth has three appointments this morning.

BOB: What? He never grants interviews!

MARGE: He's going to see these people. They must be pretty important. (*Reading*) Evelyn Farrell, City Hospital. Mary Ellsworth. Alice Bond.

BOB: Mary Ellsworth? Do you suppose she's a relative?

MARGE: Probably. How about the other names. Evelyn Farrell? Alice Bond? I don't recognize them.

BOB: Ellsworth has refused to meet prime ministers, presidents, kings. Why are these three people so important?

MARGE (*Mysteriously*): They must represent Ellsworth's secret past.

BOB: Don't be melodramatic! Still, this might furnish the angle we need for our story.

MARGE (*Excitedly*): And I can get exclusive pictures!

BOB: How are we going to hear the interviews, though? I have to check lines A,B, and C!

MARGE: I'm Miss Dudley's assistant. I'm going to be here when those women arrive.

BOB: Nonsense! Miss Dudley will never permit it.

MARGE (*Solemnly*): We'll have to get rid of her.

BOB: Look! I'm already involved in bribery and forgery. Murder's something else!

MARGE: I didn't mean murder. I just meant some way to get her out of the hotel for the next hour. (*She puts notepad back on desk.* MISS DUDLEY *enters left.*)

MISS DUDLEY (*Annoyed; to* BOB): You must check the Washington line at once. The Senior Senator from Maine just informed the hotel manager that he had difficulty placing a call. And Miss Ames! (*She crosses to desk, picks up contracts.*) We need Xerox copies of these contracts immediately. (*She claps hands.*) Come, come, both of you! There's so much to be done. (*Desk phone rings.* MARGE *quickly nudges* MISS DUDLEY *aside, answers phone.* MISS DUDLEY, *glares, furious.*)

MARGE (*On phone*): Yes, this is Mr. Ellsworth's suite . . . . I see — I see. . . . Yes, immediately. (MISS DUDLEY *reaches for phone, but* MARGE *backs away.*) Well, I don't know. Miss Dudley's terribly busy . . . . Perhaps it can be arranged. . . . Yes, yes, I'll tell her. (*She covers mouthpiece.*) Miss Dudley, this is Mr. Hagstrom from the Benson Art Gallery.

MISS DUDLEY (*Angrily*): I have the sole authority to answer Mr. Ellsworth's phone.

MARGE: But Mr. Hagstrom's in a dreadful hurry. He's catching a plane at noon. He has a Corot for Mr. Ellsworth's collection!

MISS DUDLEY: Not the "Milldam on the Thames"? Mr. Ellsworth's been trying to buy the "Milldam" for years!

MARGE (*Quickly*): That's the name he mentioned. He said it just came on the market. He wants you at the art gallery immediately. There are three interested buyers.

MISS DUDLEY (*Shocked*): Impossible! I can't leave now.

MARGE (*Shrugging*): I'm sure Mr. Ellsworth will be terribly unhappy if he misses this opportunity.

MISS DUDLEY: You may be right. Give me that phone! (MISS DUDLEY *grabs receiver, jiggles cradle, then slams receiver on cradle.*) The line is dead!

MARGE: The art gallery's on 57th Street. You could be there in fifteen minutes.

MISS DUDLEY (*Perplexed*): But Mr. Ellsworth is expecting visitors this morning.

MARGE: I'll be glad to help. I can take notes and have them transcribed by the time you return.

MISS DUDLEY: That's impossible. You're a stranger! Mr. Ellsworth wouldn't permit you to attend his private meetings.

MARGE (*Persuasively*): He might consider it — in view of the Corot.

MISS DUDLEY: You might be right. (*Suddenly*) I'll leave for the art gallery immediately. (*Warily*) I'm relying on your efficiency, Miss Ames.

MARGE: Leave everything to me. (MISS DUDLEY *exits right.* BOB *shakes his head.*)

BOB: You wanted to get rid of her, Marge. That art gallery call was timed perfectly.

MARGE: What art gallery? The call was from the hotel manager. Mr. Ellsworth's guests are on their way up. I waited until the manager hung up, and then I improvised that art gallery speech.

BOB: That was fast thinking.

MARGE: I'll stop at nothing! (*She pushes him toward right exit.*) Fix that A line. Washington, D.C., is waiting! (BOB *exits.* MARGE *arranges paper and pencils on desk. She picks up three sealed envelopes. Reading*) Evelyn Farrell — Mary Ellsworth — Alice Bond. An envelope for each visitor! I wonder . . . (*She walks to lamp, holds one of the envelopes in front of light.*) It's no use. I can't see a thing. (*She taps envelopes against her hand.*) Miss Dudley must have left these envelopes for the visitors. If I could open one and reseal it . . . . (*She walks to desk, picks up letter opener.* ELLSWORTH *enters left.* MARGE *does not notice him. He crosses to stand behind her.*)

ELLSWORTH: What are you doing?

MARGE (*Startled*): Oh! (*Quickly*) I — I was sorting your mail. I thought I'd open these letters and —

ELLSWORTH: It is quite evident that those letters are not addressed to me.

MARGE: I'm terribly sorry. I didn't realize —

ELLSWORTH: I dictated those letters to Miss Dudley yesterday afternoon. I will deliver them personally this morning. (MARGE *drops letters and letter opener on desk.*)

MARGE: I should have read the names. (*Quickly*) I'm Marge

Ames. Miss Dudley asked me to sort your mail, and I was only trying to help.

ELLSWORTH (*Sharply*): Where is Miss Dudley?

MARGE: She left me in charge of your clerical duties, sir. She's gone out.

ELLSWORTH (*In disbelief*): Miss Dudley left the hotel without my permission?

MARGE: She — she didn't have time to tell you. A Corot has just come on the market. "The Milldam on the Thames"!

ELLSWORTH (*Delighted*): The "Milldam"?

MARGE: Yes. Miss Dudley couldn't overlook the opportunity to try to get it for you.

ELLSWORTH: A Corot? A new Corot? Yes, it will be perfect for my collection.

MARGE: She'll be back shortly. I can take notes until she returns. Remember, my credentials have been cleared by E.I.C.

ELLSWORTH (*Grudgingly*): Well, I was prepared to cancel my morning engagements, but they are important.

MARGE (*Brightly*): The three callers are here now. I told the hotel manager to have them wait outside.

ELLSWORTH: Very well. I'll see them. (*He walks to desk, sits, picks up envelopes and stares thoughtfully at them.*) Send in Miss Farrell first.

MARGE: Yes, sir. The lady from City Hospital.

ELLSWORTH (*Quickly*): How did you know that?

MARGE: Oh — oh, Miss Dudley showed me the list of your appointments before she left.

ELLSWORTH: Yes, Miss Dudley would think of that. (MARGE *goes off right and re-enters with* MISS FARRELL. MARGE *offers her a chair near desk, sits in another chair and takes notes throughout the interview.*)

MISS FARRELL (*To* ELLSWORTH): It's so good of you to see me,

Mr. Ellsworth. I'm Evelyn Farrell, from the economic planning board of City Hospital.

ELLSWORTH: I am an extremely busy man, Miss Farrell. Please confine your remarks to four minutes. (*He glances at his watch.*)

MISS FARRELL: The board held an emergency meeting at the hospital, and all the members agreed that I should see you during your New York visit. That is, everyone except our chairman, a man I've never met.

ELLSWORTH (*Waving his hand*): Spare the preliminary details. What is your business?

MISS FARRELL: The business of most hospitals, I'm afraid. We're building a new addition, and we are soliciting contributions from private citizens.

ELLSWORTH (*Curtly*): Wealthy citizens, you mean.

MISS FARRELL: Well, we don't like to think of ourselves as a mercenary group, but you are one of the world's richest men.

ELLSWORTH: Yes, the third richest man, to be precise. Miss Farrell, Ellsworth Enterprises controls my charitable donations. I do not concern myself personally with such matters.

MISS FARRELL: But I would like your personal assurance of a contribution.

ELLSWORTH: Never! Your request is completely unreasonable.

MISS FARRELL: I hardly feel that requesting help for the sick and needy could be called unreasonable.

ELLSWORTH: You may have your definition, Miss Farrell, and I will have mine. (*Stands*) Good day, Miss Farrell. I don't see any reason to continue this interview. (MISS FARRELL *stands.* ELLSWORTH *hands her one of the sealed envelopes.*) I believe the contents of this envelope will explain many things. You may read it at your convenience.

MISS FARRELL: Thank you for your time, Mr. Ellsworth. I can

give the board the complete details of our interview — but there's one thing.

ELLSWORTH: Yes?

MISS FARRELL: I don't know what to tell the people who need our help. (*She exits.* ELLSWORTH *shrugs.*)

ELLSWORTH: Everyone has a cause these days.

MARGE (*Impatiently*): It was such a worthy cause. I have no right to say that, but an addition for the hospital —

ELLSWORTH (*Coldly*): It is evident that you know little about my methods. You must understand the situation before passing judgment.

MARGE: I'm sorry, Mr. Ellsworth. (*He glances at watch.*)

ELLSWORTH: Show in my next visitor, if you please. Mary Ellsworth.

MARGE: Yes, Mr. Ellsworth. (*She exits and immediately re-enters with* MARY ELLSWORTH, *who crosses toward* ELLSWORTH, *smiling and extending her hand.*)

MARY: Effingham! Oh, it's so good to see you again. (*He draws away from her.*) Oh — I forgot. No bodily contacts. (*She sits in chair by desk.*)

ELLSWORTH (*Musing*): Let me see. Is it four or five years since I've seen you and Bruce?

MARY: Almost five years.

ELLSWORTH: You're looking well. Whatever my brother lacked in business judgment, he compensated for in the choice of an attractive wife.

MARY: Please, Eff, don't hold Bruce's failure against him.

ELLSWORTH: Why not? Bruce always did what he wanted — at the expense of everyone else. After all, he was the first Ellsworth to enter the world of commerce and industry.

MARY: Bruce always wanted to help you, but you were always so independent, so —

ELLSWORTH (*Quickly*): Obstinate? (*Angrily*) Enough! I was left with the sole responsibility for our parents while he foundered in the business world. He did not care for my ambition — for the things I wanted. (*He sits back, reflects.*) That's all changed now. My empire is flourishing while Bruce faces financial disaster.

MARY: Bruce is ruined, Eff! He put his money, all his holdings, into the manufacture of a new turbine engine. It failed.

ELLSWORTH (*Coldly*): How foolish! He should have diversified his investments.

MARY: Bruce still believes in the turbine. He knows it has great potential, but he has no money left to invest in it.

ELLSWORTH: Frustrating, but the situation hardly interests me. I have bought a company that holds a patent on a turbine. If I were to help Bruce, I would be competing with my own interests.

MARY: Please, Eff! If Bruce fails now, it will kill him! (*She sobs.*)

ELLSWORTH: No hysterics, please. I suggest that Bruce have patience. Perhaps something favorable will develop.

MARY (*Brokenly*): There isn't time. Bruce's creditors are threatening foreclosure. (MARGE *clears her throat.* ELLSWORTH *glares at her.*)

ELLSWORTH (*To* MARGE): Is something wrong, Miss Ames?

MARGE: No, no. I'm sorry.

ELLSWORTH: Did you wish to say something?

MARGE: I have no right, I know, but (*Boldly*) your brother — this is his life's work! Something should be done! Someone should help him. (ELLSWORTH *pounds on desk and rises, upsetting his chair.*)

ELLSWORTH (*Furious*): You shouldn't have come to me at all, Mary. My clerk is evidently an expert in such matters. You should have sought her advice.

MARGE: I didn't mean to interfere, Mr. Ellsworth. (*She smiles at* MARY.) I know your husband's business will succeed, somehow.

MARY (*Weakly*): Thank you. (*Stands*) I'm sorry I took your time, Eff. I thought you might be able to help Bruce. I thought . . .

ELLSWORTH (*Sarcastically*): At least your visit was not wasted. You received sound advice from my clerk!

MARY: I received something more than that. She was kind and understanding. But I suppose those things have no place in your financial world. (*She runs toward right.*)

ELLSWORTH (*Calling*): Mary! (*She stops, turns.*)

MARY: Yes? (*He picks up an envelope, holds it out to her.*)

ELLSWORTH: Perhaps this letter will explain a few things. (*She takes envelope.*)

MARY: It's too late for explanations. It's too late for many things. (*She exits.* MARGE *looks sheepishly at* ELLSWORTH, *then straightens his chair and puts her pad and pencil on desk.*)

MARGE: I suppose you want me to leave now.

ELLSWORTH: I need a stenographer. You may as well stay until Miss Dudley returns.

MARGE: Yes, sir. (*She picks up pad and pencil.*) You have a third appointment —

ELLSWORTH: Yes — Alice Kramer. I haven't seen her in twenty years. (MARGE *glances at steno pad.*)

MARGE: Her name is Bond. Alice Bond.

ELLSWORTH: Her married name. She was Alice Kramer in our high school days.

MARGE: You knew her then? How interesting! (*She touches her pendant.*)

ELLSWORTH (*Lost in thought*): Yes, I knew Alice then and I thought that she — that someday — (*Quickly*) What is this — a personal interview? Show in Alice — Bond. And stop playing with that necklace. It makes me nervous. (MARGE *quickly drops her hand.*)

MARGE: Yes, sir. (*She crosses right, exits and re-enters followed by* ALICE BOND. ELLSWORTH *smiles, starts to walk toward her, extending his hand. Then he stops suddenly and drops his hand.*)

ELLSWORTH: Alice — Alice Kramer. It's good to see you again.

ALICE (*In strained voice*): Thank you, Eff. But, remember, my name is Alice Bond, now.

ELLSWORTH: Yes, you married Ralph Bond. (*He offers her chair. They sit.* ALICE *wrings her hands nervously.*) I suppose you've come to see me about Ralph.

ALICE: Oh, yes, yes! You must help me find him! (ELLSWORTH *signals to* MARGE.)

ELLSWORTH: Miss Ames, I'd like to conduct this interview in private.

ALICE (*Waving her hand*): That won't be necessary, Eff. I'll only take a few moments of your time. Ralph disappeared a week ago. He left for work that morning, and I haven't seen him since. I've been frantic with worry!

ELLSWORTH (*Calmly*): You must be patient.

ALICE: My patience is gone. Ralph and I have never been separated, not for a day, since our marriage. I know that something dreadful has happened to him!

ELLSWORTH: Are you familiar with his work?

ALICE: Oh, yes. Ralph has been in plant efficiency work since he graduated. He seemed happy enough, though he's always been waiting for his one big chance — but that's unimportant now. Please — please help me find him!

ELLSWORTH: Did you go to the police?

ALICE (*Nodding*): Yes, but it's just another missing persons case to them.

ELLSWORTH: What do you want of me? How do you think I can help?

ALICE: You're an important man. Your investigators — all the important contacts you have — I know you'll be able to find him.

ELLSWORTH (*Curtly*): I'm sorry, Alice. There's nothing I can do.

ALICE: Oh, I don't believe that. If you will only give me some encouragement, some hope. I know you can find him!

ELLSWORTH: I told you to have patience. Everything will be all right.

ALICE (*Quickly*): You know something about Ralph. Something's happened to him!

ELLSWORTH: Please, Alice —

ALICE (*Hysterically*): Why won't anyone tell me about my husband? What — what do you know?

ELLSWORTH: You must have confidence in me.

ALICE (*Standing*): Confidence! You were never interested in anyone but yourself. You resented Ralph — because I married him.

ELLSWORTH: Alice!

ALICE: Well, Ralph offered me much more than you could. You were too busy building the Ellsworth empire to worry about minor matters like friendship — or love. I won't take any more of your precious time. I'm leaving now — and I'm going to find Ralph. He needs me.

ELLSWORTH (*Slowly*): Being needed is an important thing. If a man is needed, he is never lonely.

ALICE: Don't tell me you're lonely, Eff? You — the third richest man in the world? No, you have everything you ever wanted.

ELLSWORTH: Everything . . . (*He picks up an envelope and hands it to* ALICE.) Go now — and read this letter. (*He waves impatiently, glances uncomfortably at* MARGE. ALICE *exits right.* ELLSWORTH *adjusts his scarf.*) That concludes the interviews, Miss Ames. (MARGE *slams steno pad and pencil on desk.*)

MARGE: I think there's a great deal more, Mr. Ellsworth.

ELLSWORTH: I beg your pardon?

MARGE: You could have helped those people — and you refused!

ELLSWORTH: That is none of your concern.

MARGE: No, but it's your concern. What about Miss Farrell? You could have made a handsome endowment to the hospital and helped many needy people.

ELLSWORTH: Your philosophy doesn't interest me.

MARGE: Then what about Mary Ellsworth? She's your brother's wife. You could have bolstered his business, offered him new contracts, financed his plant until he succeeded. How could you refuse to help your own brother?

ELLSWORTH (*Coldly*): Bruce is a poor business man. He is not capable of supervising a plant.

MARGE: There are experts in that field. You could have found an advisor to put his business back on its feet. (ELLSWORTH *tightens his fists.*)

ELLSWORTH: I suggest that we conclude this interview, Miss Ames.

MARGE (*Defiantly*): Not yet! I can't help thinking about Ralph Bond. You know something about him.

ELLSWORTH (*Sharply*): What made you assume that?

MARGE: You were aware of the purpose of Alice Bond's visit. She sensed it, too. If you know where her husband is, tell her. You have no right to make her suffer. (ELLSWORTH *stands, turns away.* MARGE *grabs his arm.* 'He spins around in astonishment.*)

ELLSWORTH: You touched me!

MARGE (*In contempt*): Oh, I forgot! No bodily contacts! (*Scornfully*) You're a cruel, egotistical man who thinks of nothing but power and greed!

ELLSWORTH (*Suspiciously*): Who are you, anyway? What have you done to Miss Dudley? (BOB *enters right.*)

BOB: Line A is now in working order.

ELLSWORTH: Confound Line A! (ELLSWORTH *storms left.* BOB

gestures helplessly at MARGE. ELLSWORTH *opens door, left, calls.*) Allison! Allison! (ALLISON *enters with drawn gun.*)

ALLISON: Yes, sir?

ELLSWORTH (*Pointing to* MARGE): This young woman! She has no right to be here.

ALLISON: I checked her papers, sir. She's been cleared by E.I.C.

ELLSWORTH: She's an impostor, I tell you! (*He fingers his glasses nervously.*) Why won't anyone give me a moment's peace! (*To* ALLISON) Contact the other guards. Have all entrances and exits guarded. No one is to enter — or leave — my private suite.

ALLISON: Yes, sir.

ELLSWORTH: And locate Miss Dudley immediately. I'll find out what's going on here! (*He pounds his fist in his hand.*)

ALLISON: Right away, sir. (*He exits.*)

BOB (*Innocently*): Is something wrong with the telephone service, Mr. Ellsworth?

ELLSWORTH (*Impatiently*): Get on with your work! (*Suddenly*) What are you doing here? You're supposed to be working on the lines outside. (*Coldly*) Are you an imposter, too? (MISS DUDLEY *enters right. Gasping for breath, she points to* MARGE.)

MISS DUDLEY: Mr. Ellsworth — that woman is a fraud! The one who was supposed to be my assistant is downstairs with the hotel manager.

ELLSWORTH: I knew it!

MISS DUDLEY (*Breathlessly*): The real assistant received a call from a woman impersonating me who told her not to report for work today. I'm going to call the police!

MARGE (*Sighing*): That won't be necessary, Miss Dudley. I'm Marge Ames of City College, and I came here to get a story for our campus newspaper. (*She removes pendant, places it on desk.*) That is my camera. You can destroy the film.

ELLSWORTH: But your credentials!

MARGE: They were forged. I read an article about the E.I.C. and tried to make my own credentials.

ELLSWORTH: You must have had help. You couldn't have engineered this plan unaided.

MISS DUDLEY (*Nodding*): Yes, you have a confederate. (ELLSWORTH *and* MISS DUDLEY *turn accusingly to* BOB.) You arrived together. Do you know this girl? (BOB *nods, removes tape recorder from belt.*)

BOB: It was a good try. Yes, I'm Bob Holland, editor of the college paper. This story meant everything to Marge and me. (*He puts tape recorder on desk.*) You can destroy the tape. (*To* MARGE) I guess there won't be a story now.

MARGE: I don't care. Someday, a story about the third richest man in the world will be published. (*Defiantly*) Then people will know what a cruel, selfish man he is!

MISS DUDLEY: This is a police matter.

MARGE: You're right, Miss Dudley. I'm prepared to face the consequences. (MISS FARRELL, MARY ELLSWORTH *and* ALICE BOND *enter right, holding envelopes.*)

MISS FARRELL (*Softly*): Mr. Ellsworth, we'd like to speak to you.

MARY: The guards didn't want to let us in, but the hotel manager persuaded them that we had visited you earlier.

ELLSWORTH (*Weakly*): I've seen too many people this morning.

MARY: We owe you an apology, Eff.

ALICE (*Nodding*): Why didn't you tell me about Ralph?

MISS DUDLEY (*Sharply*): Ladies, Mr. Ellsworth's schedule is filled for the rest of the day!

ELLSWORTH: Just a minute, Miss Dudley. These reporters wanted an exclusive story. (*To* MARGE) Maybe these ladies can give you some more facts for your article.

MISS FARRELL: This letter you gave me explained so many

things. I never realized that you were the chairman of the hospital board!

MARGE: The chairman?

ELLSWORTH: I was represented at the meetings, but I demanded anonymity. If the general public discovered that I believed in charitable work, I'd be hounded for the rest of my life.

MISS FARRELL (*To* MARGE): Mr. Ellsworth has contributed more than ten million dollars to the hospital during the past year.

BOB: Ten million dollars!

MISS FARRELL: If it weren't for Effingham Ellsworth, there'd be no City Hospital. (*She turns.*) Mr. Ellsworth, can you ever forgive me?

ELLSWORTH: I wish to remain the anonymous chairman of the board. That is my only stipulation.

MARY: Your letter to me explained the purpose of your trip to Europe. You're planning a merger of your turbine plant with Bruce's company. The merger will help Bruce to continue his work. It will assure his success!

ELLSWORTH (*Coldly*): A man can't live in the past. Yes, I am going to help him.

MARY: But why didn't you tell Bruce?

ELLSWORTH: I wanted to complete the merger before telling him. I didn't want him to be disappointed again. If anything went wrong — well, no, I couldn't let that happen to my brother. (*To* ALICE) And I suppose you know that your husband is involved in the merger, too.

ALICE (*Nodding*): Ralph is at your brother's turbine plant now, working as an efficiency expert. You hired him to handle the technical details.

ELLSWORTH: Yes. It's time I did something for you and Ralph. He's very talented, and this will give him a chance to prove himself.

ALICE: But I've been so worried. Why didn't you tell me?

ELLSWORTH: Secrecy was our primary concern. If my plans had been discovered, it might have ruined the chances for the merger. Besides, I didn't want you and Ralph to think that I was offering charity.

ALICE: I've always been so proud — so foolish.

ELLSWORTH (*Gruffly*): The merger will be completed within twenty-four hours. That is the purpose of my European trip. Ralph is flying to New York today. You'll meet him at the airport, if you hurry.

ALICE: I'll never forget you, Eff. (*She kisses him on the cheek.*)

ELLSWORTH: It's all right, Alice. Go now — to your husband.

MARY: Bruce and I will be waiting for you when you return from Europe. We must make up for the years we've lost.

ELLSWORTH: I'd like to know my brother and his wife again.

(MISS FARRELL, MARY ELLSWORTH *and* ALICE BOND *exit right.*)

MARGE: What can I say, Mr. Ellsworth?

BOB: I have a few things to say. We've been the mean and cruel ones, Marge. We thought of nothing else but our story. We didn't care what our story would do to Mr. Ellsworth's life. We didn't think that our publicity could destroy all his good work in a second.

MARGE: You're right, Bob. (*To* ELLSWORTH) I don't know what you're going to do with us, but you don't have to worry — there's not going to be any story.

ELLSWORTH: I was hoping you'd make that decision.

MARGE: And I learned a lesson today. A good reporter must get all the facts before drawing conclusions.

ELLSWORTH: I think you'll make a good newspaperwoman with that attitude, Miss Ames.

MISS DUDLEY (*Hoarsely*): But, Mr. Ellsworth, surely you're not going to let them go unpunished!

ELLSWORTH: Why not? I think they learned a lesson today.

MARGE: But there must be something I can do for you, Mr. Ellsworth.

ELLSWORTH (*Simply*): What could you possibly do for me? (MARGE *walks upstage, throws open draperies. Light floods room, as if from sun.*)

MARGE: Open your eyes as well as your heart! (ELLSWORTH *turns away from window, shielding his eyes.*)

ELLSWORTH: It is too soon for me to accept the whole world — and its light. Just let me try to find it a little at a time. Then, perhaps, I'll never live in the shadows again. (*He turns toward window as the curtains close.*)

THE END

Production Notes

THE THIRD RICHEST MAN IN THE WORLD

Characters: 3 male; 6 female; 4 male or female for guards, nurse, and doctor.

Playing Time: 35 minutes.

Costumes: Ellsworth wears a smoking jacket, ascot, and sunglasses. Bob wears a telephone lineman's outfit, including a hard hat, work shirt and trousers. He wears a large belt on which are attached a telephone receiver, wires, various tools, and a disguised "tape recorder." Marge wears an everyday dress, and a necklace with a big pendant on it. Miss Dudley, Miss Farrell, Mary and Alice wear attractive dresses or suits, and carry purses. Doctor, Nurse, and Maid are in appropriate uniforms. Allison and the Guards are in dark shirts and trousers, and have guns in holsters.

Properties: Steno pad, pencils, paper, blueprints, contracts, pen, etc., for desk; identification papers for Marge; wrist watches for Miss Dudley and Ellsworth; three envelopes; aerosol can.

Setting: Elegant living room of a large suite in a hotel in New York City. There is a large window in the rear wall, covered with draperies. City skyline can be seen behind the window. Down right there is a large desk, with several chairs arranged near it. A telephone, intercom, and various papers, etc., are on desk. Other chairs, table lamps, rugs, complete furnishings. There are exits left and right.

Lighting: Subdued lighting, with bright sunlight effect whenever draperies are opened, as indicated in text.

Sound: Telephone, as indicated in text.

Once Upon a Midnight Dreary

Terrifying creatures and eerie voices frighten the visitors to a deserted Southern mansion . . . .

Characters

JUDGE LIVINGSTON
JEFF CARSON, *the first heir*
MADGE, *his wife*
BOB, *Judge's son*
PROFESSOR JOHN GRANGER, *the second heir*
VALERIE, *his wife*
TOM, *Judge's son*
BETSY CARSON, *the third heir*
LINDA, *her friend*
ZOMBIE
CAT MAN

SCENE 1: THE ZOMBIE

TIME: *Evening.*

SETTING: *Drawing room of the Bayou House, gloomy Southern mansion. Furniture is covered with dust sheets.*

AT RISE: JUDGE LIVINGSTON *stands center, surveying room. He crosses to fireplace, up right, touches statue of black cat on mantel, nods. He goes down left, shakes corner of sheet covering sofa, and frowns as if at dust. He walks to French window up center, opens it, and stares out into night. Ani-*

mal's cry is heard from offstage. *Leaving window open, he
walks downstage and picks up book on table near sofa.*

JUDGE (*Reading*):

"Once upon a midnight dreary, while I pondered, weak
and weary,

Over many a quaint and curious volume of forgotten lore —

While I nodded, nearly napping, suddenly there came a
tapping,

As of some one gently rapping, rapping at my chamber
door."

(*Closes book*) "The Raven," by Edgar Allan Poe. (*Heavy
pounding is heard from offstage.* JUDGE *exits right. He re-
enters shortly, accompanied by* JEFF *and* MADGE CARSON.
JEFF *carries suitcase.*)

JEFF (*As they enter*): I know we're terribly late, Judge Livingston, but we took the wrong turn-off. (*Drops suitcase near
sofa*)

MADGE (*Nodding*): Leave it to Jeff. We went almost ten miles
out of our way before I could persuade him to turn back.

JEFF (*Slightly annoyed*): O.K., Madge, we found the right road
— and here we are. (*He glances around, shivers.*) I think we
should have stayed on that wrong road.

MADGE (*Slowly*): Such a desolate, lonely old place.

JUDGE (*To* JEFF): Your late uncle, Edward Carson, preferred
the solitude of Bayou House. He found a certain enchant-
ment in the desolation — in the swamps that encircle
this place.

JEFF: Sounds crazy, if you ask me. And the terms of his will!
I couldn't believe what you wrote me.

JUDGE: It was specified that all of your uncle's heirs should
sleep a full night in this house, or forfeit their share of the
inheritance. (*He glances at wristwatch.*) It's just a little before midnight now. If you had arrived fifteen minutes later,
you would have lost your chance.

JEFF (*Sighing*): Well, we made it, but we're not going to do much sleeping.

MADGE (*Soberly*): I may never sleep again. (*She walks upstage, glances through French window.*) Look at the mist rising from the swamp. It's like a veil of evil creeping toward the house.

JEFF (*Joining her*): It's a swamp fog, nothing more. We'll probably catch our death of cold, and we'll have to spend our first inheritance check on antibiotics. (*To* JUDGE) Did you write my sister and my cousin the terms of the will, too?

JUDGE (*Nodding*): Professor Granger and his wife are scheduled to arrive tomorrow night. Your sister, Betsy, will arrive from college to spend the third night at Bayou House. (JEFF *and* MADGE *join* JUDGE *downstage.* JUDGE *rubs his hands together.*) As your executor, I've arranged it all. (*Suddenly*) But it's time for me to leave. According to the will, you and your wife must remain here alone, until eight o'clock tomorrow morning.

JEFF: We'll be here.

JUDGE: One word of caution — the swamp is dangerous. There are bogs — treacherous beds of quicksand — from which no one has ever returned . . . . You must beware of the swamp.

MADGE: I assure you, we won't leave the house!

JEFF: Do you live far from here, Judge Livingston?

JUDGE: About five miles. My house is on the other side of the bayou. I live with my sons Bob and Tom.

JEFF (*Brightly*): Why don't you stay here for the night? With this heavy fog, and the mean turns in the road, you might have an accident.

JUDGE: The terms of the will forbid my staying.

MADGE: But what about the stone house? You could stay there.

JUDGE (*Quickly*): The stone house? What do you know about the stone house?

JEFF: We passed it as we turned into the driveway that leads to this place. It looks like a caretaker's cottage.

JUDGE (*Thoughtfully*): Yes, a caretaker . . . . (*Soberly*) You must never go into that house. There are many things associated with it, and — well, there are some things that cannot be explained. (JUDGE *turns to exit.* JEFF *grabs his sleeve.*)

JEFF: Hold on, Judge Livingston! I'm a free-lance mystery writer, remember? I'd like to hear about the caretaker's house.

MADGE: Jeff, please! I have goose bumps already.

JUDGE: You must remember that your uncle, Edward Carson, was a strange man.

MADGE: He'd have to be strange to live in this place.

JUDGE: He traveled throughout the world — writing, lecturing, and seeking information about obscure corners of the globe. In fact, he knew many secrets of the occult.

JEFF: What's that have to do with the stone house?

JUDGE: He had a caretaker, a man named Abner Benson, who lived in that house.

MADGE: Yes?

JUDGE (*To* JEFF): Benson worked for your uncle for many years. There are many bayou people who think he still serves this house.

JEFF: Great! We won't be alone, after all. I'll call old Abner and he can start a roaring fire in the fireplace.

JUDGE: You don't understand. Abner Benson has been dead for ten years.

MADGE: But you said —

JUDGE: Yes, I know. Some people think that Abner Benson still protects this place. (*Sound of animal baying is heard offstage.*)

JEFF (*Laughing*): My inheritance even comes with its own private ghost!

JUDGE: Abner Benson is not a ghost. No, the villagers believe that he is among the living dead. When he is called by Edward Carson, he leaves the stone house to do his master's bidding.

MADGE: I've read about the creatures who are neither living nor dead. They're called — zombies.

JEFF: What garbage! Leave it to the superstitious people in the bayou to believe in such nonsense.

JUDGE: Yes, our modern world disputes such theories, but Edward Carson was a strange man. He had mysterious powers.

JEFF (*Scoffing*): And I suppose he had some way to ward off the threat of a — zombie. Black magic — mumbo jumbo — some other foolishness. (JUDGE *walks to table, opens drawer, takes out gun.*)

JUDGE: Your uncle kept this gun as protection. It's a special gun. It fires silver bullets — the only bullets that can send a zombie back to the land of the dead.

MADGE: Please put it away! (*She covers her eyes.*)

JEFF (*Laughing*): There's nothing to fear. If our friend the zombie decides to leave his resting place, I'll merely get the gun. (*He holds his hand as if holding gun.*) Bang! Bang!

JUDGE: It's not that simple. A man who kills a zombie must pay a fearsome price. They say he himself turns into a zombie! (JEFF *slaps his forehead.*)

JEFF: Now I've heard everything. (*Pointing*) Is that gun loaded? (JUDGE *nods.*) Well, if there's a prowler tonight, I'll take care of him, zombie or no zombie! (JUDGE *shrugs, returns gun to drawer, closes drawer.*)

JUDGE: It's getting late.

JEFF: One thing more. How did my Uncle Edward summon this — zombie — from the world of the dead to do his bidding? (JUDGE *walks to fireplace, lifts bell with wooden handle from mantel.*)

JUDGE: He rang this bell. Many people have heard it pealing across the bayou, and there are some who say they saw Abner Benson emerge from the stone house — years after he died!

MADGE: Please, Judge, put that bell down. (*He puts bell on mantel.*) I want to leave this house tonight!

JEFF: Are you crazy? My share of the estate is over one hundred thousand dollars!

MADGE: But I'm afraid!

JEFF: Superstitious nonsense is not going to frighten me. Zombies — the occult — why, we'll laugh about it tomorrow morning, and we'll be a great deal richer. (JUDGE *walks to exit.*)

JUDGE (*Turning*): I will be here a little after eight, tomorrow. Remember, do not leave this house. And I suggest you bolt all the doors. (*He nods, exits right.*)

JEFF: Judge Livingston is what I call a little bundle of sunshine.

MADGE: I still think we should leave.

JEFF: Oh, Madge! Here — I'll build a fire myself. That bayou fog is soul-chilling. (*He walks to fireplace, studies bell. He reaches for it.* MADGE *quickly crosses to him.*)

MADGE: Jeff! Put that bell down! (*Startled, he turns, dropping bell, which rings.*) It rang! The bell rang! (*She stares at French window.*)

JEFF (*Grinning*): Why did I have to marry such a superstitious woman?

MADGE: Judge Livingston warned us.

JEFF: I'm afraid the Judge is as bad as the villagers. (*He touches her arm.*) Madge, you're trembling.

MADGE: Please — please take me away.

JEFF: Pull yourself together. Look! It's only one night. We're here together and nothing can harm us.

MADGE (*Dully*): The bell rang. The bell that calls Abner Benson from the stone house. A man who's been dead for ten years!

JEFF (*Angrily*): Stop it, Madge! (*He turns, takes bell off man-*

tel, strides to French window. He throws it open, rings bell loudly. He continues to ring bell as MADGE *joins him.*)

MADGE (*Hysterically*): You don't know what you're doing! You — you don't know what's out there! (JEFF *continues to ring bell furiously.*)

JEFF (*Shouting hoarsely*): Abner Benson! We need you! Come here at once! (JEFF *laughs shrilly, throws bell aside.*) There! I hope you're convinced that there are no zombies.

MADGE (*Weakly*): Oh, Jeff — I'm frightened. (*She walks down center, sits on sofa.* JEFF *joins her.*)

JEFF: And now I'm going to see to that fireplace. (*He crosses to fireplace, drops to his knees, looks into grate.*) Of all the rotten luck. There's no firewood. (*He straightens, joins* MADGE.) There must be some wood, maybe near the kitchen stove. I'll be right back.

MADGE: Don't leave me, Jeff. I couldn't stand it.

JEFF: You're acting childish. Who knows? Maybe this old house will belong to us someday. We mustn't let anything scare us away.

MADGE: But the stone house —

JEFF (*Quickly*): And we haven't seen a single zombie. (*He pulls her to her feet. Cheerfully*) I think a blazing fire will do wonders for this gloomy old room. (*He exits quickly.* MADGE *starts after him, then stops and turns to fireplace. Animal baying is heard again. She shivers, walks to French window, prepares to close it. Her hand freezes on door as sound of footsteps is heard from offstage.* MADGE *stifles a scream. Footsteps grow louder.* BOB, *dressed as zombie, appears at window. His hands and face are chalk-white.*)

BOB (*Slowly*): You — called — me? (BOB *enters, hands outstretched.* MADGE *retreats, screaming hysterically. She covers her face with her hands. Slowly,* BOB *turns, exits through French window.* MADGE *continues to scream.* JEFF *re-enters quickly.*)

JEFF: Madge! Madge! (*Shaking her*) What's the matter with you?

MADGE (*Breathlessly*): Out — out there! I saw him! He tried to touch me. The zombie! (*She screams again.* JEFF *releases her.*)

JEFF (*Suddenly*): Sh-h-h! (*Low*) Yes, someone is out there. Footsteps. I hear them, too.

MADGE: The spirit of Abner Benson!

JEFF: Whoever it is will have a tough time explaining why he's trespassing on my property. (*He pats her reassuringly.*) Maybe it's just an animal.

MADGE: No, I saw him. His face was so deathly pale — his eyes were blank and horrible!

JEFF: I'm going to prove to you that it wasn't a zombie. (*He takes gun out of table drawer, releases safety catch, steps toward French window.*)

MADGE: Please don't go out there!

JEFF: If there is a wild animal, I have protection. (*He scoffs.*) And I'm not afraid of turning into a zombie!

MADGE: But, Jeff! The Judge told us that's what would happen if you shot it. Please, stop! (*He exits. She stands stiffly by window.*)

JEFF (*Offstage*): Who — what are you? (*Sound of scuffle is heard.* MADGE *draws back fearfully. There are several gunshots, then silence.* JEFF *re-enters. He carries gun at his side. He walks slowly downstage and drops it into drawer.*)

MADGE: Jeff — what was it? What happened out there?

JEFF (*Slowly*): I don't know. I saw something on the fringe of the swamp. I called, but no one answered. I fired the gun. I kept firing, and — it's all over.

MADGE: Are you all right? How do you feel?

JEFF (*Slowly*): I'm very tired. It's been a long day and I need to rest. (*He walks to chair by fireplace. It is a high-backed swivel chair, turned away from audience. He sinks into chair.* NOTE: *While seated out of sight.* JEFF *rumples his hair and applies chalk to his face and hands.* MADGE *takes deep breath.*)

MADGE (*Regaining composure*): Jeff, I'm terribly sorry I was so foolish. My nerves — I'm upset. (*She attempts a smile.*) Imagination! Of course I didn't see a thing. You were right. We'll laugh about this tomorrow. Tomorrow! (*She steps closer to chair.*) It was an animal. Yes, that's it, of course. You fired at some animal in the swamp. (*Her voice rises.*) I didn't see a thing. There was no zombie. I was foolish. Forgive me. Please, forgive me! (*Slowly* JEFF *turns chair to face audience. His face and hands are white.* MADGE *gasps at his zombie-like appearance, screams in terror)* Jeff! What's happened to you? Why are you looking at me like that?

JEFF (*Slowly*): You — called — me? (MADGE *screams again, faints and slumps into his arms. Slowly, he carries her out French window. Offstage clock chimes twelve times as curtain slowly falls.*)

* * * * *

SCENE 2: THE CAT MAN

TIME: *The following night.*
SETTING: *Same as Scene 1.*
AT RISE: JUDGE LIVINGSTON *stands at table downstage, reading from book.*

JUDGE (*Reading*): "The cat followed me down the steep stairs and, nearly throwing me headlong, exasperated me to madness." (*He closes book.*) "The Black Cat," by Edgar Allan Poe. (VALERIE GRANGER *enters right. She wrings her hands.*)

VALERIE: Oh, Judge Livingston, I'm so glad you've come!

JUDGE: Your husband's telephone call worried me. I was afraid that something had happened to Professor Granger.

VALERIE: John? No, he's all right, I suppose. We arrived at Bayou House this afternoon. It was a frightful trip. I always hated this place. (*She holds onto sofa for support.*) And my heart — I'm so very tired. (JUDGE *helps her to sit on sofa.*)

JUDGE: There! That's better. You must relax, Mrs. Granger.

VALERIE: Relax — in this place? Oh, I'm sorry we ever heard of Edward Carson and his terrible will.

JUDGE: Your husband is one of Edward Carson's three heirs. By the terms of his uncle's will, Professor Granger must come here. (VALERIE *waves her hands.*)

VALERIE (*Quickly*): I know! I know! We must spend the night in this dreadful place!

JUDGE: And it's almost midnight. You and Professor Granger must remain here, while I return to my house.

VALERIE: Please don't go yet. Maybe you can tell me what happened to Jeff and Madge Carson. I'm so worried about them!

JUDGE: Ah, yes! A pleasant couple. I saw them last night. Jeff Carson was the first heir to spend the night in Bayou House.

VALERIE: But where are the Carsons? They were supposed to meet us here this afternoon.

JUDGE: A change in plans, perhaps. (*Pauses*) Yes, that's it, of course. They probably returned to town after fulfilling the terms of the will.

VALERIE (*Impatiently*): I don't believe that. We wanted to discuss the settling of the property. They wouldn't have left without telling us, without leaving some word. (JOHN GRANGER *enters. He is a serious, middle-aged man with a trim goatee. He carries a suitcase.*)

JUDGE: You'll hear from Jeff and Madge in a few days.

JOHN (*As he enters*): I'm not so sure of that, Judge Livingston.

(*He puts suitcase on table.* JUDGE *stands.* JOHN *indicates suitcase.*) Does it seem logical that they would have left without taking their suitcase?

JUDGE: Where did you find that?

JOHN: It was in this room. It had not been moved to the bedroom upstairs, and its contents were undisturbed. The clothing, the toilet articles — nothing had been touched.

VALERIE: Why didn't you tell me about the suitcase, John?

JOHN: I didn't want to disturb you, my dear. (*To* JUDGE) Valerie hasn't been well. Her heart — no excitement.

VALERIE: My pills. Where are my pills?

JOHN: They're upstairs. Don't be alarmed. I'll get them in good time. (VALERIE *stands slowly.*)

JUDGE: I'm sure the Carsons must have forgotten the suitcase.

JOHN: I told you the things hadn't been touched. I don't believe they spent the night in this house.

JUDGE: I'm certain that they did. They wouldn't violate the terms of the will.

JOHN: I suppose not. (*Sighing*) It was unfortunate that I missed Jeff. I wanted to discuss the possibility of buying his interest — and his sister's — in the estate. I would like to own Bayou House.

JUDGE: You want to live in this house, do you?

JOHN (*Nodding*): Yes. The old place fascinates me. There is a certain mystery — a quiet horror — a tantalizing charm that compels me to remain in Edward Carson's house.

VALERIE: John, I wish you'd stop talking like that. You know I could never live in this place. I dread staying here tonight!

JOHN (*To* JUDGE): My wife is theatrical — very dramatic. (*With scorn*) She conjures visions of evil and dread — things that go "bump" in the night. (*He places his arm around* VALERIE.) My dear, you will learn to love this house. It will enable me to conduct my work . . . my experiments.

JUDGE: Experiments?

JOHN: I suppose I have followed in the footsteps of Edward Carson. I, too, am a student of the occult. (*He picks up book.*) And I share the old man's enthusiasm for the writings of Edgar Allan Poe.

JUDGE (*Nodding*): Poe — the master of the macabre.

JOHN (*Reciting*): "Once upon a midnight dreary, while I pondered, weak and weary —" Yes, I'm certain that Edward Carson was inspired to write his strange will after reading "The Raven."

JUDGE (*Impatiently*): If you will kindly tell me why you called me here tonight, I'll be glad to help you. I must leave in a little while in order not to violate the terms of the will.

JOHN (*Suddenly*): I am interested in the tale of the old stone house and the caretaker, Abner Benson. I remember Benson when I visited Bayou House as a little boy. He was a harmless old man. (*Smiles*) I doubt that he had any supernatural powers.

JUDGE: What else do you remember?

JOHN (*Slowly*): Benson had a cat . . . . A large, black cat.

JUDGE: Yes, I've seen the cat around the place.

JOHN (*Strongly*): A cat is an amazing animal — a harbinger of evil. Its mysterious powers were known to the ancient Egyptians. Edgar Allan Poe wrote one of his most famous short stories about the sinister creature of the night.

JUDGE (*Nodding*): Yes, I was just reading the story called "The Black Cat."

JOHN: Whatever became of Abner Benson's cat? I'm interested in the animal. I'd like to find out.

JUDGE: I don't know anything about the cat. It's dead, I suppose. Abner Benson's been gone for ten years, so I'm sure the cat is dead.

JOHN (*Slowly*): I wonder. Do you think it's possible for a man's spirit to possess the body of a cat? Perhaps Abner Benson lives out there — in the bayou — in the body of his cat.

VALERIE: John, how can you say such things? Please stop talking about that black cat. I can't stand it! (*She clutches arm of sofa.*)

JUDGE (*Sternly, to* JOHN): I must agree with Mrs. Granger. I know you've both had a hard day and a long drive, and I feel there's no purpose in continuing the discussion if it upsets your wife. If you'll excuse me, I'll go now. (*He moves right.*)

JOHN: Very well, Judge Livingston. We will obey Edward Carson's will.

JUDGE: I'll call you in the morning. If there's anything you need, I'll be at my home.

JOHN: Thank you, Judge Livingston. (JOHN *bows gallantly.* JUDGE *exits.*)

VALERIE: You were terribly rude to Judge Livingston, John!

JOHN (*Musing*): On the contrary. I think he knows more about Abner Benson's cat than he admitted. He's a cagey character! Judge Livingston knows a great deal about this house. (JOHN *goes to fireplace, strokes statue of black cat.*) This black cat — what a perfect conversation piece for this old house! (*He returns to table and looks at book.*) And a copy of Edgar Allan Poe's works. How convenient!

VALERIE: What are you talking about?

JOHN: It's a little too prearranged. (*Slowly*) I think we're going to have an interesting evening. A very interesting evening, indeed. (VALERIE *sinks back wearily on sofa.*)

VALERIE: It's too much for me. All this excitement — this house. Where are Jeff and Madge Carson?

JOHN: Who knows? (*Laughs*) Maybe the black cat carried them off into the swamp.

VALERIE (*Shrilly*): John, please! (JOHN *walks behind sofa, stares down at her.*)

JOHN: Be calm, my dear. After all, Edward Carson has made me a very rich man, and there are so many things to do with that money. Travel — research — yes, I'll be able to do things in the future that were never possible before. (*Suddenly*) What was that? (VALERIE *stands.*)

VALERIE: I didn't hear anything.

JOHN: I thought I heard something out on the bayou. It sounded like — the cry of a cat!

VALERIE: No!

JOHN: But of course there's nothing here that can hurt us. (*He walks to French window, opens it.*) Ah, a perfect night. The night of the full moon! A cat loves to stalk its prey on such a night.

VALERIE: Why are you frightening me this way? (*She gasps*) My pills — I must have my pills. They're in my purse, in the bedroom upstairs. Please — please get them for me.

JOHN: In good time. (JOHN *cocks his head.*) Ah, I hear the cat again. It's crying — out there.

VALERIE: I don't hear anything. Oh, please, John! (*She grabs his arm for support.*)

JOHN: You are frightened. I will dispel your fear. I'll go out there and find the animal. You'll see that it is nothing more than a harmless cat — and we'll be able to laugh at our fears.

VALERIE: Don't leave me. (*Gasping*) Please get my pills.

JOHN: In a little while, my dear. (*He exits through French window. Slowly,* VALERIE *struggles downstage, grasping furniture for support. She finally reaches sofa, collapses. Loud cry of a cat is heard offstage.*)

VALERIE (*Weakly*): John — John! (*She tries to rise, but falls back on sofa. She is motionless.* JOHN *re-enters. He walks slowly to sofa, stares at* VALERIE, *nods his head.*)

JOHN: Dear Valerie, you were so foolish. (*Coldly*) Such a simple-minded fool. Do you think I intended to share Uncle Edward's money with you? No, my dear. This is my first opportunity to do the things I always wanted — make a name for myself in research. You see, Valerie, you were never able to understand. (*He touches her arm.*) Don't you admit that I gave a good performance tonight? Calling Judge Livingston — inquiring about Abner Benson's cat — recalling the works of Edgar Allan Poe. It was all my idea, and I played the part well. (*Nods*) I knew about your weak heart. And if my little scene didn't kill you — well, there's always the lonely bayou — the alligators — and the quicksand. Yes, everything went perfectly. (*Offstage, clock chimes twelve times.* JOHN *smiles.*) Midnight. It's time for me to telephone Judge Livingston and tell him of my wife's unfortunate passing. (*Offstage, cat's cry is heard.* JOHN *listens intently.*) How appropriate. Now, why couldn't we have heard that cat before? It would have added realism to my performance, and I wouldn't have had to imitate a cat's cry when I stepped through the French window. (*He nods, smiles.*) Such is fate, Valerie. (*Cat cries again. Cry is closer and louder.* JOHN *frowns.*) The cat is closer to the house. Well, I'll fix that. I won't let anything frighten me away! Nothing will stand in my way. Nothing! (*He rushes to French window, throws both doors wide open.* TOM, *dressed in cat man costume, is suddenly framed in French window. He wears gloves with claws.* TOM *approaches* JOHN *with arms upraised.* JOHN *screams, retreats to back of sofa.* TOM *pounces on* JOHN, *pulls him to floor behind sofa. Clawed hands rise several times.* JOHN's *hoarse screams trail off. All is silent. Curtain.*)

*   *   *   *   *

SCENE 3: OF GHOSTS AND EMBERS

TIME: *The third night.*
SETTING: *Same as Scene 1.*

AT RISE: *Stage is in darkness, except for lamp on table which shines on* LINDA's *face, as she sits reading.*

LINDA (*Dramatically*):

"Ah, distinctly I remember it was in the bleak December,
And each separate dying ember wrought its ghost upon
   the floor."

(LINDA *laughs.* BETSY *enters right. She carries tea tray. She snaps switch on wall. Overhead lights go on. She puts tray on table.*)

BETSY (*Testily*): For heaven's sake, Linda, isn't it bad enough to spend the night in this haunted house without listening to you recite "The Raven"?

LINDA: It's the perfect atmosphere, Betsy. (*Solemnly*) "Quoth the Raven, 'Nevermore.' " (*Normal voice*) Gee, I'm glad you invited me along.

BETSY: I didn't know whether I could swing it. I called Judge Livingston and he gave me permission to invite a guest for the night. (*Shivers*) I couldn't have stayed in this place alone.

LINDA (*Dreamily*): I'd stay anywhere to get your inheritance. Imagine, all that money!

BETSY: It's not that much. Remember, my inheritance will be split with my brother, Jeff, and my cousin, John Granger.

LINDA: They've already spent a night in this house, haven't they?

BETSY: That's right. I thought I'd hear from Jeff today, but his home number didn't answer.

LINDA: Don't worry. He'll show up at Livingston's office tomorrow morning when the inheritance is divided among the three of you. (LINDA *roams around room.*) There's something compelling about this place. (*Slowly*) A house in the middle of the bayou.

BETSY (*Disconsolately*): I don't see anything romantic about a swamp.

LINDA: You have no imagination. This place turns me on. Why, I can almost feel the ghosts of the past rising from the mist — creeping, crawling to reach the house.

BETSY: There you go again. (*She gestures.*) Have some tea.

LINDA (*As she pours*): Do you remember your Uncle Edward?

BETSY: Vaguely. I visited this place years ago. He was a strange man — a sad, lonely man with brooding eyes and a black moustache. I don't think he was a happy man.

LINDA (*Slowly*): That description of him . . . . Why, you make him sound like Edgar Allan Poe.

BETSY: What a ridiculous idea!

LINDA: Not at all. It fits perfectly. (*She gestures at mantel.*) There's the black cat, and the bell. Don't you remember Poe's poem, "The Bells"? (LINDA *recites.*) "How the danger sinks and swells, by the sinking or the swelling in the anger of the bells — of the bells — bells! Bells! Bells!" (BETSY *upsets her teacup.*)

BETSY: Stop it! Stop it! (LINDA *puts her cup down.*)

LINDA: Gee. I didn't mean to frighten you. I was just clowning.

BETSY (*Regaining composure*): It's all right. (*Slowly*) My uncle was a lot like Edgar Allan Poe. There's so much mystery — so much horror — in this house that I don't want to think about it. Promise that you'll stay close to me tonight.

LINDA: Sure I will. Nothing's going to happen. Tomorrow we'll laugh at ourselves — and our foolish fears. (*From off-stage, sound of drum beating rhythmically is heard. Girls freeze.*)

BETSY: What's that?

LINDA: I don't know. It seems to be coming from the bayou. (*Drumbeat continues throughout scene.*)

BETSY: But that's impossible. Nothing lives out there on the bayou. It's infested with alligators. And those pits of quicksand! (*She walks slowly to French window, opens it.*) Such a steady beat! (*She sways in time to beat.* LINDA *joins her at window.*)

LINDA (*Thoughtfully*): It's almost like a heartbeat.

BETSY: You thought of that, too? (LINDA *nods.*) What does it mean?

LINDA (*Suddenly*): "The Tell-Tale Heart"!

BETSY: What?

LINDA: It's foolish, I know, but it reminds me of Poe's story, "The Tell-Tale Heart." The man who committed murder, and the heart of his victim that kept on beating after death.

BETSY (*Terrified*): No!

LINDA (*Quickly*): Of course, it's ridiculous. There has to be a perfectly logical explanation. It might be an animal, or a car motor, or a hollow log — it might be anything.

BETSY: What are we going to do? I can't leave now. I must remain for the night.

LINDA (*Determined*): Neither of us is going to leave. And we're going to get to the bottom of this thing. (*She steps closer to French window.*)

BETSY (*Panicky*): We're not going out there!

LINDA: We have to trace that sound.

BETSY: But the bayou is treacherous. If we wander off the driveway, we'll be lost in the swamp. (*She grabs* LINDA'*s arm.*) Don't you see? Someone wants us to go out there — something is waiting to kill us!

LINDA: Well, we'll show them we're not easily scared. Didn't I see a flashlight in the kitchen?

BETSY (*Nodding*): Judge Livingston left one in case anything happened to the lights.

LINDA: That's all we need. I'll be right back.

BETSY: Please don't go! (LINDA *gives her a smile of assurance, exits right.* BETSY *looks out through opened French window, shivers, turns her back to opening. Suddenly,* TOM LIVING-

STON, *dressed as cat man, appears in opening. He reaches his clawed hand toward* BETSY, *almost touching her shoulder. There is a crash offstage and* LINDA*'s muffled voice is heard.* BETSY *quickly hurries down left.* TOM *exits through French window, unseen.* LINDA *enters, carrying flashlight.*)

LINDA: I pulled the cabinet drawer out too far and dropped the flashlight.

BETSY: Never mind that now. Does it work? (LINDA *tests light.*)

LINDA: It works fine. (*Drumbeat stops.*) Those beats! They're gone! (BETSY *sighs, relieved.*)

BETSY: I'm so glad. I couldn't have listened to them much longer. (*Suddenly*) I think we should leave now.

LINDA: Don't be ridiculous! Nothing is going to frighten us away.

BETSY: I don't care about the inheritance. I don't care about anything! I want to get out of this house! It's evil! (*Suddenly, jangling of bells is heard from offstage.* BETSY *freezes.*) Bells! Do you hear them? Out there — bells!

LINDA (*Slowly*): "By the sinking or the swelling in the anger of the bells —" (*Offstage, bells grow louder.*)

BETSY (*Hysterically*): I'm leaving now! (*She rushes to French window.* LINDA *follows, grasps* BETSY*'s arm.*)

LINDA: Don't be foolish. You can't run blindly out there. The bayou —

BETSY (*Quickly*): If you won't come with me, I'll go alone. The car — it's parked on the other side of the house. (*She exits quickly.*)

LINDA (*Calling*): Betsy — no! The swamp! Wait for me! (*She exits.*)

BETSY (*From offstage*): I missed the path! Linda! Linda!

LINDA (*From offstage*): I'm coming, Betsy! Don't go out there — don't! (LINDA *screams. Gradually her screams trail off. Sound of bells stops. After brief pause,* JUDGE LIVINGSTON *enters right. He walks to table, opens book, reads.*)

JUDGE (*Reading*):

> "Once upon a midnight dreary, while I pondered, weak
> and weary,
> Over many a quaint and curious volume of forgotten
> lore —"

(*He closes book, nods.* BOB, *as zombie, and* TOM, *in cat man's outfit, enter through French window.* JUDGE *smiles.*) Ah — Bob! Tom! Well done, my boys. Yes — very well done, indeed. (BOB *wipes his face, removing a streak of chalk. He smooths his hair.* TOM *removes cat man's headgear, places it on table.*)

BOB (*Soberly*): We didn't plan to commit murder.

JUDGE (*Reprovingly*): Murder? No one was murdered, Bob. Edward Carson's heirs were victims of their own imaginations. (*He smiles.*)

TOM: It was our fault. (*He points to French window.*) Those girls ran blindly into the swamp. They're gone — forever.

JUDGE: Unfortunate, I will admit, but there's one consolation: Not one of the inheritors lived up to the will. Not one spent a full night in Bayou House! (JUDGE *sits on sofa, sighs.*) Take Jeff Carson. He ran out firing a gun at you, Bob, thinking you were the zombie.

BOB: He might have killed me.

JUDGE: Nonsense! Would I have taken that chance with my own son's life? No, the "silver" bullets were really blank cartridges. A stage gun.

TOM: I guess Carson and his wife were lost in the swamp, too. (*Bitterly*) We caused it all. We're responsible.

BOB: Why, Dad? Why is Edward Carson's house so important to you?

JUDGE: Edward Carson's will is an interesting document. The entire estate remains under my control if the heirs fail to follow the terms of the will. Five hundred thousand dollars.

Yes, the estate would be mine — if there were no heirs to claim it.

BOB (*Slowly*): We didn't know that you would gain by the will.

TOM: And what about John Granger?   I think he deliberately tried to kill his wife.

JUDGE: He planned to frighten her to death. She had a weak heart.

TOM (*Nervously*): But I didn't kill John Granger. I came into the room to frighten him. I jumped on him, and he fell behind the sofa. I raised my arms a few times, to frighten him, but he was dead before I touched him. I swear it!

JUDGE: A victim of his imagination. Ironic, indeed.

TOM (*Dazed*): I must go home. I must think.

BOB (*Shaking head*): I don't want to think. We've done a terrible thing!

JUDGE: A good night's sleep will do you good. You'll see things in a different light in the morning. (*Sighs*) I'll join you at home later. I must close Bayou House for the last time.

TOM: Dad's right. We should go home tonight, Bob. We'll talk it over. Maybe in the morning, we'll go to the police —

JUDGE: I don't think that would be smart. After all, you were my accomplices. Now go along. Everything will be all right when you get home. (TOM *picks up cat man's mask, exits.* BOB *stares around room, shakes his head, exits.* JUDGE *walks to mantel. He rubs hand across statue of cat.*) The black cat! (*He picks up bell, laughs.*) The bells! (*He takes bell to opened French window, rings it loudly, calls hoarsely.*) Abner Benson, can you hear me? (*He continues to ring bell, finally throws it aside. He walks downstage, touches book. Footsteps are heard from offstage.* JUDGE *snaps to attention, turns to French window.* ZOMBIE *enters.*)

ZOMBIE: You — called — me?

JUDGE: Bob, if this is your idea of a joke — (*He crosses to* ZOMBIE.)

ZOMBIE: I — am — here — now — for — you! (JUDGE *touches* ZOMBIE'*s face, shrieks, pulls his hand away, wipes it against his coat.*)

JUDGE (*In disbelief*): You — you're not Bob! You — you're a — (*He backs away, right.* CAT MAN *appears at right entrance, and reaches out clawed hand in* JUDGE'*s direction.* JUDGE *screams, retreats center.*) Tom — Tom — is that you? Why are you doing this to me? (CAT MAN *screams savagely, advances with claws stretched forward.* JUDGE *retreats.* ZOMBIE *walks slowly forward, blocking* JUDGE'*s exit.* JUDGE *looks quickly at two creatures, screams again, falls to his knees, covers his face with his hands.* CAT MAN *and* ZOMBIE *continue their slow approach toward kneeling* JUDGE. *Offstage, clock begins to chime twelve times as curtain falls.*)

THE END

ONCE UPON A MIDNIGHT DREARY

Characters: 7 male; 4 female.

Playing Time: 40 minutes.

Costumes: Modern dress, for all but Bob, Tom, Zombie and Cat Man. Bob and Zombie wear faded shirts and trousers, chalk-white makeup. Tom and Cat Man wear black, furry suits, cat's-head masks with red, glowing eyes, and claws with gloves.

Properties: Book; statue of black cat; bell; suitcase; gun; tea tray with cups; flashlight.

Setting: Drawing room of Bayou House, gloomy southern mansion. French window is up center. Fireplace is up right, and there are several objects on mantel — statue of cat, bell, etc. Down center there is a long table, with lamp and book on it. At left is sofa, covered with dust sheet. Other chairs, tables, similarly covered, complete furnishings.

Lighting: Dim, night lighting. In Scene 3, only table lamp is on at beginning of scene, as indicated in text.

Sound: Animal bays and cries, footsteps, drumbeat, bells, chiming of clock, as indicated in text.